What People Are S
Chicken Soup for the

"Nourishment for the heart and mind should not end at age sixty. *Chicken Soup for the Golden Soul* provides inspiration for maintaining a healthy lifestyle throughout the golden years of our lives."

Denton A. Cooley, M.D.
pioneer heart surgeon
president and surgeon-in-chief, Texas Heart Institute

"*Chicken Soup for the Golden Soul* is a collection of inspirational and encouraging stories which are very welcome in our present-day culture. There is so much negativity in what we read and hear every day that an uplifting book of this nature is truly worth reading."

Tom Osborne
former head football coach, University of Nebraska
and author of *Faith in the Game*

"An inspirational collection of heartwarming stories about people over sixty living life fully with purpose and joy. A must-read for people of all ages."

Dr. Helen K. Kerschner
president, The American Association for International Aging
and The Beverly Foundation

"The *Chicken Soup for the Golden Soul* stories gave me so many smiles and laughs. This wonderful book makes us aware that we are not alone and love is the answer."

Jane Powell
actress, *Seven Brides for Seven Brothers*

"Jesus taught with stories—some parables, some allegories, some just factual accounts—but all short. He knew we could only digest truth, like *Chicken Soup*, in small servings, but how nourishing!"

Pat Boone
entertainer

"I think all of the *Chicken Soup* books have the faith to tell people that their problems are important and that there is always a light at the end of the tunnel."

Ralph Emery
Ralph Emery Television Productions
radio and TV personality and author

"*Chicken Soup for the Golden Soul* is the Golden Rule in book form. Read unto others as you would have them read unto you."

Bil Keane
cartoonist/creator, *The Family Circus*

"*Chicken Soup for the Golden Soul* is a powerful reminder that the quality of life is determined by one's attitude. A must-read for anyone wishing to enrich their years after sixty!"

Ruth Matheson
general director, Leadership Management International, Canada
Canadian Woman Entrepreneur, 1999

"A priceless treasury of uplifting stories straight from real life. Kindness, caring and hope will fill the heart of every reader."

Dr. Robert H. Schuller
founding pastor, Crystal Cathedral Ministries

"Ah! Can we ever have too much *Chicken Soup* for souls? I think not. This golden helping heals the soul and warms the spirit."

Karen Ross
producer and host, Chicago's *The Karen Ross Show*

CHICKEN SOUP
FOR THE
GOLDEN SOUL

Chicken Soup for the Golden Soul
Heartwarming Stories About People 60 and Over
Jack Canfield, Mark Victor Hansen, Paul J. Meyer, Barbara Russell Chesser,
Amy Seeger
Published by Backlist, LLC,
a unit of Chicken Soup for the Soul Publishing, LLC. www.chickensoup.com

Front cover design by Andrea Perrine Brower
Originally published in 2000 by Health Communications, Inc.

Back cover and spine redesign by Pneuma Books, LLC

Distributed to the booktrade by Simon & Schuster. SAN: 200-2442

Publisher's Cataloging-in-Publication Data
(Prepared by The Donohue Group)

Chicken soup for the golden soul : heartwarming stories about people 60
and over / [compiled by] Jack Canfield ... [et al.].

p. : ill. ; cm.

Originally published: Deerfield Beach, FL : Health Communications, c2000.
ISBN: 978-1-62361-088-3

1. Older people--Conduct of life--Anecdotes. 2. Middle-aged persons--
Conduct of life--Anecdotes. 3. Anecdotes. I. Canfield, Jack, 1944-

BJ1690 .C45 2012
158.1/28/0846   2012944784

PRINTED IN THE UNITED STATES OF AMERICA
on acid free paper
23 22 21 20 19   06 07 08 09 10 11

CHICKEN SOUP
FOR THE
GOLDEN SOUL

Heartwarming Stories About People 60 and Over

Jack Canfield
Mark Victor Hansen
Paul J. Meyer
Barbara Russell Chesser
Amy Seeger

Backlist, LLC, a unit of
Chicken Soup for the Soul Publishing, LLC
Cos Cob, CT
www.chickensoup.com

Let me start with my generation—with the grandparents out there. You are our living link to the past. Tell your grandchildren the story of the struggles we had, at home and abroad. Of sacrifices freely made for freedom's sake. And tell them your own story as well—because every American has a story to tell.

President George Bush
State of the Union Address, 1990

Listening children know stories are there. When their elders sit and begin, children are just waiting and hoping for one to come out, like a mouse from a hole.

Eudora Welty
One Writer's Beginnings

Contents

3. ACROSS THE GENERATIONS

4. CELEBRATING LIFE

5. STILL LEARNING

6. ON LOVE

7. ON OVERCOMING

8. A MATTER OF PERSPECTIVE

"At my age, I don't mind a little memory loss.
I keep forgetting I'm over sixty."

Introduction

"To every thing there is a season, and a time to every purpose under the heaven."

Ecclesiastes 3:1

These timeless words have emboldened countless individuals during the ups and downs of life. Stories passed from person to person and from generation to generation have offered consolation and inspiration for all seasons of life.

Wise storytellers through the ages inspired their listeners and helped them find direction and purpose in life. Storytellers reawakened people to their own spirituality, afforded them the courage to dream wonderful possibilities and embraced making a heart connection.

For *Chicken Soup for the Golden Soul,* we selected stories that encircle the heart and then captivate it. Some stories tell about enjoying satisfying relationships across generational lines, retiring and refocusing interests and energy, relishing the milestones of change and leaving behind what has been outgrown. Many stories deal with grandparenting and mentoring, while others focus on the realities of growing older. Our hope is that all the stories stimulate thinking on how to spend our days for maximum meaning and enjoyment.

As we sorted through the literal mountains of stories received for consideration in *Chicken Soup for the Golden Soul*, we were reminded of the importance of passing along to future generations the wisdom gleaned in life. We realized anew the importance of savoring each moment in our lives. We became mindful of how some of our greatest growth occurred during our darkest hours. We have found a serendipity that enables us to face the future with openness and trust, ready to receive whatever our Creator has in store for us.

We invite you to cherish all of life's seasons, the warm and the cold, the dark and the bright—for they are the best preparation for making the "growing older" years even more rewarding than you ever thought possible. It is never too late to discover richness and tranquillity in life.

"Tell me a story." These sweet words of children around the world and across the ages echo the heart of all of us. We hope *Golden Soul* inspires you to tell your own stories to the younger people in your life—and to the people who are "young at heart."

Through *Chicken Soup for the Golden Soul*, we celebrate life with you. Read the stories one at a time. Let them soothe your soul, tickle your funny bone and rekindle your spirit. Pass them on to others.

Grow old along with me! The best is yet to be, the last of life, for which the first was made.

Robert Browning

1

STAYING YOUNG AT HEART

As long as you can admire and love, then one is young forever.

Pablo Casals

Risky Business

What I've dared I've willed . . . and what I've willed, I'll do.

Herman Melville

A woman who tells her age will tell anything, according to Oscar Wilde, so I have no intention of saying how old I am. But I must admit I'm no longer in the first flush of youth. In fact, name almost any World War II song, and I can probably sing it all the way through.

That gives you some idea of why I felt so foolish when I bought the motor scooter.

Even as I wrote out the check, I couldn't believe I was actually making such a reckless purchase. True, I had thought for years what fun it would be to have a motor scooter. "Whatever for?" hooted family and friends.

"To explore little back roads," I told them.

"You can do that in the car," they said. Yes, but on a scooter I'd be able to pause and look at a wildflower or listen to the gossipy voice of a stream.

"You'll get yourself killed," family and friends said. That's exactly why I'd never made a serious move toward getting a scooter. I knew as well as anyone that cars come swinging around curves and there you are, tossed in the air like a matador on the horns of a bull.

So, why then, when a friend suggested we stop at a showroom, did I find myself purchasing one of the dangerous contraptions? Granted, the little scooter was as neat and trim as a folded paper airplane, and it came in my favorite shade of blue. It was also quiet and easy to ride, the salesman assured me. But these were foolish reasons.

The real reason was that I somehow felt I had to call my own bluff. I'd said for years that I wanted one; here was my chance. If I flunked it, I had a feeling my life would begin to close down. I'd watched it happen to other people—the desirable job not taken because it meant a scary move to a new city, the exciting chance to go whitewater rafting passed up because the boat might overturn—and each time I'd seen the person's life grow narrower, more restricted, as though closing one door had slammed other unknown doors shut.

I wrote out a check for the scooter.

The next step was to apply for a learner's permit. When I handed my driver's license to the young blonde behind the desk, she checked it indifferently until she came to "Date of Birth." Her eyes leaped to my face. A derisive smile twitched the corners of her mouth. "Aren't you a little old to be joining the Hell's Angels?" she drawled.

I couldn't have agreed more the first time I took the machine on the road. I was as nervous as a squirrel's tail. Anxiously, I kept reminding myself where the accelerator and brakes were located. A car was coming up behind me so I veered over to the side. I was slipping on gravel! I stamped on the floor. *Where was the brake? Why was I going so fast?*

After the car passed, I found panic had frozen my hand on the accelerator. And the brakes were not on the floor but on the handlebar. As soon as I somehow figured out how to stop, I got off and walked the scooter back home.

I tried again the next day and the one after. On the fourth day, I relaxed just enough to make a delightful discovery: I could smell the countryside—the grasses and daisies and fresh mud and wild roses. And I could see their sources. The landscape wasn't a movie unreeling rapidly but a tapestry of stitched leaves and branches and blades and petals. That is, if I could drag my eyes from the road long enough to snatch a look.

In search of a safe place to practice, I discovered a long, paved lane that led to a factory. After the factory closed and on weekends, I had the road to myself to do figure-eight turns. When I grew bored with patient circling, I took off for the factory, wheeled around and sped back. Every day I went faster, leaning into curves, dipping and swooping. And when I slowed, I laughed with joy. I had no idea that hurtling into the wind, unprotected, free, could be so exhilarating.

One day, with growing confidence in my little purring machine, I ventured as far as the village two miles downriver. I put the scooter up on its stand and took a bag of leftover rolls to the river's edge to feed the ducks. I was vaguely aware of two little boys eyeing the scooter. Suddenly, one was at my elbow. "Him and me," he said, nodding toward his companion, "we'll trade you our bikes for your scooter."

I started to laugh, but his freckled face was perfectly serious. I answered gravely, "It's a handsome offer, but I'm afraid I don't have much use for two bikes."

He nodded. He could understand that. But he didn't go away. "Where do you live?" he asked. "What's your name? How fast does the scooter go? What did it cost?"

When my supply of rolls was gone, the ducks wandered off, but Brian and Lou stayed another half-hour.

Something felt odd as we chatted. Then I realized it was exactly that: We were chatting. They weren't shy little boys. I wasn't a remote, grown-up lady. I was the owner of a marvelous toy, and that erased the gulf between us.

Neighbors seemed to feel the same thing. When I passed on my scooter, they smiled and waved and often called out, "How ya' doin'?" At first I thought it was because I looked so funny in my white helmet, horn-rimmed bifocals, and leather gloves and jacket on the hottest days (for protection in case I got knocked down). But when I took my eyes off the road, all I saw in their faces were warmth and a sort of vicarious pleasure in my adventure.

I knew I'd really been accepted, though, when a teenager roared by in his souped-up Chevy and yelled, "Go for it, lady!" His smile was broad and approving.

"I did!" I shouted after him. *And I'm glad,* I've thought a thousand times since. The scooter has indeed taken me on unexpected paths. It's brought me new adventures. But most of all, it makes me feel that all the doors of my life are still wide open. Anything is possible.

Riding it is risky, sure; I haven't changed my mind about that. On the other hand, one of the friends who was most vocal about the dangers of a scooter has fallen in the bathtub and broken her arm. Another, a widow who was going back to college until she grew afraid of being laughed at by younger students, has fallen into a deep depression.

I think of them, and I wonder if the only thing more dangerous than taking a risk is not taking it. Maybe, as Garrison Keillor has remarked, you're supposed to get reckless as you grow older. That way you keep saying yes to life. And perhaps saying yes, not being safe, is the real point of life.

Jo Coudert

Time Out

In the name of God, stop a moment, cease your work, look around you. . . .

Leo Tolstoy

I live high in the hills and my body is getting old. One day I was out in my garden fussing with weeds and grew tired. I decided to lie back on the grass and rest like I used to when I was a small boy.

I woke up some minutes later with a neighbor I had never met leaning over me, all out of breath, asking me if I were okay. He had looked out his window two blocks up the hill and saw me lying on my back on the grass, looking, I am sure, like the victim of a stroke or heart attack, and had run all the way down the hill to check on me.

It was embarrassing, but it was also so wonderfully touching. After we had it all sorted out, he let out a deep breath and lay down on the grass beside me. We both stayed there very quietly for a while and then he said, "Thank you for deciding to take your nap out on the lawn where I could see you. The sky is such a beautiful thing, and I cannot remember the last time I really looked at it."

Random Acts of Kindness

The Age of Mystique

How old would you be if you didn't know how old you are?

Leroy Satchell Paige

On my fiftieth birthday, my older daughter gave me a pin that said "Fifty is nifty." I wore it to work that day, and what fun it was! All day, people kept saying things to me like, "Anita, you don't look fifty," or "Why, Anita, you can't be fifty," and "We know you can't be fifty."

It was wonderful. Now, I knew they were lying, and they knew I knew, but isn't that what friends and co-workers are for? To lie to you when you need it, in times of emergency, like divorce and death and turning fifty.

You know how it is with a lie, though. You hear it often enough, and you begin to think it's true. By the end of the day, I felt fabulous. I fairly floated home from work. In fact, on the way home, I thought: *I really ought to dump my husband.* After all, the geezer was fifty-one, way too old for a young-looking gal like me.

Arriving home, I had just shut the front door when the doorbell rang. It was a young girl from a florist shop, bringing birthday flowers from a friend. They were lovely. I stood in my doorway holding the flowers and admiring them, and the delivery girl stood there, waiting for a tip.

She noticed the pin on my jacket and said, "Oh, fifty, eh?"

"Yes," I answered, and waited. I could stand one last compliment before my birthday ended.

"Fifty," she repeated. "That's great! Birthday or anniversary?"

Anita Cheek Milner
Excerpted from Chocolate for a Woman's Soul *by*
Kay Allenbaugh

Strike Out or Home Run?

It ain't over till it's over.

Yogi Berra

Everyone said the Yankees would lose this game. It was the fourth game of the 1996 World Series. Now the score was 6–0 with Atlanta winning. I lay in bed half awake.

Forget it, I thought, as I turned off the radio and fell asleep. But when I awoke, I immediately turned on the radio. It was the eighth inning now, the score 6–3, the Yankees making a comeback. *But what chance did they really have?* the realist in me asked.

What chance did I have? I thought as I lay there in the dark. When you have had cancer, you're always fighting the statistics, always hoping for complete recovery. When you're a widow, you're always fighting against loneliness. I felt like the Yankees in the fourth game of the World Series. That night, I didn't think I had a chance, either.

And then the Yankees hit the home run with two men on base. I jumped out of bed. I ran into the kitchen and wolfed down a sandwich and had a drink. The dog thought it was time to go out and play. I let him into the backyard. The cats thought it was morning. I fed them. All the lights blinked on in the house. I was fully awake. I was shouting. I was talking aloud, as if there were others in the room. "Come on, Yankees!" I yelled.

And then they did it in the tenth inning. They put the game away. I was laughing, running around the house and jumping on the sofa, and telling the dog and the cats: "They did it! They really did it!" I had not been a baseball fan before, but I vowed I would be a Yankee fan forever, because now I understood about baseball.

My husband had been a passionate baseball fan. He would sit, sometimes by the radio, sometimes by the television. He would talk to the radio, talk to his favorite team. If they were doing well, he smiled. If they were doing poorly, he cursed the set, cursed the players, threw the newspaper on the floor. He never went through the game alone. There were always friends to call, back and forth a dozen times, through all the innings. If it was a victory, they rejoiced together. If it was a defeat, they mourned. And, of course, they went to games with hoagies and sodas packed away, enough food for a week; fathers took sons and daughters, and mothers wondered what this excitement was all about.

I was envious of my husband's baseball passion when springtime came. There was nothing outside my home and family that possessed me so fully. My husband knew baseball better than he knew me. His mother told me he had loved baseball as a boy, and the love had continued into manhood.

I never understood about my husband and baseball, about his baseball cards, about his dream to attend just one spring training camp in Florida, about the pride on his face when he wore his team's baseball cap.

I never understood about baseball until the Yankees

won the fourth game of the 1996 World Series. The odds were against them. Nobody thought they had a chance, certainly not to come back from a 6-0 deficit.

There were times when the bases were loaded against them, and their pitcher threw the ball anyway. There were times when the batter was up at bat, and it looked bleak, but it was his turn, and that's all there was to it. There were times when the score turned sour, and there didn't seem to be a reason to even try, but try they did.

Many times I feel the bases are loaded in my life. The odds pile up against me. I just don't want to pitch that ball. It seems futile. But every day, I get the opportunity to pitch the ball again. The bat's in my hand, and it's my turn up at a new day. I can hit the home run if I believe it, and sometimes I do and sometimes I don't.

Those Yankees didn't care about the people who didn't believe in them, and I'm sure they didn't care about the statistics. They believed in themselves, in the game and in the unpredictability of life.

I thought about it that night, why I felt so good, so energized, why I was celebrating, why that good feeling remained with me. Now I understood why my husband loved baseball.

Life is just one big baseball game. That was the secret he knew. You never can tell what the outcome is going to be until the very last inning.

Perhaps tomorrow will be the day I hit my own home run.

Harriet May Savitz

The Long Ride

Life is like a bicycle. You don't fall off unless you stop pedaling.

Claude Pepper
U.S. Congressman

Betty Olsen was just settling down to enjoy the golden years with her husband. The last of their five children was about to leave home. The couple had plans to travel. But then after thirty-three years of marriage, he sprung a little surprise on her. "I'm leaving," he announced. He had found someone else, twelve years younger.

The pain rattled her entire soul and body. Life seemed over, at least the life she had known for the last three decades. "Starting over at age fifty-five won't be easy," Betty said. But she decided it would do her no good to feel sorry for herself. So she got busy. She joined a speaking program, became a volunteer at the American Cancer Society and trained as a docent at a local art museum. She played bridge and tennis, worked at the local blood bank, and got recertified as a nurse.

But no matter how busy Betty kept, her heart remained cold and lonely. Nothing really captured her spirit. Then one day, two friends asked her to go on a bike ride. Not just any bike ride, but a metric century ride—a sixty-four-mile journey up and down the hills of Gilroy, California.

The couple didn't tell Betty, then sixty, the distance of the ride. "Or I would never have gone," she laughs. Betty had poked around town on a bike before, but that was about it.

The threesome hit the road together with a pack of other riders. As Betty huffed and puffed up the hill, she couldn't believe the breathtaking beauty of the country-side—the sage thickets, the velvet green colors of the brush and creeksides. Nothing compared to experiencing the wildflowers, the sweet, dank smell of woods, even people's front yards. That's when Betty became enraptured with biking. She had determined when her marriage came crashing down that she was going to find new frontiers, new worlds to explore, new dreams to dream. She exclaimed, "Life really begins at sixty!"

The enthusiastic novice joined two bike clubs and started to travel everywhere by bicycle. First, she biked one hundred miles in the Inland Passage of Alaska where she saw bear footprints and golden eagles in flight, and watched cruise ships from a mountaintop. The next summer she traveled to New Zealand. But these rides weren't enough for Betty. She wanted to try something more challenging. Like biking twenty-five hundred miles or so.

Her first long-distance undertaking was a cross-country ride from San Diego to Jacksonville, Florida—an eighty-mile-a-day, five-week trip. Her children were terrified, and her sister told her, "Don't do that. It's too strenuous."

Betty admits, "I, too, was uncertain I could make it!"

But nothing could stop Betty, and she had no regrets when she found herself amid towering pine trees and fields of bluebonnet lupines. "I had never seen anything like it in my life!" she observed. In addition to the awesome sights, Betty loved stretching her limits and discovering new sources of inner strength. Invigorated, she convinced her forty-three-year-old son to tag along with her on some of her shorter rides, like the fifty-mile Tierra Bella.

Now seventy-three-years young, Betty has completed a total of three cross-country trips, biked through forty-seven states, and visited thirteen national parks. She estimates she's done a total of seventy thousand miles on her bike since she started these great adventures.

Betty has made dozens of biking friends, packed forty pounds of gear in intense Sierra Club hikes and has been asked to remarry twice. "I turned both gentlemen down," she says, "because they weren't into biking or hiking." Betty thinks she needs someone a bit more on the active side.

Her riding spirit and intense journeys—which include a trip from San Francisco to Washington, D.C., and from the state of Washington to Maine—have captured the interest of many journalists who have written her story a half-dozen times. "I find it's an exhilarating fatigue," she has said. "I feel so healthy. I'm in better shape than I've ever been. It's been a cure for loneliness. I have many friends. It's not too strenuous. When you travel, you have no yard work, no shopping, no cooking, no meetings and no housework. And I'd like to get to know more of the history of our country." Biking obviously is also helping Betty get to know herself better.

This paragon of health—physical and mental—has seen sights other people never see in their lifetimes. Once when touring in Yellowstone, with all the bikers riding single file, a herd of buffalo joined them across the river trotting single file, too. In Costa Rica, she came eyeball to eyeball with a monkey swinging through the trees right toward her. One summer, she saw swarms of stunning butterflies in the Ozarks.

These magnificent, life-enriching experiences are why

Betty probably didn't quit bike riding even after she got shot in the Napa Valley. She was at the very end of a bike line when a teenager shot her with a pellet gun. She was hospitalized for two nights, but doctors concluded that removing the pellet was too dangerous and decided to leave it where it was.

Within two weeks, this gallant lady—pellet intact—was back on her bike, cruising the Eastern Sierras. She had learned not to let a little detour stop her from exploring her newfound world. "Biking is so fulfilling," she explains. "I just don't have enough time to do all I'd like to do. I'd like to get to the garden, for example, but the weeds get there faster. I really love being with my children and my family, but I think biking adds a new chapter in my life.

"When I rode the Oregon Trail, the Santa Fe Trail and the Natchez Trail, I felt like the pioneers." She enthusiastically adds, "I hope my newfound discoveries will rub off on the rest of my family."

Who knows? Maybe some of her family members are ready to embark on new journeys in their own lives to broaden their horizons. Two of her teenage grandsons are joining her in the Tierra Bella, and her young granddaughters were at her house the other day when they said excitedly, "Grandma, let's go for a long bike ride."

Betty hoisted the exuberant grandchildren, one onto a tricycle and the other onto a two-seat banana bike. She hopped onto her twenty-four speed bicycle, and together they rode an entire five blocks before the kids were exhausted. They enjoyed the exhilaration of a short journey that may well be their first taste of what it is like to embark on life-expanding expeditions—just like Grandma.

Diana L. Chapman

Annual Checkup

Never go to a doctor whose office plants are
dead.

Erma Bombeck

The call came as expected. It was from Ellen at Davis
Clinic. Time for my annual checkup. The tragic time had
rolled around again. Spending eight hours being poked,
gouged, pitied and x-rayed is no picnic. Have you ever
noticed that the nurse always gets in a lead bunker for her
protection but leaves your quivering body exposed?

I guess checkups are necessary as we pass through
infancy, adolescence, adulthood and over-the-hillhood.
After you turn sixty, it's all maintenance, though.

As I entered the clinic, I was met by Ellen with that supe-
rior, expectant look. She wanted me to sign a release form
so they would not be responsible for anything they did.
They wanted to know who would be responsible for the
bill if I didn't make it. They also wanted to know where the
remains should be sent. She wanted to know if they could
use any of my parts that happened to be good. (At that
point, I would not need them anymore, she assured me.)

She then handed me a mimeographed list of terrible diseases, and she wanted me to mark the ones I had experienced in the last twelve months. I always mark four or five good ones to give them something to do in the back room. Remember, you are presumed to be senile or you would not be there.

Then a little girl (young enough to be my granddaughter) wanted some additional information. "Dr. Thorn, have you ever shot illegal drugs by needle, even once?" I shook my head. "Tested positive for the AIDS virus?"

"No," I said.

She continued. "Have you given money for sex anytime since 1955?" Then, "Have you had sex with a man? With a prostitute?"

"No, no, no, none of the above." If they are going to give my parts away, they want them without blemish.

She then asked, "Are you married to Jessie Holder Thorn?" I indicated that I was. She said that she wanted to ask me this before, but she did not want to get too personal.

I was then given a sack and ushered into a small dressing room. Being alone, I opened the sack and found the notorious hospital gown. Medical science can give you new joints and organs, but they still have the same gowns they used back in the days of antiquity. One size fits anything—car, chair or table. It is easy to walk into them but impossible to tie the strings in the back. If you can, you have no business being at the doctor's office. If you try and can't, you might have to stay an extra week. I've learned the secret: Just take the gown off, lay it on the floor and tie the strings. Then you can slither into it. This ingenuity shows that the passing of years has not entirely dulled my intellect.

The nurse came in and told me she needed to take my blood pressure. She said, "Have a seat on that metal stool." The cold stool sent my blood pressure sky high. No one has normal blood pressure in a doctor's office.

With a sneer she handed me a little jar and informed me that she needed a specimen. When she returned to the room, she noticed that the jar was dry. She cooed, "Now don't you worry, many men your age have this problem."

"My age nothing, I can't get the lid off the jar." The human body is a marvelous contrivance, but it does get a little frayed as time goes on.

There came a stout knock on the door. "Come in," I said. In walked a woman in a white robe. I noticed by the nametag that she was a medical doctor. She informed me that she was here to give me my physical. If they are going to give somebody else my body parts, I guess they wanted to check them out.

She demanded that I take off my robe.

"Doctor, I have never felt this good in my life and everything is working," I whined. Again she demanded that I take off my robe.

"What are you doing?" she screamed.

"Getting down on the floor so I can get out of this gown," I responded.

There I stood with only my clinic identification bracelet, which identified for them that I was a male.

"Do you have any questions before I leave?" questioned the doctor.

"Just one. Why did you knock?"

Apparently I passed the annual checkup and am still alive with all my parts. You can survive anything except death.

Norman Cousins talked about "that apothecary inside of you," by which he meant the medicine of humor. When this medicine works, muddled thinking clears. Solomon said, "A cheerful heart is good medicine; but a crushed spirit dries up the bones" (Proverbs 17:22).

I believe that the Apostle Paul was more than inspired when he wrote, "A man ought to examine himself . . ." (1 Corinthians 11:28).

W. E. "Bill" Thorn

Daily Prayer

Dear Lord—
I'm proud to say, so far today
I've got along all right;
I have not gossiped, whined or bragged,
Or had a single fight.

I haven't lost my temper once,
Or criticized my mate,
I have not lied, I have not cried,
Or loudly cursed my fate.

So far today I've not one time
Been grumpy or morose,
I've not been spiteful, cold or vain,
Self-centered or verbose.

But, Lord, I'm going to need Your help
Throughout the hours ahead,
So give me strength, Dear Lord, for now
I'm getting out of bed.

John T. Baker

2

SHARING
WITH OTHERS

To do for the world more than the world does for you—that is success.

Henry Ford

The Rich Family

Give, and it will be given to you. A good measure, pressed down, shaken together and running over, will be poured into your lap. For with the measure you use, it will be measured to you.

Luke 6:38

I'll never forget Easter 1946. I was fourteen, my little sister, Ocy, was twelve and my older sister, Darlene, was sixteen. We lived at home with our mother, and the four of us knew what it was to do without. My dad had died five years before, leaving Mom with no money and seven school-aged kids to raise.

By 1946, my older sisters were married and my brothers had left home. A month before Easter, the pastor of our church announced that a special holiday offering would be taken to help a poor family. He asked everyone to save and give sacrificially.

When we got home, we talked about what we could do. We decided to buy fifty pounds of potatoes and live on them for a month. This would allow us to save twenty dollars of our grocery money for the offering. Then we thought that if we kept our electric lights turned out as much as possible and didn't listen to the radio, we'd save money on that month's electric bill. Darlene got as many house- and yard-cleaning jobs as possible, and both of us baby-sat for everyone we could. For fifteen cents we could buy enough cotton loops to make three potholders to sell for a dollar. We made twenty dollars on potholders. That month was one of the best of our lives.

Every day we counted the money to see how much we had saved. At night we'd sit in the dark and talk about how the poor family was going to enjoy having the money the church would give them. We had about eighty people in church, so we figured that whatever amount of money we had to give, the offering would surely be twenty times that much. After all, every Sunday the pastor had reminded everyone to save for the sacrificial offering.

The night before Easter, we were so excited we could hardly sleep. We didn't care that we wouldn't have new clothes for Easter; we had seventy dollars for the sacrificial offering. We could hardly wait to get to church! On Sunday morning, rain was pouring. We didn't own an umbrella, and the church was over a mile from our home, but it didn't seem to matter how wet we got. Darlene had cardboard in her shoes to fill the holes. The cardboard came apart, and her feet got wet.

But we sat in church proudly. I heard some teenagers talking about our old dresses. I looked at them in their new clothes, and I felt rich.

When the sacrificial offering was taken, we were sitting in the second row from the front. Mom put in the ten-dollar bill, and each of us kids put in a twenty-dollar bill.

We sang all the way home from church. At lunch, Mom had a surprise for us. She had bought a dozen eggs, and we had boiled Easter eggs with our fried potatoes! Late that afternoon, the minister drove up in his car. Mom went to the door, talked with him for a moment, and then came back with an envelope in her hand. We asked what it was, but she didn't say a word. She opened the envelope and out fell a bunch of money. There were three crisp twenty-dollar bills, one ten-dollar bill and seventeen one-dollar bills.

Mom put the money back in the envelope. We didn't talk, just sat and stared at the floor. We had gone from feeling like millionaires to feeling poor. We kids had such a happy life that we felt sorry for anyone who didn't have our Mom and our late Dad for parents and a house full of brothers and sisters and other kids visiting constantly. We thought it was fun to share silverware and see whether we got the spoon or the fork that night. We had two knives that we passed around to whoever needed them. I knew we didn't have a lot of things that other people had, but I'd never thought we were poor.

That Easter day I found out we were. The minister had brought us the money for the poor family, so we must be poor, I thought. I didn't like being poor. I looked at my dress and worn-out shoes and felt so ashamed—I didn't even want to go back to church. Everyone there probably already knew we were poor!

I thought about school. I was in the ninth grade and at the top of my class of over one hundred students. I wondered if the kids at school knew that we were poor. I decided that I could quit school since I had finished the eighth grade. That was all the law required at that time.

We sat in silence for a long time. Then it got dark, and we went to bed. All that week, we girls went to school and came home, and no one talked much. Finally, on Saturday, Mom asked us what we wanted to do with the money. What did poor people do with money? We didn't know. We'd never known we were poor. We didn't want to go to church on Sunday, but Mom said we had to.

Although it was a sunny day, we didn't talk on the way. Mom started to sing, but no one joined in, and she sang only one verse.

At church we had a missionary speaker. He talked about how churches in Africa made buildings out of sun-dried bricks, but they needed money to buy roofs. He said one hundred dollars would put a roof on a church. The minister added, "Can't we all sacrifice to help these poor people?" We looked at each other and smiled for the first time in a week.

Mom reached into her purse and pulled out the envelope. She passed it to Darlene. Darlene gave it to me, and I handed it to Ocy. Ocy put it in the offering.

When the offering was counted, the minister announced that it was a little over one hundred dollars. The missionary was excited. He hadn't expected such a large offering from our small church. He said, "You must have some rich people in this church." Suddenly it struck us! We had given eighty-seven dollars of that "little over one hundred dollars."

We were the rich family in the church! Hadn't the missionary said so? From that day on, I've never been poor again.

Eddie Ogan

The Secret Benefactor

There's a delight that comes with helping other people.

Paul Newman

As a chauffeur for several years in the early 1910s, my father saw his affluent employer anonymously meet the needs of numerous people, aware they would never be able to repay him.

One instance stands out in my memory of the many stories my father shared with me. One day, my father drove his employer to another city for a business meeting. On the outskirts of town, they stopped for a sandwich lunch.

While they ate, several boys rolling hoops passed by their "Tin Lizzie." One of the boys limped. Looking more closely, my father's boss observed that the boy had a club-foot. He stepped out of the car and caught up with the boy.

"Does that foot give you a lot of trouble?" the man asked the youngster.

"It slows down my running some," the boy replied. "And I have to cut up my shoe to make it comfortable. But

I get along. Why're you asking me these questions?"

"Well, I may be able to help get that foot fixed. Would you like that?"

"Sure," he said. The youngster was positive but a little confused by the question.

The ever-efficient businessman wrote down the boy's name and returned to the car. Meanwhile, the boys picked up their hoops and continued down the street.

As my father's employer got back in the car, he said, "Woody, the boy who limps . . . his name is Jimmy. He's eight years old. Find out where he lives and get his parents' names and address." He handed my father the boy's name on a piece of paper. "Go visit his parents this afternoon and do your best to get their permission to let Jimmy have his foot operated on. We can do the paperwork later. I'll take care of all the costs."

They finished their sandwiches, and my father drove his employer on to the business appointment.

It didn't take long to get Jimmy's home address from a nearby drugstore. Most everyone there knew the boy with the clubfoot.

The small house Jimmy and his family called home needed paint and repair. Looking around, my father noticed tattered shirts and patched dresses hanging on the clothesline attached to the side of the house. A discarded tire hanging from an old piece of rope on an oak tree served as a swing.

A woman in her mid-thirties responded to the knock on the rusty screen door. She looked tired, and her furrowed features betrayed a life of hardship.

"Good afternoon," my father greeted her. "Are you Jimmy's mother?"

She frowned slightly before responding. "Yeah. Is he in trouble?" Her eyes scanned my father's starched collar and pressed suit.

"No, ma'am. I represent a wealthy man who wants to get his foot fixed so he can play like all his friends."

"What's the catch, mister? Ain't nothing free in this life."

"This is no tease. If you'll let me explain it to you—and your husband, if he's around—I think I can make it clear. I know this is sudden. I don't blame you for being suspicious."

She looked at my father once again, and, still hesitant, invited him inside. "Henry," she called out in the direction of the kitchen, "come in here and talk to this man. He says he wants to help get Jimmy's foot fixed."

For almost an hour, my father explained the plan and answered their questions. "If you're willing to let Jimmy have these operations," he concluded, "I'll send you some permission papers to sign. Again, we pay all costs."

Perplexed, Jimmy's parents looked at each other. They still weren't sure about all this.

"Here's my card. I'll write you a letter when I send the permission papers. The things we have discussed, I'll put in the letter. If you have any more questions, call or write me at this address." This seemed to give them a little more assurance. My father left. His mission was accomplished.

Later, my father's employer got in touch with the mayor with a request to send someone to Jimmy's home to reassure the family that this was a legitimate offer. Of course, the name of the benefactor was not mentioned.

Soon, with permission papers signed and in hand, my father took Jimmy to an excellent hospital in another state for the first of five operations on his clubfoot.

The operations were a success. Jimmy became a favorite of the nurses on the orthopedic ward at the hospital. Tears and hugs were shared all around when Jimmy left for the last time. They gave him a gift as a final gesture of their care . . . a new pair of shoes, specially made for his "new" feet.

Jimmy and my father got to be great friends as they traveled back and forth from the hospital. On the final trip home, they sang songs, talked about what Jimmy could do now with his fixed foot and shared silent times as they approached his house.

A smile flooded Jimmy's face when they arrived at his house and he stepped out of the car. His parents and two brothers stood clustered on the weathered front porch.

"Stay there," Jimmy yelled to them. They stared in amazement as Jimmy walked toward them. His limp had vanished.

Hugs, kisses and smiles surrounded the returned youngster with the "fixed foot." His parents shook their heads and grinned as they watched. They still could not believe that a man they had never seen would pay a large sum of money to have a foot corrected for a boy he did not know.

* * * *

The wealthy benefactor removed his glasses and wiped tears from his eyes when the homecoming was described to him. "Do one more thing," he said. "Near Christmas time, contact a good shoe store. Have them invite every member of Jimmy's family to their store to be fitted for a new pair of shoes of their choice. I'll pay for them all. Let them know I will do this only once. I don't want them to become dependent on me."

Jimmy became a successful businessman before his death a few years ago. To my knowledge, Jimmy never knew who paid for his foot surgery. His benefactor, Mr. Henry Ford, always said it's more fun to do something for people when they don't know who did it.

Woody McKay Jr.

They Call Me "The Umbrella Lady"

It takes both rain and sunshine to make a rainbow.

An Apple a Day

There wasn't a cloud in the sky that warm June morning when my friend Carole and I started out for a day of shopping. We had learned of a quilt shop which showcased the wares of nearby artisans. Carole's heart was set on finding a blue-and-white Dresden plate quilt to put the finishing touch on her guest bedroom.

We parked the car next to the only traffic light in town, armed with fabric swatches and paint chips. But next door, a ladies' boutique lured us inside where we admired the most exquisite collection of rainwear we had ever seen. As I ran my fingers across the vinyl-laminated floral chintz umbrella, I heard myself exclaim: "These are the most gorgeous umbrellas.... Why, they're just like an old-fashioned flower garden."

A sales clerk hastened to my side. "Perhaps you'd like to try one of them out," she suggested. I opened the oversized canopy. Underneath its protective bouquet, I felt wonderfully carefree and sheltered from the whole world.

But with new tires to buy, there was no money for expensive umbrellas. Besides, even if I could afford one, it wouldn't be a practical purchase.

Back in the sixth grade, I'd once eyed a beautiful, pink, frilly umbrella in a department store window. "Safety patrols need nice umbrellas," I'd explained to Mother.

"Safety patrols need serviceable umbrellas, not flimsy parasols," she countered. "Besides, you might lose it." How I'd wanted to own something pretty as well as practical.

"Thanks for showing me the umbrella," I wistfully muttered to the boutique clerk and headed next door to the quilt shop, a few steps ahead of Carole.

When my friend's steps caught up with mine, I noticed a long, slender box underneath her arm. "This is for you," she said softly. "I've never seen you look so longingly at anything before."

"But Carole, it's not Christmas. It's not even my birthday. You were going to buy a quilt today."

"Look, there won't always be sunshine in the sky like today," she answered convincingly. "And when the rain comes, I want you to think happy thoughts of friendship."

I tossed the umbrella's box in the back seat of the car and placed my treasure beside me for the long drive home. It smelled like a brand-new toy, and I felt as cared for as a little girl tucked in bed with her teddy bear. I rolled down the car window, shut my eyes and inhaled the pure mountain air.

I didn't understand it, but in the weeks that followed, I found myself thinking a lot about umbrellas. I couldn't pass a dime-store display without lingering for a second look, and suddenly I noticed all the broken, frayed and faded umbrellas people all around me carried. Sometimes, warm and dry inside my car during a storm, I'd see folks with no umbrella at all. When I spotted a lady dashing to her car with a plastic bag over the top of her head or an elderly man with umbrella spokes that refused to cooperate, it was as if God was saying to me: "Why not start an umbrella ministry, Roberta? You just give the umbrellas away and trust me to do the rest."

"You want me to give away umbrellas?" I asked God one day. "What if someone thinks that I am the one who doesn't have sense enough to come in out of the rain?"

About that time, my comfortable office at work was temporarily moved outdoors to a trailer with no canopied breezeway. During rainstorms, water collected on the roof and poured down in torrents as I came and went, despite the oversized umbrella Carole had given to me. I began to think incessantly about umbrellas.

Gingerly, I purchased only one umbrella at a time to test the waters of this new venture. First, I gave an umbrella to an acquaintance facing surgery. "Into each life some rain must fall. I hope that sunny days are ahead," I explained. As it turned out, her surgery wasn't successful, and I felt utterly foolish. Then she sent me this note: "Thanks for that beautiful umbrella. I can't explain it, but each time I look at it, I feel so loved."

Soon after, a friend whose son had left home telephoned. "Could you just come and spend the evening with me?" she asked. I took her an umbrella, and without saying a word, I prayed that God's "son"shine would touch her home and shield her from the storms.

As time went on, I discovered wonderful umbrellas on sale at record low prices. I discreetly stashed some in a hallway closet and tucked others in a sack in the back seat of my car. "Please show people that you are the real source of these umbrellas," I prayed. And, with few words exchanged, the recipients amazingly understood that the umbrellas symbolized both friendship and God's blanket of protection.

It had seemed at first to be the kind of undertaking I could keep hidden, camouflaged in the secret corners of my heart, my closet and my car. I chose my umbrella recipients with precision—people whose paths never crossed, out-of-towners and total strangers; a colleague who had lost her job; a friend who moved to a new city; an innkeeper who operates a bed-and-breakfast establishment; a farmer selling tomatoes at a roadside stand; friends facing a monsoon of difficulty and passersby who seemed to need a bit of encouragement.

But unbeknownst to me, the word of my "umbrella fixation" leaked out. One day, I ran into shelves of lovely umbrellas at a nearby glassware outlet. "I have a feeling you're the umbrella lady," the manager quipped with a curious glance at my armful of finds. "I've heard all about you, and do I have a deal for you! They got us mixed up with another company and sent us their overstock of umbrellas." I scooped up another one, featuring a perky apple motif, sure to charm any teacher.

The following week, a retired teacher from Arizona telephoned me. "I read your recent article on the teacher in one of the crafts magazines," she explained. "I'll be passing through West Virginia, and I'd like to meet you."

After we arranged our meeting, I asked a friend, "What do you think about me giving her an umbrella? I just bought that one with red apples splattered all over it."

"I wouldn't do that if I were you," she said. "It doesn't seem very professional. And, besides, you've never even met her before. She'll think you're crazy."

So, dressed in the "proper" clothes and prepared to say the "proper" words, I drove to the restaurant where we were to meet. As I opened my door, the skies opened in a sudden downpour. After I located the teacher in the lobby, she admitted with a lighthearted laugh: "Can you believe I forgot to pack an umbrella? Where I live, we haven't had any rain for weeks."

I instantly regretted having no umbrella for her. *Why had I not trusted my own instincts? Why had I sought someone else's opinion and allowed another person to put a damper on my umbrella ministry?*

The next morning, I wrapped the frivolous apple-print umbrella with *practical* plain brown paper, tied it up with a piece of heavy, *serviceable* twine, and addressed it to my new friend. I was certain she, too, could use something pretty as well as practical.

"Another umbrella?" the postmistress queried when I placed it on the counter. By now, she was familiar with the contents of my ubiquitous, long, slender boxes. "Oh, this one's bound for Arizona," she chuckled, as the relentless rain poured outside. "An umbrella headed for the desert . . . now, *that's* a new one."

I smiled to myself at the wonder of how an umbrella—such a simple object—when received unexpectedly can brighten just about anyone's day and help people from all walks of life feel cared for and protected. Never again, I promised myself, would I allow anyone to squelch an inner prompting to reach out to someone else, no matter how trivial it seemed. This time it had been a compelling urge to give away umbrellas, but in the future there would be other ideas, other opportunities, and I must never disregard them.

When I turned on the car radio, I heard the weatherman's grim prediction: "More rain expected tomorrow, for the third day in a row."

But I've been growing rather fond of precipitation. For hidden deep in my heart is God's bright forecast: "Continued showers of blessing."

Roberta L. Messner

A Million-Dollar Smile

The only ones among you who will be really happy are those who will have sought and found how to serve.

Albert Schweitzer

"You don't love me. No one loves me," the little girl whispered, her lower lip quivering and her hollow eyes dropping to the floor. Uncombed hair, wrinkled and soiled clothes, chapped hands and ragged fingernails were all convincing evidence that she perhaps was right. But she did not look much different from many of the other children in her class. Most came from a decidedly poverty-ridden neighborhood where broken couches sat on front porches and junk cars rusted in front yards.

The response of the sad little girl stunned Bernard Rapoport, a tall, slightly stooped octogenarian with a commanding presence. He was the leader of one thousand volunteers spending one hour a week helping children learn to read. The hour he had just spent with this little girl was a struggle—for her and for him. Learning to read was obviously not high on her list of priorities.

Wanting to encourage her, he had said, "I love you." The ravages of poverty and neglect had taken their toll on her, and she had given her honest reply to this well-intentioned man.

Poverty was nothing new for Bernard Rapoport. He grew up in it. "But being poor was different when I was a kid," he says, "for there was hope we could improve our lot in life." The son of a Russian-born Jewish Bolshevik, Rapoport counts himself lucky. His parents, deprived of higher education themselves, placed great value on learning and knowledge. "In a house of less than one thousand square feet, we had a library—one room was entirely dedicated to books," he remembers.

His parents' emphasis on education and hard work paid off. Rapoport finished high school and went on to college where he studied hard, attending class in the morning and working on a job until early evening. Then in 1942 he married Audre, now his wife of fifty-five-plus years. With a twenty-five-thousand-dollar loan from her family, he founded an insurance company. With Rapoport's business know-how and his Herculean appetite for hard work, his company succeeded beyond anyone's expectations. It provided Rapoport a good living, but even more important, in his estimation, is that it provided him a "good giving." Over the years, he and Audre have given millions of dollars to worthwhile causes, and in 1997 they were named among the top twenty-five philanthropists in the United States.

Hard times taught Rapoport hard lessons—and gave him a tender spot for those in need. After he had grandchildren, he became acutely aware of the destitute situation of many younger children. "I knew from my own experience that education is vital to success—and reading is basic for succeeding in school and in almost anything," Rapoport points out. Believing that education is the escape from the clutches of poverty for the sad little girl and other victims of poverty, Rapoport says, "There's a big chasm between failure and success, and education is the bridge."

Before one of Rapoport's granddaughters was six, she had her own desk in his corporate headquarters. One day she was visiting her grandfather and sitting at her desk when one of several top executives passing through the area asked her what her job was. "I run the company," she replied. The executive said, "I thought your grandpa ran the company."

"Well, he does," the granddaughter replied matter-of-factly and then added, "but I run him."

This granddaughter is not the only child who has captured Rapoport's heart. Rapoport wants to share his big heart with other children not so fortunate as his own grandchildren. When he learned that one thousand third-graders in the most economically depressed areas of his hometown could not read at grade level, he was sure he could find one thousand tutors, people who would give one hour of their time each week to help these children learn to read. This all-out volunteer effort became known as Waco One Thousand.

Rapoport's fervor for helping children is infectious. Following his lead, many of his employees are active members of his efforts to help children learn to read. While tutoring some young children, several volunteers noticed the obviously hand-me-down, ill-fitting, rag-a-tag shoes that most of the elementary school children wore. They joined forces with other Rapoport employees, raised approximately six thousand dollars and gave every child in that elementary school a new pair of name-brand tennis shoes. An employee nearing retirement in Rapoport's home office comments, "We saw Bernard's absolute ecstasy at spending his time and money on children, and we wanted to enjoy just a little bit of the fun and fulfillment."

In spite of being well past the age that most executives retire, Rapoport travels extensively, sometimes criss-crossing the country several times a week to visit his branch offices. But he still makes it a high priority to put in his one hour of tutoring each week. He points out, "The hour that the one thousand volunteers give each week is worth at least a million dollars—to help kids learn to read and to give them the encouragement and confidence that they can learn. So it's important that each one of us be there." If Rapoport absolutely has to miss one week, he makes up for it by doubling his hours the next week.

Recently Rapoport was completing his one-hour session with a little boy. The third-grader was clutching two books he had just finished reading. Rapoport put his arm around the little boy's shoulders and said, "I love you." Only a few months ago this little boy had looked just like the discouraged, despondent little girl. But now he stood tall and proud, obviously thrilled with his accomplishment. The youngster's smile broadened into an even bigger smile as he said, "I love you, too."

Rapoport's eyes sparkled as he savored the deep satisfaction of this well-earned response. Then Rapoport said, "Now that's a million-dollar smile!"

Paul J. Meyer

Uncle Li and Sarah Wong

If I can stop one Heart from breaking
I shall not live in vain
If I can ease one Life the Aching
Or cool one in Pain
Or help one fainting Robin
Unto his Nest again
I shall not live in Vain.

Emily Dickinson

In my work with women worldwide, I hear countless compelling stories of life and death—and love. Human emotions are the same the world over. The heartfelt yearning for understanding, forgiveness, acceptance and continuity of generations is universal as revealed in this human drama unfolding in Singapore—it could've been played out in the hearts of anyone anywhere in the world.

On this particular sun-drenched morning, I was filled with anticipation as I made my way to my favorite coffee shop. Eating breakfast in a coffee shop on the way to work is quite the norm in Singapore. I sat at my customary table enjoying the steaming hot sweet coffee and *pau*, a popular

Chinese bread. Screwing up my eyes against the glare, I looked out the door where I could see the corner of the sidewalk.

Something was missing—the usual vendor was not there. He was always there—his dilapidated bicycle propped up against the lime-green Chinese shops, his pile of newspapers stacked neatly by his side. I'd miss his toothy grin, his cheery *"Chou San"* (good morning) if he did not arrive in time for me to buy my morning paper.

Most of us regulars at the coffee shop felt a real affection for him and called him "Uncle," the Chinese term of respect. His seeming poverty did not hide his wisdom and graciousness. His wizened frame and goatee beard made him look like a sage. Uncle Li seemed to lend an air of stability and constancy to my life. He may have been merely a newspaper vendor, but his cheeriness—like the song of an early-morning bird—set the tone for the day. His *"Chou San"* brought a smile to all who bought a paper from him. Lighthearted banter constantly floated from his corner into the coffee shop.

Studying Uncle Li and his customers was my favorite morning pastime. A lovely young Chinese woman was the most interesting of all. Always immaculately dressed, she'd park her black car by the sidewalk, hop out, daintily run over to Uncle Li, buy a paper, and with a smile and greeting, away she'd go.

The emotions that crossed Uncle Li's wrinkled face when she appeared intrigued me. His smiling face softened, and then gaiety gave way to a deeper emotion, one that I was familiar with yet could not define. I felt baffled, but on the verge of a discovery.

So, each morning, like Uncle Li, I waited for the arrival of the beautiful young woman. Black glossy hair, bobbed and fringed, encircled a creamy magnolia-colored, heart-shaped face. Her dark eyes gave her a demure look. The most striking detail of her beauty lay in her smile, which lit up her face. Each day when she left, Uncle Li's face looked like the sun shadowed by a cloud.

Suddenly brakes shrieked, shattering my reverie and alarming the traffic on the busy street. Commotion followed. I craned my neck for a better view. What had happened? Who was hit? A crowd quickly gathered, obscuring my view. The babble of voices told me nothing, and I could not determine what had happened.

Curiosity urging me, I edged my way into the spectator crowd on the sidewalk. The first thing I saw was a bicycle tangled like a piece of modern sculpture. Loosened newspapers caught by the wind scattered across the street. Passersby picked them up; others crushed them underfoot in their eagerness to get closer to the scene. "God, please don't let it be Uncle Li," I prayed. Like a coward, I retraced my steps into the coffee shop and sat down to view the frenzy through the door.

Police and ambulance sirens soon added to the hubbub. A young woman upheld like a rag doll between two policemen entered the shop. It was the young woman who drove the black car! I couldn't believe it. The policemen gazed around the room imploringly. I gently took the girl's arm and guided her to my table. Relieved, the policemen explained that witnesses said it was not her fault, for the old man had lost control and swerved into her car. I further gathered that they could not locate his relatives, but she'd agreed to pay hospital expenses.

The young woman signed a form the policemen put in front of her. They then disappeared into the crowd, and I was left with the devastated woman. With trembling hands, she grasped the cup of coffee. Closing her eyes, she drank deeply from its comforting warmth.

Only moments before this tragedy, I had felt on the fringe of events like any other spectator. But with the distraught young woman seated before me, I was drawn into the morning's drama. Her face crumpling like a child's, she broke the silence, "I can't understand how the accident happened. The bicycle struck the car; it seemed to come from nowhere. Why did Uncle Li lose control?" Shaking her head, she whispered through her tears, "How could this happen?"

Looking at me she implored, "Please, come with me to the hospital." I agreed and rang the office on my mobile phone to explain I'd be late. She kept speaking. "I have to see him. I just have to see him and tell him how sorry I am." I could understand that for peace of mind she needed to see him comfortable, out of pain and alive.

She was not in a fit state to drive, so we took a taxi. It wove through the busy office traffic to the Singapore General Hospital. During most of the ride, we sat locked in our own thoughts. I pondered the morning's events and realized I knew very little about the striking young woman, not even her name! So I introduced myself and asked her name.

"My name's Sarah Wong."

"Do you have family, and is there someone we should call?"

"No, I was an orphan and brought up by a wealthy old lady. I call her Aunty." I learned her life had been secure with nothing disruptive or hurtful except for the void in her heart because she'd never known her parents.

"My aunt is quite old, and I would not wish to distress her about the accident." Sarah fingered the little diamond cross. No doubt a gift from her aunt, a symbol of her love and generosity.

We eventually got to the hospital. Sarah was as nervous as I was—concerned at what had happened to Uncle Li. We made inquiries and were told he was in the operating theatre. Our hushed wait began. My heart ached at the sight of Sarah's pinched, pathetic face. She caught my sympathetic gaze. A tremulous smile touched her soft, young mouth; I wanted so very much to allay her fears of Uncle Li's death.

Before long, a blue-robed doctor, his mask drawn down capping his chin, approached the waiting room. We got up to greet him as he looked expectantly around the room. He must have been informed about Sarah. The doctor explained, "Mr. Li's rib cage is badly injured, but we have managed to stem the internal bleeding." The doctor continued, "The old man is frail, and his life hangs by a thread. If he lives, he'll live with pain."

Sarah softly asked, "Can we see him?" The doctor allowed us to visit Uncle Li in intensive care.

Riddled with guilt and sorrow, Sarah was blaming herself and wondering how she could have avoided the accident. Her body shuddered. I put an arm across her sagging shoulders as we came to intensive care.

We were directed to Uncle Li's bed. Numerous tubes protruding from his body made him look like a collapsed puppet. His breathing labored and harsh, I expected at any moment to hear the death rattle rumble from his throat.

I had wanted so much for Sarah's sake for Uncle Li to live. But now for his sake, I wanted him to die. He'd never ride his bike again, never sell newspapers. We'd never hear again the cheery *"Chou San."* I dug into my pocket for a crumpled tissue to wipe away my relentless tears and noisily blew my nose while my young friend stood motionless, immobilized by sorrow.

Uncle Li struggled to open his eyes. They flickered and gradually opened. I saw a hint of a smile. I also saw something else—the emotion that had eluded me seemed to come alive as he peered at the young woman's face. I felt like an outsider, intruding on an intimate moment. Feebly he lifted a hand. She reached out and held it, too choked to utter words she'd rehearsed in her mind. The old man's face gathered strength, and the emotion I'd witnessed before was now reflected strongly in his face. He said to Sarah, *"Ngo ke chai"* (my child). Emotionally she responded, *"Ahpah"* (father).

The puzzle piece fell into place, and I recognized the elusive emotion. The indefinable had become definable. It was beautiful, like the brightness of the evening star, solitary in loveliness and suspended in space. In an unforgetable moment, love passed from a dying old man and filled the void in a young girl's heart—like the love of a father for his child. Smiling peacefully, Uncle Li fell into a contented sleep from which he'd never awaken.

Sarah and I became friends, bonded together by that fateful morning. We visited Uncle Li's sister, his only remaining relative. In her home, beside his picture, was the photograph of a young woman. I was startled. The resemblance was striking! I could have been looking at Sarah. Uncle Li's sister explained that the woman in the photograph was Uncle Li's wife. She'd died at childbirth, and their baby girl was stillborn. He'd loved his young wife dearly. He would have loved and treasured his daughter. Sarah had brought them both to life again, and in return Uncle Li had given Sarah a legacy of love.

Audrey Bowie

Greater Than a Super Bowl

*There is a loftier ambition than merely to stand
high in the world. It is to stoop down and lift
mankind a little higher.*

                                        Henry Van Dyke

I coached the World Champion Dallas Cowboys from
1960 until I retired in 1988. Except for a stint as a B-17
bomber pilot in World War II, my life has been focused on
football. I loved the rush of adrenaline before a game, the
exhilaration of making a touchdown, the roar of the
crowd, the thrill of each victory, the unique experience of
playing in the Super Bowl—and winning a couple of
times.

The deep satisfaction of coaching the players to learn to
discipline themselves, to develop their skills and to work
together as a team was a driving force in my life.
Encouraging the players to pay the price for their achieve-
ments and earning the support of the fans were important
to me. But there's a part of my life that most of the millions of football fans do not know. My life centers around
God and family—and helping at-risk children.

For many years now I have served on the board of Happy Hill Farm, a children's home and special school located in the Texas hills, on the edge of the Dallas/Fort Worth Metroplex. We simply call it the Farm; it is a five-hundred-acre working farm complete with horses, cattle and most important, more than one hundred hurting, troubled children whose families are unable or unwilling to help them.

I've seen some great victories on the football field, but far greater are the victories I've witnessed in hundreds of kids since Ed and Gloria Shipman opened their hearts and home about twenty-five years ago. Some kids have survived unimaginable horrors and carry horrendous emotional scars with them. But more often than not, these battered kids leave the Farm with their lives repaired, a high school diploma in hand, ready to take on the world again.

Although each kid is special, I remember some more than others. I'll never forget John, a frail little boy living with his mother in an abandoned car in a Fort Worth garbage dump before coming to the Farm. And Frieda, a young girl who had been sexually abused by her step-father and brother. And Jack, whose father abandoned his family, leaving a single mom and a young son who wanted to die. Jack had tried to take his life before coming to live on the Farm. And Amy, whose parents were in prison. Amy would have been killed had her desperate grandmother not found Happy Hill Farm.

And then there was Tip, a great kid from a small Texas town not far from Happy Hill Farm. Tip's background was plagued with all kinds of problems, but when he slugged a teacher, a judge referred him to the Farm. Tip was only twelve, but he was large for his age. It was hard to tell that his hair was red because his father kept it shaved. "It's easier to see the lice," Tip quipped.

Tip had been labeled "white trash." Because his family's shack had no indoor plumbing, they got their drinking water from a well and bathed in a nearby creek. Personal hygiene and social skills were not high among the family's priorities. Tip was uncoordinated, unmotivated and volatile. After being sent to the Farm, he had to be taught how to use a knife and fork. Having spent so much time outdoors, he had to be coaxed to sleep indoors on a bed. I recall how Tip would ramble through the house, knocking over vases and lamps as he gestured to make a point. But Tip didn't really need to gesture because every other word coming out of his mouth was an expletive.

"I hate all these rules!" Tip screamed more than once. But there was one fate Tip would have hated worse— being confined in a juvenile jail. Because Tip had heard what it was like and concluded he wanted to stay out at all costs, he began trying to follow the Farm's rules.

Yet persuading Tip to sit in a classroom took days. Encouraging him to study at all required weeks. Replacing his profanity with more appropriate language took months and months. Perhaps the biggest challenge, though, was removing the chip from Tip's shoulder. Large doses of unconditional love and consistent discipline were required to instill in Tip trust for authority figures and society in general.

But I watched Tip slowly change. Over the years as coach of the Cowboys, I saw a lot of impressive changes, as players became more disciplined, more skilled and more motivated. But the changes I saw in Tip and other bruised and suffering kids like him were far more dramatic than anything I had seen on the football field.

Tip finally graduated from the Farm's high school. He was the first person in his large family ever to stay in school long enough to graduate. Tip was also the first male in his family not to serve time in a Texas prison. Tip's accomplishments were among the greatest points I have ever seen scored. But more championship feats in Tip's turbulent life were yet to come.

After graduating from high school, Tip went to work in the oilfields of West Texas. He saved his money and had plumbing installed in his family's house. He bought his mother a car. He helped his sisters go to school. He returned to his small hometown to work as a mechanic. Tip is now married and has four children.

The dehumanizing cycle of poverty, brutality and imprisonment has been broken for Tip. His overcoming almost insurmountable obstacles in his childhood is an incredible victory I feel privileged to have shared even a small part in. I love football—always have, always will— but mending the lives and hearts of boys and girls like John, Frieda, Jack, Amy and Tip gives me a sense of satisfaction like no other thrill. Giving them a fair chance at living their dreams is a victory far greater than a Super Bowl.

Tom Landry

[EDITORS' NOTE: *Names of children have been changed for privacy.*]

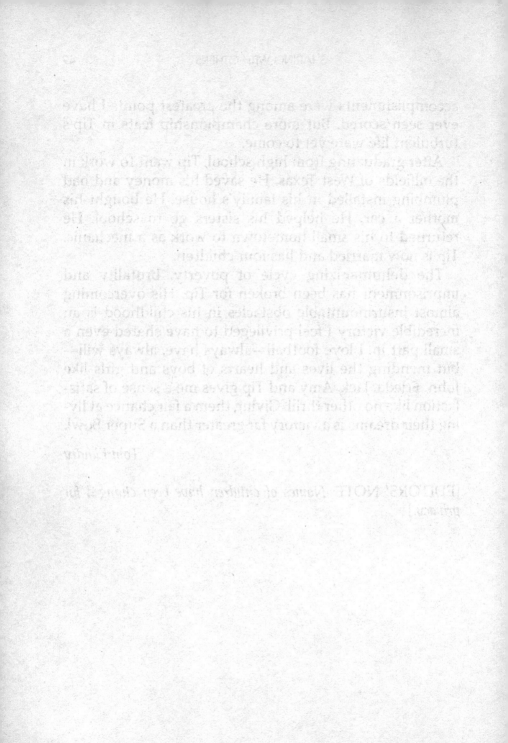

3

ACROSS THE GENERATIONS

*H*onor the old, teach the young.

Old Danish Proverb

DENNIS THE MENACE

"Look, Mom. Grandpa says I've got your old seat."

The Inventive Generation

Life is a series of collisions with the future.

José Ortega y Gasset

Once, at the University of California, a student got up to say that it was impossible for people of Ronald Reagan's generation to understand the next generation of young people. "You grew up in a different world," the student said. "Today we have television, jet planes, space travel, nuclear energy, computers. . . ."

When the student paused for breath, Ronnie said, "You're right. We didn't have those things when we were young. We invented them."

Nancy Reagan with William Novak
My Turn: The Memoirs of Nancy Reagan
Submitted by Tonette Holle

Love Is a Grandparent

If I'd known grandchildren were going to be so much fun, I'd have had them first.

Erma Bombeck

A preschooler who lives down the street was curious about grandparents. It occurred to me that, to a child, grandparents appear like an apparition with no explanation, no job description and few credentials. They just seem to go with the territory.

This, then, is for the little folks who wonder what a grandparent is.

A grandparent can always be counted on to buy all your cookies, flower seeds, all-purpose greeting cards, transparent tape, paring knives, peanut brittle and ten chances on a pony. (Also a box of taffy when they have dentures.)

A grandparent helps you with the dishes when it is your night.

A grandparent will sit through a Greek comedy for three hours to watch her grandson and wonder how Aristophanes has time to write plays when he is married to Jackie Onassis.

A grandparent is the only baby-sitter who doesn't charge more after midnight—or anything before midnight.

A grandparent buys you gifts your mother says you don't need.

A grandparent arrives three hours early for your baptism, your graduation and your wedding because he or she wants a seat where he or she can see everything.

A grandparent pretends he doesn't know who you are on Halloween.

A grandparent loves you from when you're a bald baby to a bald father and all the hair in between.

A grandparent will put a sweater on you when she is cold, feed you when she is hungry and put you to bed when she is tired.

A grandparent will brag about you when you get a typing pin that eighty other girls got.

A grandparent will frame a picture of your hand that you traced and put it in her Mediterranean living room.

A grandparent will slip you money just before Mother's Day.

A grandparent will help you with your buttons, your zippers and your shoelaces and not be in any hurry for you to grow up.

When you're a baby, a grandparent will check to see if you are crying when you are sound asleep.

When a grandchild says, "Grandma, how come you didn't have any children?" a grandparent holds back the tears.

Erma Bombeck
Submitted by Tonette Holle

THE FAMILY CIRCUS.　　By Bil Keane

"Oh no! Here comes Spencer with more
pictures of his grandparents."

Kids on Grandparents

some of them are not
so old, But I think you
are supposed to be
at least 50.

Wendy,
7 1/2

Grandpas and Grandmas
are the ones who always
love you and never yell
no matter how many
dumb things you do.

Edward, 10

I love them because that's what they're there for.

Ashley, 8 years old

When we go to Grandma's for Easter dinner everyone's there. My Aunts and Uncles and my cousins too. And we eat for hours and hours. You could bust, and everybody shouts and laughs and they tell stories. We have a great time. The food is nice but the laughing and the stories are best.

Kevin, 11

Stuart Hample and Eric Marshall

Change of Heart

Each of us can make a difference in the life of another.

George Bush

When our youngest sister was born sixty years ago, my little brother was six and I was eight. I had always been the "Big Sister" and he had always been "The Baby."

Our sister's arrival was a complete surprise to both of us. In those days no one worried much about sibling rivalry, and no "experts" told us how to deal with another child in the house. We had wise and loving grandparents, however.

I was thrilled about the baby and loved to hold her and help care for her. My brother's feelings were quite different! He looked at her briefly and left, preferring to spend the evening in his room. When I went to his room to talk to him and try to get him to play games with me, he just looked away.

"Why did they have to go and get that old baby?"

Later that night, Grandpa came over to see the new baby. As he held her, he said to my brother, "You know, she's a lot like that lamb I'm raising on the bottle. I have to take care of her and feed her often, just the way your Mama does with the baby."

My brother said, "I'd rather have the lamb" under his breath, but just loud enough for Grandpa to hear.

Even though Grandpa seemed pretty old to me (at least fifty, I figured), he could hear very well, and he heard my brother's muttered comment.

"Well," said Grandpa, "if you'd rather have a lamb, maybe we could trade. I'll give you a day to think it over, and if you still want to trade tomorrow, we'll do it."

I thought I saw him wink at Mama, but I knew I must have been mistaken because Grandpa never winked at anyone.

After Grandpa left, Mama asked my brother if he wanted her to read to him. He cuddled up beside her, and she read to him for a long while.

He kept looking at the baby, and Mama asked him to hold his little sister while she went to get a diaper. When Mama came back, my brother was gently touching the baby's smooth black hair, and as he held her hand, she grasped his finger.

"Mama, look! She's holding my hand!"

"Sure, she knows you're her big brother," Mama smiled. He held the baby for a few more minutes, and he seemed much happier at bedtime. Grandpa came back the next evening as he had promised and called my brother to talk to him.

"Well, are you ready to trade the baby for a lamb?"

My brother looked surprised that Grandpa had remembered the bargain.

"She's worth two lambs now."

Grandpa seemed to be taken aback at this breach of contract. He said that he'd have to think it over and would be back the next night to talk about it.

The next day was a Saturday, and my brother and I

spent much of the day indoors watching the baby have her bath, watching her sleep and holding her. My brother held her three more times that day. He looked worried when Grandpa came to see us that evening and called him over to talk.

"You know, I've thought about that baby-and-lamb trade all day, and you really do drive a hard bargain. I've decided, though, that the baby is probably worth two lambs. I think we can do business."

My brother hesitated very briefly before answering Grandpa. "She's a whole day older now, and I think she's worth five lambs."

Grandpa looked shocked, and he slowly shook his head. "I don't know. I'll have to go home and give your offer some serious thought. Maybe I'll have to talk it over with my banker."

Grandpa left soon after, and my brother seemed worried. I tried to get him to play some games with me, but he went to Mama's room and held the baby for a long time.

The next day, Sunday, Grandpa came to visit us in the early afternoon. He told my brother he had come early because if he had to round up five lambs and get a room ready for the baby, he'd need an early start.

My brother took a deep breath, looked Grandpa squarely in the eye and made an announcement.

"The baby is worth fifty lambs now!"

Grandpa looked at him in disbelief and shook his head. "I'm afraid the deal's off. I can't afford fifty lambs for one little baby. I guess you'll have to keep her and help your parents take care of her."

My brother turned away with a little smile he didn't know I saw, and this time I really did see Grandpa wink at Mama.

Muriel J. Bussman
Submitted by Winnie Luttrell

Minimaxims for My Godson

*Just as the wave cannot exist for itself, but must
always participate in the swell of the ocean, so
we can never experience life by ourselves, but
must always share the experience of life that
takes place all around us.*

Albert Schweitzer

Dear Sandy,

Your nice thank-you note for the graduation
present I sent you a few weeks ago just came in,
and I've been chuckling over your postscript in
which you say that such presents are dandy but
you wish someone could give you "half a dozen
foolproof ideas for bending the world into a pretzel."

Well, Sandy, I must admit I don't have any
very original thoughts of my own. But through
the years I've encountered a few ideas of that
kind—not platitudes but ideas sharp-pointed
enough to stick in my mind permanently.
Concepts that release energy, make problem-
solving easier, provide shortcuts to worthwhile

goals. No one handed them over in a neat package. They just came along from time to time, usually from people not in the wisdom-dispensing business at all. Compared to the great time-tested codes of conduct, they may seem like pretty small change. But each of them has helped make my life a good deal easier and happier and more productive.

So here they are. I hope you find them useful, too.

If you can't change facts, try bending your attitudes. Without a doubt, the bleakest period of my life so far was the winter of 1942 to 1943. I was with the Eighth Air Force in England. Our bomber bases, hacked out of the sodden English countryside, were seas of mud. On the ground, people were cold, miserable and homesick. In the air, people were getting shot. Replacements were few; morale was low.

But there was one sergeant—a crew chief—who was always cheerful, always good-humored, always smiling. I watched him one day, in a freezing rain, struggle to salvage a Fortress that had skidded off the runway into an apparently bottomless mire. He was whistling like a lark. "Sergeant," I said to him sourly, "how can you whistle in a mess like this?"

He gave me a mud-caked grin. "Lieutenant," he said, "when the facts won't budge, you have to bend your attitudes to fit them, that's all."

Check it for yourself, Sandy. You'll see that, faced with a given set of problems, one man may tackle them with intelligence, grace and courage; another may react with resentment and bitterness; a third may run away altogether.

In any life, facts tend to remain unyielding. But attitudes are a matter of choice—and that choice is largely up to you.

Don't come up to the net behind nothing. One night in a PTA meeting, a lawyer—a friend and frequent tennis partner of mine—made a proposal that I disagreed with, and I challenged it. But when I had concluded what I thought was quite a good spur-of-the-moment argument, my friend stood up and proceeded to demolish it. Where I had opinions, he had facts; where I had theories, he had statistics. He obviously knew so much more about the subject than I did that his viewpoint easily prevailed. When we met in the hall afterward, he winked and said, "You should know better than to come up to the net behind nothing!"

It is true; the tennis player who follows his own weak or badly placed shot up to the net is hopelessly vulnerable. And this is true when you rush into anything without adequate preparation or planning. In any important endeavor, you've got to do your homework, get your facts straight and sharpen your skills. In other words, don't bluff—because if you do, nine times out of ten, life will drill a backhand right past you.

When the ball is over, take off your dancing shoes. As a child, I used to hear my aunt say this, and it puzzled me a good deal, until the day I heard her spell out the lesson more explicitly. My sister had come back from a glamorous weekend full of glitter, exciting parties and stimulating people. She was bemoaning the contrast with her routine job, her modest apartment and her day-to-day friends. "Young lady," our aunt said gently, "no one lives on the top of the mountain. It's fine to go there occasionally—for inspiration, for new perspectives. But you have to come down. Life is lived in the valleys. That's where the farms and gardens and orchards are, and where the plowing and the work are done. That's where you apply the visions you may have glimpsed from the peaks."

It's a steadying thought when the time comes, as it always does, to exchange your dancing shoes for your working shoes.

Shine up your neighbor's halo. One Sunday morning, drowsing in a back pew of a little country church, I dimly heard the old preacher urge his flock to "stop worrying about your own halo and shine up your neighbor's!" And it left me sitting up, wide-awake, because it struck me as just about the best eleven-word formula for getting along with people that I've ever heard.

I like it for its implication that everyone, in some area of life, has a halo that's worth watching for and acknowledging. I like it for the firm way it shifts the emphasis from self to interest and concern for others. Finally, I like it because it reflects a deep psychological truth: People have a tendency to become what you expect them to be.

Keep one eye on the law of the echo. I remember very well the occasion when I heard this sharp-edged bit of advice. Coming home from boarding school, some of us youngsters were in the dining car of a train. Somehow the talk got around to the subject of cheating on exams, and one boy readily admitted that he cheated all the time. He said that he found it both easy and profitable.

Suddenly a mild-looking man sitting all alone at a table across the aisle—he might have been a banker, a bookkeeper, anything—leaned forward and spoke up. "Yes," he said directly to the apostle of cheating. "All the same—I'd keep one eye on the law of the echo if I were you."

The law of the echo—is there really such a thing? Is the universe actually arranged so that whatever you send out—honesty or dishonesty, kindness or cruelty—ultimately comes back to you? It's hard to be sure. And yet, since the beginning of recorded history, mankind has had the conviction, based partly on intuition, partly on observation, that in the long run a man does indeed reap what he sows.

You know as well as I do, Sandy, that in this misty area there are no final answers. Still, as the man said, "I think I'd keep one eye on the law of the echo if I were you!"

Don't wear your raincoat in the shower. In the distant days when I was a Boy Scout, I had a troop leader who was an ardent woodsman and naturalist. He would take us on hikes, not saying a word, and then challenge us to describe what we had observed: trees, plants, birds, wildlife, everything. Invariably we hadn't seen a quarter as much as he had, nor half enough to satisfy him. "Creation is all around you," he would cry, waving his arms in vast inclusive circles, "but you're keeping it out. Don't be a buttoned-up person! Stop wearing your raincoat in the shower!"

I've never forgotten the ludicrous image of a person standing in the shower with a raincoat buttoned up to his chin.

The best way to discard that raincoat, I've found, is to expose yourself to new experiences in your life all your life.

All these phrases that I have been recalling really urge one to the same goal: a stronger participation, a deeper involvement in life. This doesn't come naturally, by any means. And yet, with marvelous impartiality, each of us is given exactly the same number of minutes and hours in every day. Time is the raw material. What we do with it is up to us.

A wise man once said that tragedy is not what we suffer, but what we miss. Keep that in mind, Sandy.

Your affectionate godfather.

Arthur Gordon

"And if you ever want more advice, Daniel, my e-mail address is *grandpa@x.com.*"

From the Wall Street Journal. Reprinted by permission by Cartoon Features Syndicate.

Help for the Helper

It is one of the most beautiful compensations of life that no man can sincerely try to help another without helping himself.

Ralph Waldo Emerson

At age eighteen, I left my home in Brooklyn, New York, and went off to study history at Leeds University in Yorkshire, England. It was an exciting but stressful time in my life, for while trying to adjust to the novelty of unfamiliar surroundings, I was still learning to cope with the all-too-familiar pain of my father's recent death—an event with which I had not yet come to terms.

While at the market one day, trying to decide which bunch of flowers would best brighten up my comfortable but colorless student digs, I spied an elderly gentleman having difficulty holding onto his walking stick and his bag of apples. I rushed over and relieved him of the apples, giving him time to regain his balance.

"Thanks, luv," he said in that distinctive Yorkshire lilt I never tire of hearing. "I'm quite all right now, not to worry," he said, smiling at me not only with his mouth but with a pair of dancing bright blue eyes.

"May I walk with you?" I inquired. "Just to make sure those apples don't become sauce prematurely."

He laughed and said, "Now, you are a long way from home, lass. From the States, are you?"

"Only from one of them. New York. I'll tell you all about it as we walk."

So began my friendship with Mr. Burns, a man whose smile and warmth would very soon come to mean a great deal to me.

As we walked, Mr. Burns (whom I always addressed as such and never by his first name) leaned heavily on his stick, a stout, gnarled affair that resembled my notion of a biblical staff. When we arrived at his house, I helped him set his parcels on the table and insisted on lending a hand with the preparations for his "tea"—that is, his meal. I interpreted his weak protest as gratitude for the assistance.

After making his tea, I asked if it would be all right if I came back and visited with him again. I thought I'd look in on him from time to time, to see if he needed anything. With a wink and a smile he replied, "I've never been one to turn down an offer from a good-hearted lass."

I came back the next day, at about the same time, so I could help out once more with his evening meal. The great walking stick was a silent reminder of his infirmity, and, though he never asked for help, he didn't protest when it was given. That very evening we had our first "heart to heart." Mr. Burns asked about my studies, my plans, and, mostly, about my family. I told him that my father had recently died, but I didn't offer much else about the relationship I'd had with him. In response, he gestured toward the two framed photographs on the end table next to his chair. They were pictures of two different women, one notably older than the other. But the resemblance between the two was striking.

"That's Mary," he said, indicating the photograph of the older woman. "She's been gone for six years. And that's our Alice. She was a very fine nurse. Losing her was too much for my Mary."

I responded with the tears I hadn't been able to shed for my own pain. I cried for Mary. I cried for Alice. I cried for Mr. Burns. And I cried for my father to whom I never had the chance to say good-bye.

I visited with Mr. Burns twice a week, always on the same days and at the same time. Whenever I came, he was seated in his chair, his walking stick propped up against the wall. Mr. Burns owned a small black-and-white television set, but he evidently preferred his books and phonograph records for entertainment. He always seemed especially glad to see me. Although I told myself I was delighted to be useful, I was happier still to have met someone to whom I could reveal those thoughts and feelings that, until then, I'd hardly acknowledged to myself.

While fixing the tea, our chats would begin. I told Mr. Burns how terribly guilty I felt about not having been on speaking terms with my father the two weeks prior to his death. I'd never had the chance to ask my father's forgiveness. And he had never had the chance to ask for mine.

Although Mr. Burns talked, he allowed me the lion's share. Mostly I recall him listening. But how he listened! It wasn't just that he was attentive to what I said. It was as if he were reading me, absorbing all the information I provided, and adding details from his own experience and imagination to create a truer understanding of my words.

After about a month, I decided to pay my friend a visit on an "off day." I didn't bother to telephone as that type of formality did not seem requisite in our relationship. Coming up to the house, I saw him working in his garden, bending with ease and getting up with equal facility. I was dumbfounded. Could this be the same man who used that massive walking stick?

He suddenly looked in my direction. Evidently sensing my puzzlement over his mobility, he waved me over, looking more than a bit sheepish. I said nothing, but accepted his invitation to come inside.

"Well, luv. Allow me to make you a 'cuppa' this time. You look all done in."

"How?" I began. "I thought. . . ."

"I know what you thought, luv. When you first saw me at the market . . . well, I'd twisted my ankle a bit earlier in the day. Tripped on a stone while doing a bit of gardening. Always been a clumsy fool."

"But . . . when were you able to . . . walk normally again?"

Somehow, his eyes managed to look merry and contrite at the same time. "Ah, well, I guess that'll be the very next day after our first meeting."

"But why?" I asked, truly perplexed. Surely he couldn't have been feigning helplessness to get me to make him his tea every now and then.

"That second time you came 'round, luv, it was then I saw how unhappy you were. Feeling lonely and sad about your dad and all. I thought, well, the lass could use a bit of an old shoulder to lean on. But I knew you were telling yourself you were visiting me for my sake and not your own. Didn't think you'd come back if you knew I was fit. And I knew you were in sore need of someone to talk to. Someone older, older than your dad, even. And someone who knew how to listen."

"And the stick?"

"Ah. A fine stick, that. I use it when I walk the moors. We must do that together soon."

So we did. And Mr. Burns, the man I'd set out to help, helped me. He'd made a gift of his time, bestowing attention and kindness to a young girl who needed both.

Marlena Thompson

These Things I Wish for You

You cannot teach children to take care of them-selves unless you let them try. They will make mistakes; and out of these mistakes comes wis-dom.

H. W. Beecher

We tried so hard to make things better for our kids that we made them worse.

For my grandchildren, I'd know better.

I'd really like for them to know about hand-me-down clothes and homemade ice cream and leftover meat loaf. I really would.

My cherished grandson, I hope you learn humility by surviving failure and that you learn to be honest even when no one is looking.

I hope you learn to make your bed and mow the lawn and wash the car—and I hope nobody gives you a brand-new car when you are sixteen.

It will be good if at least one time you can see a baby calf born and you have a good friend to be with you if you ever have to put your old dog to sleep.

I hope you get a black eye fighting for something you believe in.

I hope you have to share a bedroom with your younger brother. And it is all right to draw a line down the middle of the room, but when he wants to crawl under the covers with you because he's scared, I hope you'll let him.

And when you want to see a Disney movie and your kid brother wants to tag along, I hope you take him.

I hope you have to walk uphill with your friends and that you live in a town where you can do it safely.

If you want a slingshot, I hope your father teaches you how to make one instead of buying one. I hope you learn to dig in the dirt and read books, and when you learn to use computers, you also learn how to add and subtract in your head.

I hope you get razzed by friends when you have your first crush on a girl, and that when you talk back to your mother you learn what Ivory soap tastes like.

May you skin your knee climbing a mountain, burn your hand on the stove and stick your tongue on a frozen flagpole.

I hope you get sick when someone blows smoke in your face. I don't care if you try beer once, but I hope you won't like it. And if a friend offers you a joint or any drugs, I hope you are smart enough to realize that person is not your friend.

I sure hope you make time to sit on a porch with your grandpa or go fishing with your uncle.

I hope your mother punishes you when you throw a baseball through a neighbor's window, and that she hugs you and kisses you when you give her a plaster of paris mold of your hand.

These things I wish for you—tough times and disappointment, hard work and happiness.

Lee Pitts

4

CELEBRATING LIFE

*B*e glad of life because it gives you the chance
   to love and to work and to play and to look
   up at the stars.

Henry Van Dyke

A Novel Experience

The rapture of being alive is the true experience of life.

Source Unknown

After I boarded the plane in Atlanta for the flight to Spokane, I eagerly opened a highly recommended novel. I anticipated seven relaxing hours of good reading. Just as the attendants were closing the doors for takeoff, a late passenger rushed on, breathlessly looking for her seat. Before I finished thinking, *I hope it's not the empty seat next to me,* the tiny bundle of energy plopped down right beside me and exclaimed, "Gracious, I thought I could never make this flight!" I closed my book and didn't open it again for the rest of the flight.

Her name was Thelma. She was from New York and was dressed stylishly. Her enthusiastic explanation of her life's work at a children's center in upstate New York captivated me. I could feel Thelma's dedication as she shared one story after another about the children. Her delightful sense of humor shone through as she described her all-out efforts to fill the role of surrogate grandmother to the many hurting children.

Thelma also told me of her daughter's recent tragic death from breast cancer and that she was flying to Spokane for a reunion with her son-in-law and his family. She was eager to meet and hold a new great-grandson and to see the lovely new home of her son-in-law on Lake Pend'Oreille, Idaho.

Thelma was obviously coming to terms with her daughter's death. She emphasized that her daughter had not wanted her to mourn but to continue her worthwhile work of helping children without parents. I silently prayed, *If I am ever faced with losing a child, let me handle it with her kind of courage, grace and dignity.*

I confided in Thelma that my trip to Spokane was one of compassion. Our youngest daughter, Debbie, had just divorced after twenty-two years of marriage and needed a "Mom fix." Debbie and I had talked endlessly by telephone, and mother's intuition told me she needed loving arms to hold her, along with words of encouragement.

As the plane landed, Thelma and I were astounded that the flight had passed so quickly. We exchanged addresses, promising to write. At the gate we each walked into the arms of waiting loved ones and turned to wave good-bye to each other.

My daughter and I had a wonderful visit. We shopped for items Debbie needed in her new apartment. We talked long into the nights, discussing her plans for the future. Debbie had decided to continue her photography business but needed my reassurance. I agreed that she had made a sound decision. Debbie's two children were in college, and it seemed for the first time in many years my daughter had the complete freedom to think and plan for herself. She held fast to the hope for renewed happiness. Winging my way back to Atlanta, I was confident that

Debbie would be just fine in her new life. I knew that a loving man who would appreciate her qualities was somewhere in her future.

Months later a ringing telephone hurried me into the kitchen, and a breathless voice said, "Hi, Mom! I have some exciting news for you. I've been dating a man who is great fun and loves to dance. His name is Don. And he's asked me to marry him. He's a widower with four grown children, a darling little grandson, and he has a beautiful new home on Lake Pend'Oreille, Idaho."

Flashing lights went off in my memory! I asked Debbie, "Would it be possible to call Don and ask him if he has a mother-in-law named Thelma, from New York?" I knew the answer before her return call.

Thelma's son-in-law Don and my daughter Debbie were married at the lovely home on Lake Pend'Oreille on March 7, 1993. Thelma carried on with her life after her daughter's death, and by her example she encouraged Don to go on living as well. The results? Debbie has a wonderful husband—every mother's dream for her daughter.

As for the bestselling novel I planned to read on that milestone flight from Atlanta to Spokane? Well, I eventually read it, and it was okay. But that opportune meeting with Thelma was just the beginning of a beautiful, unfolding story of life, love and family—much better than a book!

Phyllis S. Heinel

Together We Can Make It

We are all like one-winged angels. It's only when we help each other that we can fly.

Luciano deCrescenzo

Bob Butler lost his legs in a 1965 land mine explosion in Vietnam. He returned home a war hero. Twenty years later, he proved once again that heroism comes from the heart.

Butler was working in his garage in a small town in Arizona on a hot summer day when he heard a woman's screams coming from a nearby house. He rolled his wheelchair toward the house, but the dense shrubbery wouldn't allow him access to the back door. So the veteran got out of his chair and crawled through the dirt and bushes.

"I had to get there," he says. "It didn't matter how much it hurt."

When Butler arrived at the house, he traced the screams to the pool, where a three-year-old girl was lying at the bottom. She had been born without arms and had fallen in the water and couldn't swim. Her mother stood over her baby screaming frantically. Butler dove to the bottom of the pool and brought little Stephanie up to the deck. Her face was blue, she had no pulse and she was not breathing.

Butler immediately went to work performing CPR to revive her while Stephanie's mother telephoned the fire department. She was told the paramedics were already out on a call. Helplessly, she sobbed and hugged Butler's shoulder.

As Butler continued with his CPR, he calmly reassured Stephanie's mother. "Don't worry," he said. "I was her arms to get out of the pool. It'll be okay. I'm now her lungs. Together we can make it."

Seconds later the little girl coughed, regained consciousness and began to cry. As they hugged and rejoiced together, the mother asked Butler how he knew it would be okay.

"When my legs were blown off in the war, I was all alone in a field," he told her. "No one was there to help except a little Vietnamese girl. As she struggled to drag me into her village, she whispered in broken English, 'It okay. You can live. I be your legs. Together we make it.'"

"This was my chance," he told Stephanie's mom, "to return the favor."

Dan Clark

A Second Chance

The question is not whether we will die, but how we will live.

Joan Borysenko

Sitting up in the hospital bed, Buddy smiled and reassured his wife, Ruth, "I'll be waltzing you across the dance floor again soon." Ruth nodded and squeezed his hand a little tighter. Looking at the man she loved, she knew this ordeal had frightened him much more than he would ever show. But Buddy was not the kind of man to let a thing like a mild heart attack dampen his spirits. Instead, he was making a concerted effort to put everyone at ease. Besides, the doctors assured him that he could go home in a few days. So Buddy's mood was even more jovial than usual, joking and winking at his wife.

That changed in an instant as Buddy's expression suddenly went blank. He called out, "Ruth, everybody, come closer—quick!" He then quietly began to recite his confirmation verse, and continued with the Lord's Prayer, asking everyone to say it with him. Then, Buddy looked up at his family and said, "This is it—I love you all. Good-bye . . ."

Ruth cried out, "Help him!" as she felt his hand go limp in hers. The room was immediately filled with doctors and nurses, and the panic-stricken family was pushed from the room. Ruth watched helplessly from the hall.

Buddy was watching, too, but not from the hall. Floating above all the commotion, he was looking calmly down at the frantic scene. Suddenly, he felt himself being pulled through a tunnel of brilliant light. He could see the most beautiful view up ahead. It was like nothing he had ever seen before, and he knew it was not a dream.

Ahead, he saw a mountain covered with flowers from the foot to the peak. Each bloom exploded in brilliant color, and not even the tiniest blossom was hidden from view by leaves or stems. At the bottom of the mountain, Buddy saw a figure cloaked in pure light at the center of a group of people. Buddy knew he was in the presence of God.

A little girl wearing a nightgown stood nearby. The child smiled up at him, then walked to the figure whose arms were outstretched to greet her. Buddy began walking toward the shining figure, an overwhelming sensation of peace and joy growing stronger with each step. Then, with only a few feet to go, he could go no farther. The figure put up a hand and spoke, "Stop, it's not time. Go back."

Buddy's eyes fluttered open. For an instant the light still filled his hospital room, but then it was gone. Past the doctors and nurses Buddy could see his worried family, and he smiled. Ruth blew him a kiss, looked up and whispered, "Thank you."

"It was a massive heart attack." That was the doctor's diagnosis the day all Buddy's vital signs had indeed stopped. Triple-bypass surgery was successful a week later, and in time Buddy regained his strength and his health.

But from then on that vision was never far from him, and neither were those words: "Stop, it's not time. Go back."

Ruth and Buddy knew more than ever that each day they had together was a special gift. Dozens of family members and friends were invited to a golden celebration for their forty-fifth wedding anniversary instead of waiting for a fiftieth anniversary to celebrate their long marriage. At the toast, Ruth told everyone, "Buddy and I believe that as long as you are celebrating together, every year is golden."

Buddy enjoyed each day with renewed appreciation. The smell of fresh-cut grass, the taste of iced tea on a hot summer day, the laughter of a friend, offering comfort by letting someone cry on his shoulder—these were things far too precious to take for granted.

Twelve years later, while he was resting in the shade of his favorite tree, Buddy's spirit left his body again. Without a doubt, that shining figure spoke to him in a strong, reassuring voice, "Come with me. Now is the time," and welcomed him home with outstretched arms.

I remember walking in at my dad's funeral and seeing more people in that church building than I had ever seen there before. People were standing in the aisles and outside the doors of the sanctuary. Everyone spoke of the glimpse of heaven Daddy had seen for a moment more than a decade before. The thought was comforting in facing the awful pain of his death, but I noticed something more about life, too.

Although I knew my dad was a special person, I had no idea until his funeral how many other people felt the same way. I realized that a successful life is measured by how you live and love in the time you are given. Daddy was given a second lease on life and made the most of it, not by getting busier, but by enjoying it more fully. And spending it on people. That's what second chances are for.

Renae Pick

Happy Anniversary

Reflect upon your present blessings. . . .

Charles Dickens

Often, after she finished her solitary supper, she would just sit at the kitchen table in no hurry to enter the rest of the house which seemed even emptier at night. She would remember how everyone used to rush off after they had eaten—the boys up to their rooms and Peter to his favorite TV news programs.

Always so much to do and it seemed at times the boys would never grow up so she could have at least a little time to herself. Time for herself. Oh my, she had lots of time now, big blocks of time which filled so little space in her life. Especially now with Peter gone.

They had planned to travel a little after the boys all left, only Peter had been part of a different plan. She would give anything to have those frenzied days back again, but of course it was impossible. There was her volunteer work and the house work and the occasional baking for bake sales, but she missed the noise and she would have been happy to hear the angry voices in the midst of a fight. "Ma, he took my shirt without asking" and "Ma, he won't let me study." Ma, Ma, Ma. Sometimes she had wanted to throttle them, and now she wanted only to hug them and hold them close. She looked at babies on the street and felt sad, remembering when her arms were also full.

She was being especially silly tonight, and she had told Charlotte, one of her neighbors who had dropped by earlier, that today would have been her fortieth anniversary and they had talked of a special celebration this year. Foolish woman. After Charlotte left she had baked the chocolate blackout cake that had been a favorite of Peter's, and there it sat in the refrigerator, awaiting its trip to the table.

Last year the boys had all called, and they had laughed and talked about the big forty and how they would all celebrate, only there was nothing to celebrate now. In fact, no one had called, but you really couldn't observe a wedding anniversary with half a couple, could you? At least that's what she had said to Charlotte, who kind of clicked her teeth at her and looked sad.

Feeling sorry for herself, was she? *Come on, gal,* she scolded herself, let's get our act together and have a big slice of cake and maybe some treats for Max, who must have read her mind because he began to bark. Poor old Max. He had been Peter's dog, waiting for him by the door each night till he came home. Some nights he still waited at the door which never opened, jumping up and barking at the slightest noise.

Like tonight. What was he barking at? He thought he owned the street, maybe even the world, but certainly anything on this block was his terrain. Tonight something was setting him off. So she walked over to the window to see what it was. There was only a car. "For heaven's sake, Max," she admonished, "we're not the only people on the street." Maybe Mrs. Boris, another neighbor, was having company. She had a big family and they came often to visit their parents.

But Max kept right on, and she thought she heard a noise at the door. Never fearful of the dark or the unknown, she went to the door, flung it open and said, "See, Max—there's no one—oh my Lord!" They were standing there, the three of them, and they yelled, "Surprise, surprise" and suddenly there were hugs and kisses everywhere—her boys had come home.

"I didn't think you'd remember and besides, with Dad . . ." Her voice trailed off in a blur of tears.

"Ma," that was Josh's voice, "you and Dad were always here for us, always in our hearts and our memories, and every anniversary will be our special day." The others nodded, and now the tears were rolling down her face. "Hey, Ma, where's the cake?" That was Chuck's voice. "We want to party." Suddenly she smiled and ran back to the kitchen, thanking the divine force that had directed her to bake her cake today and had given her three wonderful sons.

Evelyn Marder Levin

A Matter of Life and Death

*D*o *not complain about growing older—many*
are denied the privilege.

Robert Russell

My mother's wedding ring and some of her other personal valuables were in my purse. Happy and grateful
that my mother had come through heart surgery successfully, I was going to the hospital to pick her up. Carey, my
happy-go-lucky two-year-old son, was with me in the car
as I maneuvered through Houston's busiest freeway
exchange. Then something happened that marked 1976 as
the year that changed my life—a terrifying explosion. I
remember it with every breath I take—literally.

Traffic came to a riveting halt. Stunned by the sudden
shock of it all, I jumped out of the car with Carey right
behind me. A strange stench choked me and stung my
eyes, and then a huge cloud of toxic fumes enveloped
Carey and me. I grabbed Carey and darted back into the
car and closed the door. All the while, Carey was screaming, "Help me, Mommy. I hurt!" Frantic, I wrapped Carey

in my suit jacket and lay on top of him, trying to protect him from the deadly fumes. Between passing out and throwing up, I tried to honk the horn in desperate hopes that someone would hear it and rescue us. Finally, after I hit the windshield wipers, someone pointed rescuers our way.

Later we found out that the highway holocaust had been caused by a truck pulling a large tank of anhydrous ammonia. The hitch broke, causing the trailer and tank to fall off the upper freeway and onto the lower freeway where I was driving. Fourteen people were killed instantly, and more than two hundred hospitalized. Carey and I were the only two survivors in the area where the explosion had ripped the freeway apart.

After the accident, Carey spent two-and-a-half months in the hospital, and I was there for more than a year. After that, live-in nurses stayed in my home for about two-and-a-half years. Carey and I both received around-the-clock love and attention from my husband. Before the accident, we all enjoyed a wonderful life. We climbed mountains, we went on trips and family outings together, and we even enjoyed our routine workaday life. But in 1976, all that changed. I was an invalid, blind, unable to breathe on my own and certainly not able to care for my two-year-old, my other children, nor my husband.

After a couple of years, I began getting better even though I still took antibiotics every day and breathing treatments three or four times daily. Then I'd suffer set-backs so serious the doctors would call all my family in to be with me while I died. But each time I miraculously rallied.

Different parts of my body gave out at different times. For example, I was blind a great deal of the time until I had a two-cornea transplant. Coping with blindness when I had enjoyed such an active life before the accident was an agonizing struggle, but my lungs—damaged from breathing the toxic fumes—posed the most life-threatening challenges.

The time had come when there was no longer a choice. I simply could not breathe on my own anymore. I was in the hospital for two months on a ventilator, but the doctors said they couldn't consider me for a lung transplant because I was in such poor condition.

I refused to give up hope. Too many people were praying for me. God had already worked numerous miracles in my life—just to be alive was the greatest one.

As I lay in the hospital teetering on a tightrope between life and death, I was told that a donor had been found.

I asked my husband Don to call our minister for me to talk to before I went into the operating room. My husband could not find our minister, so I asked him to find John Morgan, my brother's minister. When John came into my room, he said to me, "You are not going to believe this! Something has happened that I'm not going to tell you about until you wake up after your surgery." I was curious, of course, but I was simply too weak to interrogate him. John prayed with me that I would make it through surgery even though I was in critical condition.

After the surgery, when it looked like I was going to survive, my husband explained to me the miracle John had alluded to. "Last Sunday when we prayed in church for you, a young man and his family were there. His name was Jason. Later that day, Jason was shot and killed in a tragic act of violence. Jason is your donor."

Don filled in more details. "Jason's parents would not have even thought about Jason's being a donor if John had not prayed specifically for you that morning in church and mentioned your name." My husband continued, "Numerous people were on the waiting list—some for over a year. But Jason was the right size for you and the right blood type and had all the other technical compatibilities. Mickey, you were the only one right for Jason's lungs."

One day when I was still in the hospital recuperating from the transplant, a man came into my intensive care room and asked Don, "Is Mickey Johnson your wife?"

Of course, my husband responded, "Yes." The man explained, "My father is in the hospital here, too, and I have come to see him." He then said, slowly and deliberately, "I was also Jason's schoolteacher." He continued, "I brought all these letters Jason's classmates wrote to your wife."

I cried as I read each letter. They were the most beautiful testimony to a teenager—or anybody—I had ever read. They talked about what a fine young man Jason was and how thrilled he would be that he was able to give life to me if he had to die. My heart almost broke with sadness for Jason's family. How could I ever thank him and his family for the joy that my own life had been extended because of his priceless gift?

I later found out that Jason was born in 1976, the same year as that freeway explosion. The same year that *changed* my life *gave* me life.

* * * * *

As a grandmother, I still have aches and pains, but they are merely reminders of the privilege of growing older. Like George Burns once said, "Growing older is not always golden, but it sure beats the alternative."

Mickey Mann Johnson
Submitted by Jane Meyer

Hindsight

The difference between genius and stupidity is that genius has its limits.

Albert Einstein

I came across an article about a sixty-year-old woman who went up a mountain that any novice skier should have avoided. No one would have blamed her had she stayed behind. At twelve below zero, even Frosty the Snowman would have opted for the warm fire. Hardly a day for snow skiing, but her husband insisted. So she went.

While waiting in the lift line, she realized she was in need of a restroom, *dire* need of a restroom. Assured there would be one at the top of the lift, she and her bladder endured the bouncy ride, only to find there was no facility. She began to panic. Her husband had an idea: Why not go into the woods? Since she was wearing an all-white outfit, she'd blend in with the snow. And what better powder room than a piney grove?

What choice did she have? She skied past the tree line and arranged her ski suit at half-mast. Fortunately, no one could see her. Unfortunately, her husband hadn't told her to remove her skis. Before you could say, "Shine on harvest moon," she was streaking backwards across the slope, revealing more of herself than she ever intended. (After all, hindsight is 20/20.) With arms flailing and skis sailing, she sped under the very lift she'd just ridden and collided with a pylon.

As she scrambled to cover the essentials, she discovered her arm was broken. Fortunately her husband raced to her rescue. He summoned the ski patrol, who transported her to the hospital.

While being treated in the emergency room, a man with a broken leg was carried in and placed next to her. By now she'd regained her composure enough to make small talk. "So, how'd you break your leg?" she asked.

"It was the darndest thing you ever saw," he explained. "I was riding up the ski lift and suddenly there was this crazy woman skiing backwards, at top speed, with her ski suit down around her knees. I couldn't believe my eyes, so I leaned over to get a better look. I guess I didn't realize how far I'd moved. I fell out of the lift."

Then he turned to her and asked, "So how'd you break your arm?"

Retold by Max Lucado

The Door Prize

We are all God's extension cords, taking His light and song to the dark and empty places of our world.

Roberta L. Messner

I already regretted my promise to Mrs. Saunders, the coordinator of the annual charity Christmas bazaar. "Would you donate the door prize this year, dear?" she persuaded. "There's *nothing* like a wonderful door prize to draw shoppers to a bazaar."

With only three weeks until Christmas, the uncompleted task hung over my head like a frost-brittled tree limb. I wanted to craft something really special, but now on the eve of the bazaar, as I sat at my kitchen table, inspiration eluded me. The next thing I knew, I was crawling in the attic, praying for a quick dose of creativity. I grabbed a tabletop evergreen tree and two boxes of would-be treasures and trudged back to the kitchen. *Perhaps some holiday music would put me in a festive mood,* I thought as I snapped in a Christmas cassette.

I rummaged through a box labeled "Old Dolls." Before

long, I was singing the familiar words: "Joy to the world. . . ." I gazed down at the pile of nearly two dozen dolls I'd purchased years ago at a flea market. I cradled in my hands a Japanese doll in a royal blue kimono; a Native American family with a brown felt teepee; a "Miss Liberty" doll bedecked in red, white and blue; and a quartet of dolls in Scandinavian attire.

Suddenly something deep within me suggested: Craft a "Joy to the World" tree! One by one, I wired the dolls to the evergreen branches until they nearly sagged from the weight of them all. A few of the dolls were in pieces. Painstakingly, I re-strung their arms and legs with a pair of tweezers and some rubber bands. One black-haired doll with darting eyes and a Spanish costume was forever falling apart despite my efforts. As I cupped her in my hands to re-string her limbs a third time, I felt a kinship with women all over the world who, just like me, need the spirit of Christmas to put them back together.

Just then my friend Betsy walked through the door to check my progress. Soon we both were full swing into the project. "How about using some of these dried flowers?" Betsy suggested, pointing to the bouquet of cockscombs, baby's breath and sweetheart roses hanging from the kitchen ceiling beams. Next we added snippets of ribbon and lace.

"What are we going to do about that bare spot in the middle?" Betsy asked. The two of us combed the house for the crowning touches . . . a small world globe from my desk, topped with a velvet bow retrieved from the wreath hanging over my mantel.

Together we stood back and smiled at our handiwork. "That's the prettiest tree I've ever seen," Betsy concluded. The next morning, I carefully packed our "Joy to the World" tree in my car. On impulse, I dashed back into the house and grabbed an extension cord, a portable tape player and the tape of "Joy to the World."

When I arrived at the bazaar, everyone was in the holiday spirit. A lady dressed in a cashmere coat tapped me on my shoulder. "This tree reminds me of all my travels," she said as she stirred her cider with a cinnamon stick. An aproned craftswoman strolled over. "I'm ordering one of these trees for my granddaughter in Germany," she announced. Then the gingerbread cookies lady joined in. "I'm going home with this tree."

Before long, the room was packed with shoppers gazing at the never-to-be-duplicated tree. Moments before the drawing, a tiny woman with tired eyes and a dingy gray coat exchanged fifty cents for a ticket stub. Her neatly braided hair, coiled tightly into a bun, framed a face stripped of everything except determination.

"We came into town to buy feed for the livestock, and I talked my husband into stopping here," she said. "Had a little egg money left to spend."

The woman admired the satin angels, homemade jellies and a fruitcake baked to resemble a holiday wreath. Just then she spotted the tree. "That tree, the dolls!" she cried. "All my life I've wanted a purty doll. Only doll I ever did have was the one my Ma made out of corncobs. Is someone gonna win *all* them dolls?" she asked with a faraway look in her eyes.

I flipped on the cassette player, and the melody of "Joy to the World" filled the room. All eyes but hers were now on the box of ticket stubs, and on the hand that would draw the winning number. From all over the room, I heard the blurring of voices. "That tree is mine . . . ," "No, it's mine. . . ."

But the tiny woman never took her eyes off the tree. "My grandson Willie, he lives up the holler from our place," she said. "He's real smart in book learnin'. Why, he could recite every one of them countries on that map."

Then came the long-awaited announcement. "The door prize goes to number 1153." I glanced down at the gnarled hands that held the winning ticket and squeezed her thin shoulders.

"You won the tree!" I cried.

"You mean it's *my* ticket? I ain't *never* had nothin' nice as this." Tears rolled down her wrinkled cheeks.

I unplugged the lights and tape player and wound the extension cord. "Am I gonna get that music box and long cord, too?" she asked. "I'm settin' that tree in the winder and we only have one outlet in the room. I shore could use that extra cord."

"Of course . . . it's Christmas," I answered. A rusted yellow pickup truck pulled up in front, and a man wearing high-bibbed overalls and a plaid flannel shirt jumped out. "Sadie, what in thunderation you got there?" he hollered.

"Pa, I won this tree!" Quickly, he rearranged a shovel, tire chains and sacks of feed to make room in the truck.

I waved good-bye as the clunking truck disappeared into the violet evening sky. In my mind's eye, I envisioned the tree given a place of honor in the window of a humble, dimly lit cabin in the heart of the mountains. The folks who lived there were a happy sort, I told myself. Not world travelers, but hard workers, content with what they had. Black smoke would likely billow from their chimney into the nippy December air as the family gathered around the tree. "Look Granny, here's Japan," perhaps Willie would say, pointing to the globe that once sat on my desk. And Josie, still fascinated with that extension cord, would plug in the twinkling lights and her "music box."

Yet, I'm convinced that I was the real winner that night. While I never saw Josie again, she had helped me discover how to take light and song to the dark and empty places of our world.

Roberta L. Messner

Red Shoes with Gold Laces

On with the dance! Let joy be unconfined.

Lord Byron

Gilda was a dancer,
a ballroom dancer,
her billowing skirts,
held to a tight waist,
by a belt made of
a rainbow of tiny conch shells.
Gilda wore red shoes, with gold laces.

When invited to come play bridge,
even with the luring promises
of meringue coconut cream pie
at the end of the bidding wars,
Gilda would apologize, say her thanks,
and instead go dancing in her
red shoes with gold laces.

Some nights folks at the condo
convoyed to the bingo palaces,

They'd come home smelling from
cigarettes, their fingers tainted
with bingo markers, and sometimes money.
But Gilda preferred to go dancing,
in red shoes with gold laces.

That's where Gilda and Bill met.
His dancing uniform was a tie
with Nittany Lions on it.
His shoes were old U.S. Navy issue,
with leather soles that could slide,
and never step on the toes of a woman
in red shoes with gold laces.

They slow-danced, an easy, gliding song.
He felt her soft skin and looked into her eyes
but Bill kept his distance,
hummed Glenn Miller in her ear,
and smelled her cologne,
something as old
as his GI Bill college days.
What was that name? It drifted
through memories, White Shoulders,
and he dipped his new Gilda deep and low,
Gilda kept her sweet-smelling balance
Safe in red shoes with gold laces.

And could that Gilda jitterbug.
Her grin picked up the spinning mirrored ball.
Bill didn't throw her over his shoulder,
nor did she leap up to wrap her legs around his hips,
but for the first time out,
he had no doubt that this was a dancer,
Gilda of the red shoes with gold laces.

Bill knew she was here alone,
There was no wedding band on her pale hand,
so he asked in between sets, about where
love had two-stepped right by her,
Just as it had polka-ed all over him,
She answered, not with vanity,
and not with false modesty.
Her eyelids fluttered like a muted tombstone,
"That husband just didn't dance enough."
She made it clear that if the new ones don't,
"I simply fox trot out of here, and go home alone,
in my red shoes with gold laces."

A whole dance card later,
Back at her place, trim and neat,
Bill undid those gold laces for her,
Softly, to the rhythm of a Sinatra
tune that danced in his head.
Then Bill kissed those toes
that had twinkled under that soft red leather.
He could tell she liked her feet
Held in reverence like an icon.
Gilda Hoffman kissed Bill on his ear,
And whispered in it, breathlessly,
That he sure knew how to dance,
even if he had never owned
a pair of red shoes with gold laces.

                                        Sidney B. Simon

5

STILL LEARNING

As we acquire more knowledge, things do not become more comprehensible but more mysterious.

Albert Schweitzer

Profile of a Prime-Timer

Life before sixty is nothing but a warm-up.

Bill Hinson

We true prime-timers were here before the Pill, the population explosion and disposable diapers. We were here before we were called "senior citizens."

We were here before TV, penicillin, polio shots, antibiotics and open-heart surgery. Before frozen food, nylon, Xerox, radar, fluorescent lights, credit cards, ballpoint pens, Frisbees and fiber optics.

For us, time-sharing meant togetherness, not computers or condos. Coeds never wore jeans. Girls wore Peter Pan collars. We were here before panty hose and drip-dry clothes, before icemakers and dishwashers, clothes dryers, freezers and electric blankets. Before men wore long hair and earrings and before women wore tuxedos.

We were here before Ann Landers, Grandma Moses and the Kinsey Report. We were here before facelifts, tummy tucks, liposuction and hair transplants. We thought cleavage was what butchers did. We were here before sex changes. Before Viagra. We just made do with what we had.

We were here before computers. A mouse pad was where the mice hung out. To log-on was to add wood to fire. A chip was a piece of wood. Hardware meant hardware, and software wasn't even a word. A hard drive was a long, grueling journey. A CD was something you invested in. Windows were for looking out of. A virus was a flu bug that people caught. Backing up was what you hoped never happened to your toilet, especially when you had company.

We were here before vitamins, Jeeps, pizza, Cheerios, instant coffee, decaffeinated anything, light anything and McDonald's. We thought fast food was what you ate during Lent. If we had been asked to explain VCR, CIA, NATO, UFO, PMS, GNP, MBA, BMW, SDI, NFL, PSA and ATM, we'd have said "alphabet soup."

We prime-timers are a hardy bunch when you think of how our world has changed, all we have learned and the adjustments we have made. I'm pretty proud of us.

Let's keep in touch. Just e-mail me, send a fax, leave a message on my answering machine or call me on my cell phone. If I don't answer, tell my voicemail you called—after the beep, leave your name, your number and a brief message, and I'll get back to you as soon as I can. If you need me quickly, call my pager. If all else fails, come on over to my house, take a seat in one of the rockers on my porch and we'll visit the old-fashioned way—face to face and in person—and let the rest of the world go by.

Nardi Reeder Campion

Matchless Moments

Some great moments occur from time to time in life. When you do all you can to enable others to have great moments, you'll be blessed with some matchless moments yourself.

E. H. Kinney

I have enjoyed many matchless moments in my life. But very few occurred while I was seven and eight years old. Diagnosed with polio, I was placed in a room with about thirty-five people, each in our own iron lung. I cried a lot because nobody, not even my mother and father, could visit me, much less talk to me or give me a hug. Contracting polio and possibly even spreading it to other people was a constant fear. Even the nurses avoided contact with us. One night, I lay in my own vomit all night because I was too sick and scared to ask for help.

When the doctor came to check on me the next morning, he pulled me out of the iron lung, placed me on the cold hardwood floor and began cleaning me off. He hugged me and told me God loved me. He began crying, and I cried with him. I'll never forget that experience. I was a terribly frightened, sick little boy, and it was one of the few matchless moments that year.

Finally, I was allowed to return home. After being there only a few days, a doctor and nurse came to the house to inform my parents that tests indicated I had tuberculosis. The choice was returning to the hospital or being quarantined in my home. I chose home. Being restricted to my bedroom was better than the iron lung, but being isolated from my friends and family was still very difficult. On Christmas, I remember my daddy knocking on my window. When I looked out on the fresh snow covering the ground, I saw that his footprints spelled the words, "I love you, Tommy." Another matchless moment I desperately needed.

By the time I returned to school a few years after being diagnosed with polio, I found I had forgotten much of what I had learned. Still, I was excited to be able to go back to school. But on my first day back, the teacher ordered me, "Tommy, come and sit right in the front." I was a big kid at a little desk, and I was embarrassed and didn't want everybody looking at me. Then the teacher said, "Let's see what all you've learned while you have been goofing off, while you've been sick or whatever your problem was." Then he told me to write the word "cat" on the blackboard. By then I was so scared I don't think I could have spelled my own name. I tried to talk with the teacher, but he wouldn't listen. Instead he ordered me out of the class, "You're misbehaving. Get out of here!"

I never went back to school, and I did not learn to read until my two sons were adults. Not knowing how to read and write put me at a distinct disadvantage for many years, and I was constantly plagued by it. But I worked hard and made a very good living. In fact, this once-illiterate sixtyish-plus millionaire wrote a book about it. Going from an illiterate to the author of *The*

Millionaire's Secret: Miss Melba and Me was another match-less moment in my life.

While many people my age were retiring, I dedicated myself to encouraging other illiterate adults to learn to read and write. And that's what I've been doing fervently since 1992. I have given over six hundred talks and have told many stories about how lives have been changed when illiterate adults have learned to read and to write. Encouraging those who can read and write to tutor those who cannot has also brought some matchless moments.

One of my favorite audiences to speak to about literacy is prisoners. Eighty percent of prisoners in the United States cannot read. My being able to offer encouragement to prisoners who have learned to read and write has provided some matchless moments for me—and hopefully some for them.

At a recent prison GED graduation this was true for one particular prisoner and for me. The graduates were hard-core criminals, so I was closely guarded everywhere I went. The prisoners were shackled, and fully armed guards stood inside and outside the large room where graduation was to take place. The graduates were seated to my right as I approached the podium. After the warden introduced me, he instructed under his breath, "Under no circumstances are you to hand over the microphone or get near one of these prisoners."

"No, sir, I won't," I said, assuming he meant the prisoners were dangerous. He made it sound as if one misguided yell over the public address system would incite a riot.

I congratulated the men, and the ceremonies continued with awards and diplomas presented. This hard-core group would never be released from prison, but it was obvious they desired a better life by being able to read about places they would never be able to visit.

During the question-and-answer session, one of the

toughest-looking prisoners stood and asked if he could approach the podium. I glanced over at the warden, who shook his head no. I looked back at the young man. He had tears in his eyes but didn't seem to care. He knew this could be the last time he'd ever have any contact with the outside world. "But Mr. Harken, I just want to say something to my grandfather," he said.

Again, I looked at the warden. Again, he shook his head. When I turned back to the prisoner and saw the pleading look in his eyes, I couldn't stop myself from assuring him, "You bet! Come on over."

"Thank you, Mr. Harken," he said as he walked toward the podium. The little-boy expression on his face reflected gratitude and sincerity—and fright. I was convinced beyond a shadow of a doubt that he was harmless. His hand shook as he reached for the microphone, wiped his eyes and cleared his throat.

"I want all of you to know that my grandfather is the elderly gentleman over there wearing the old faded overalls. I'm sure he remembers back when I would make fun of him and of his clothes," the young man spoke from his heart.

"Grandpa, I will never get out of here because I didn't do things the way you advised me to," he said. "But I got this GED diploma because I wanted to show you I could do something right for a change. I love you, Grandpa. I'm sorry."

As his voice trailed off, I took the microphone back and told the grandfather to come up and give his grandson a big hug. I looked to the warden, then to the guards. There wasn't a dry eye in the place.

Another matchless moment! One I will never forget.

Tom Harken

Mr. Kindrick's Pearl of Wisdom

Is not wisdom found among the aged? Does not long life bring understanding?

Job 12:12

If wrinkles signaled lessons learned, then Bennett Kindrick must have known it all. At eighty-two, Bennett had every reason to consider himself a graduate of the classroom of life. But on this particular Sunday morning, Bennett's face shone with the schoolboy brightness of a new insight.

And well it should! For I was the preacher that morning, and I had worked all week to string together the most dazzling pearls of wisdom ever displayed before this usually passive group of pew-sitters. That morning I preached the splendor of heaven to folks I thought were hopelessly bound to earth. Surely this inspirational message was the source of the brightness in Bennett's eyes.

After the service, I greeted him at the door. "So, Mr. Kindrick," I asked, "what did you learn today that has you so excited?" The question zinged from my lips like fishing line from an angler desperate for the compliment of a bite.

"Is it that obvious? I've been this excited since last Friday morning." He continued, "You see, I've been studying a particular passage of scripture for fifty years, and just this week, it finally made sense to me."

Realizing that Bennett's brightness had nothing to do with my message, I soon understood that it was he who was offering me a jewel—the truth that learning is a life-long process. The revelation that dawned in Bennett's heart at age eighty-two could not have happened if he had given up learning at age thirty-two. What if he had stopped trying to understand that verse at age forty-two, or fifty-two or even seventy-two? The truth in that scripture verse might have escaped him. Only on that great Friday, after eight decades of experience and preparation, could he have been prepared to grasp that pearl of wisdom.

Bennett's revelation encourages me never to tire in my quest for insight. I realize now that to give up trying to understand new things today is to forfeit lessons that can only be learned tomorrow.

When I got home after talking to Mr. Kindrick that morning, I rushed to look up the scripture verse he had been studying all those years. The verse made no sense to me.

Well, maybe when I'm eighty-two....

Dudley Callison

"My Grandpa says you learn most
everything after you think you know it all."

Cramming for Finals

Fortune favors the prepared mind.

Louis Pasteur

A ninety-six-year-old lady was a faithful attendant at my women's club Bible studies. She came with her lessons prepared and knew all the answers. One day a tactless member asked her, "Why do you work so hard on these lessons when you're so old and it doesn't matter?"

Little Bess Elkins looked up and said confidently, "I'm cramming for my finals."

Florence Littauer

It's Never Too Late

The highest reward for a person's toil is not what they get for it, but what they become by it.

John Ruskin

With a flick of a tassel, my lifelong dream was fulfilled. At the age of sixty-eight, I graduated from college—with honors.

It was a triumphant, yet bittersweet achievement. I'd had a loving, happy marriage, filled with travel, friends and children. Then my husband died. I had never done anything on my own. Ever.

I realized I could sit at home and cry over my loss, or I could do something I had wanted to do all my life. I could go to college.

It was the scariest decision I've ever made.

Even then, making that decision was one thing. Actually doing it was another. I was so nervous my first day of school. I was terrified. Could I find my way around? Would I stick out like a sore thumb? Would the professors think I was a dilettante? Would I be able to do the work? What if everyone was smarter than I?

At the end of the first day, I was so tired.

But I was also elated. I knew I could do it. Although it was hard, the exhilaration of learning new things was worth it. My love of art led me to major in art history. It was a joy to spend my days listening to experts.

One of my unexpected pleasures was being with the other students. The age difference wasn't a problem, although it was a shock at first having kids call me by my first name. They were delightful; we discussed our classes, studied and walked together. One young man even taught me how to use computers. Best of all: No one talked about cholesterol.

I also received a great deal of attention from many of my teachers (most of whom were young enough to be my children). I suppose they weren't used to seeing a student get so excited about their lectures. As time went on, many used me as a resource. In history class, no one else knew what living through the Depression was like. I did, and I was asked to talk about my experiences.

Many of my acquaintances thought I was crazy. Sometimes I thought so, too. The papers, exams, the hours of research, the mad dashes to get across campus in time for the next class, the exhaustion. However, it didn't deter me from fulfilling all the academic requirements, including physical education. I was determined to do whatever it took to get my diploma.

My daughters were very supportive. Talk about role reversals. We planned our visits around *my* school vacation schedule. They helped me with my homework. They commiserated when I talked about a difficult professor and told me to stop worrying so much about getting good grades. (They swore I was getting back at them for all the times they had called me in a panic when they were in school.)

In addition to classroom study, I learned I could study abroad by taking school-sponsored tours during the summer. One trip took us through Eastern Europe (before the fall of Communism); on another, we explored art in Italy. I had traveled a great deal with my husband, but never by myself. I was apprehensive about going on the first trip alone. However, I met some wonderful people who took me under their wings. I had mastered another step in being on my own.

Little did I know that my college experience would provide knowledge that doesn't come from books. Looking back, I realize that going to school kept me young. I was never bored. I was exposed to new ideas and viewpoints. Most important, I gained confidence, realizing I can accomplish things by myself.

The day before my husband died, he asked me if I would go back to college. He was telling me to go on with my life and fulfill a dream. On my graduation day four years later, I walked across the stage to accept my diploma. I could feel him giving me a standing ovation.

Mildred Cohn
Excerpted from Chocolate for a Woman's Soul *by Kay Allenbaugh*

"Way to go, Mildred!"

Used by permission of Vern Herschberger.

An Even Greater Lesson

How you and those dear to you live earns your reputation; how you and those dear to you face death reveals your character.

John William Russell III

Warm, friendly, attractive, gifted. That described Julie, one of my all-time favorite students from human development courses I taught at the University of Nebraska. She was a delightful person and an ideal student.

I remember Julie coming to the front of the classroom after class one autumn day in September 1976. While most of the other students hurriedly left to enjoy the balmy weather or to relax at the student union, Julie remained to ask questions about the next week's exam. She had obviously already done some serious studying. Several other students overheard her questions and joined our conversation. Julie's winsome personality drew people to her.

Julie never made it to the exam. The day after our conversation, she was tragically struck by a large concrete truck as she biked through an intersection near campus. I was stunned to hear that Julie lay unconscious and motionless in a hospital across town from the campus where only hours before she was talking with friends, laughing, making plans for the future.

Only minutes before the accident, Julie and her mother had enjoyed one of their customary daily telephone conversations. Her mother recalls their last conversation. "Julie was so bubbly. At a store near the campus, she had seen an outfit she wanted to wear on a special date the next day. I told her to go ahead and buy it. She didn't take her car because she would lose her parking place on campus. Instead, she jumped on her bike to go buy the new outfit. The accident happened just a short distance from the sorority house where she lived." My thoughts cried out to Julie—*You cannot die, Julie! You're every professor's dream—and every parent's. You have so much to offer. So much to live for.*

Nurses silently came and went from Julie's room. Her parents stood nearby in quiet desperation. Then the attending physician entered the room, cleared his throat, and said to Julie's parents and two brothers, "Your Julie has only a few hours to live." He felt the freedom to ask, "Would you consider donating some of Julie's organs?"

At that same hour in a neighboring state, Mary leaned forward, struggling to see better in her small, cluttered living room. Her eyes followed every movement of her lively two-year-old. This devoted mother was storing up memories to savor when she could no longer see her child. Mary was going blind.

Several states away, John had almost finished six hours on the dialysis machine. This young father was reading to his two sons while his immobilized body was connected to a life-giving "artificial kidney." Doctors had given him a grim prognosis of only weeks to live. His only hope was a kidney transplant.

At the same time in the Lincoln, Nebraska, hospital, Julie's grief-stricken parents pondered the finality of the physician's question. Their pretty brunette, brown-eyed daughter had once said she wanted to be an organ donor in the event of her death. The two parents looked at each other briefly, the anguish in their hearts reflected in their eyes. Then they turned to the physician and responded, "Yes. Julie always gave to others while she was alive. She would want to give in death."

Within twenty-four hours, Mary was notified that she would receive one of Julie's eyes, and John was told to start preparing for a kidney transplant. Julie's other organs would give life and sight to other waiting recipients.

"Julie died right after her twentieth birthday—twenty-four years ago. She left us with very happy memories," says Julie's mother, now in her seventies. "Nothing—absolutely nothing—could possibly be as heartbreaking as the death of your child," she emphasizes, "for your heart breaks again and again. At each birthday. At each holiday. At each milestone: when she would've graduated; when she might've married; when she might've been having children." Taking a slow and deliberate breath, Julie's mother says, "But Julie's life was a gift to us. Knowing that in her death, she gave the gift of life and sight to others is comforting to us, and remembering that we carried out her wishes has helped us cope with her death more than anything else."

Her voice softening, Julie's mother says, "You and Julie's other friends and teachers were an important part of her life. Your teaching influenced her life tremendously, and you remind us that our love for Julie and Julie's love for others are alive today."

As one of Julie's professors, I hold dear the thought that I may have had a small part in teaching Julie how to

live. But she—and her family—are still teaching me an
even greater lesson. How to die.

Barbara Russell Chesser

[EDITORS' NOTE: *If you are unsure about the intentions of
individual family members (regardless of age) regarding organ
donation, ask them. You may be called upon as were Julie's parents
to make a life-giving decision. In addition, make sure your loved
ones know your decision about organ donation. For more information, please ask your physician or check the yellow pages of
your telephone book under Organ Donations.*]

Remembering to Forget

If we really want to love, we must learn to forgive.

Mother Teresa

Once labeled "timid as a mouse, but brave as a lion," Clara Barton founded the American Red Cross at age fifty-one. A woman of commitment, she continued to fulfill her mission through her golden years. She did not let her age get in her way. Clara went wherever there was suffering to relieve—after battle, fire, flood, earthquake or yellow fever. At the age of seventy-seven, she was on the battlefields of Cuba for the Spanish-American War. She continued her relief work until she died at age ninety-one.

One day, someone reminded her about an offense that another person had committed against her years before. But she acted as if she had never heard of the cruel act.

"Don't you remember it?" her friend asked.

"No," came Clara's reply. "I clearly remember forgetting it."

Amy Seeger

Banana, Anyone?

Aerodynamically, the bumblebee shouldn't be able to fly. But the bumblebee doesn't know it. So it keeps flying.

Mary Kay Ash

Captain's log, Whaler's Bay, Antarctica, summer 1986, water temperature—twenty-eight degrees: *Today, we met our first iceberg, saw our first humpback whale . . . and Mr. George Blair performed his barefoot water-skiing along the beach.*

With that notable feat, "Banana" George Alfred Blair became the first person to water-ski—barefoot or otherwise—on or off all seven continents.

And that's only *one* of his spectacular accomplishments. This octogenarian is a member of the Water Ski Hall of Fame, world-champion water-skier in a number of age divisions and skill categories, eleven-time American barefoot water-ski champion, wake-boarder, noted philanthropist and banana fanatic.

George's homes in the United States and elsewhere are positively glowing with yellow. His speedboat, telephones, two Cadillacs, wet suit and skis are yellow. Each

Christmas at Cypress Gardens, he wears a yellow Santa suit and hands out gifts. His name? *Banana Claus.*

George Blair overcame his family's poverty caused by the Great Depression and survived two potentially paralyzing accidents to water-ski his way into near-legendary status in this country and abroad. During his sophomore year of college, his friends decided to go to Fort Lauderdale for Easter. Since he didn't have any money, George hopped a freight train for Florida.

"So here I was on this freight car with nothing but a can of beans. Unfortunately, there were two other hobos in the same freight car, and when they saw my can of beans, they wanted it. When I refused, they picked me up by my arms and my legs and threw me off the train. I landed on my spine."

George's back never fully recovered. His only hope was what was still considered a risky experimental procedure in 1954—a spinal fusion operation. The thirty-nine-year-old was in the hospital for more than three weeks. At home, he stayed in bed for three months. Then the doctors told him to go down to Florida and sit around in the warm waters, relax and let it mend.

Which is what he did. "I'd sit in the water every day and watch the ski school on the inland waterway," George says. "Finally, the fellow who ran the school talked me into water-skiing. I tried to beg off, saying, 'I'm too old. I've just had a terrible back operation.'

"Anyway, he did get me out, and I was successful immediately because he was a good teacher with good equipment. Before long, my wife, four daughters and I were all skiing together behind a boat at one time." Today, George can ski barefoot for fifteen minutes at a stretch. He says his feet are so tough, he'll never need a podiatrist.

In a remarkably short time, George has become one of the featured attractions at Cypress Gardens. He opens most shows by being ripped off the beach by a speedboat, rising to his bare feet, then circling the grandstands with the tow rope held in his teeth.

George attributes his seemingly inexhaustible energy to exercise and a sensible diet. One small, yet significant component to George's diet is the banana.

"Because bananas are yellow and are God's most nearly perfect food, I have an affinity for bananas," he says. He gives away about two tons of bananas each year. In September 1990, Chiquita called Banana George and asked what they could do for him. George responded, "You can start by furnishing my bananas . . . about two tons a year." When they asked where he wanted them sent, he answered, "I'll let you know." And he has. Wherever George goes, whether to perform or to compete, he calls up Chiquita and they send him bananas. *Lots* of bananas.

George says that it is getting close to time to prepare for another show at Cypress Gardens, but he has a few parting words of wisdom: "My advice to sixty-year-olds who want to be doing this is that there is hope for all of us, even me. Every day I try to do a little better. And you ought to, too. Start easy, but go for it. And set goals.

"I still have all kinds of goals. Most recently I've learned to wake board. I can't wait to test myself with the next goal, with the next accomplishment. I've got all kinds of things I want to be doing. There are not enough seconds in each minute or enough minutes in each hour, for me to do what I want to do. That's my problem."

That, and how to get rid of two tons of free bananas each year.

Robert Darden

6

ON LOVE

If you would be loved, love and be lovable.

Benjamin Franklin

What He Did for Love

. . . love knows not its own depth until the hour of separation.

Kahlil Gibran

Sam, at age seventeen, had the normal dreams and desires of a young man embarking upon adulthood. He hoped to marry a good and loving woman, to work hard and study, and to create a bountiful existence for raising a family.

But in turn-of-the-century Polish Russia, a young man couldn't always hope to achieve his dreams. The threat of the draft loomed over every male of fighting age and burdened the hearts of his parents. If a man was drafted into the Russian Army, he had little hope of ever coming home. He was drafted for life or died in service. Sam was destined to be one of those boys.

Some families accepted this fate as unavoidable and tearfully said good-bye to their sons. Others took the extreme measure of chopping off the son's right index finger—the trigger finger—making him ineligible for service, viewing mutilation as the lesser evil compared with prolonged suffering or even death. Sam decided on another course, one that held larger dangers he could not even imagine—and the promise of a good life if all went well. He chose escape.

Sam wasn't just running away from the perils threatening him in Lodz; he was running *toward* something—or rather *someone*. He had fallen in love with Gussie, a young Polish girl, shortly before her family had fled Lodz for America. Sam had received word that she was safe in New York and missed him. Sam was determined to marry Gussie and fulfill his dreams, so he prepared himself for a treacherous and courageous journey.

His parents packed him food and water for the trip, but his most vital necessity was money. If Sam wanted to cross the German border, he would have to bribe the border guard. Sam's parents gathered all their savings, tied the money into a handkerchief and hid it deep under the many layers of clothing Sam would wear for his countryside trek. When, or if, Sam made it past the border, he was to find his way to some German friends who could help him reach New York.

As Sam embraced his family the morning of his departure, he wondered if he would ever see them—or Gussie—again. To pass the time and bolster his courage during the journey, Sam concentrated his thoughts on his love for Gussie and his plans for their future. This one hope would give him the strength to complete his pilgrimage. Finally, Sam approached the German border, reached for his stash of money and froze in his tracks. He saw *two* guards at the border patrol; he had only enough money for one bribe. He couldn't possibly get through. Worse, one of the guards had spotted him, so he either had to advance or flee back home.

Gussie, Sam said to himself, *I'm doing this for you, and I know God won't let us down.* Sam prayed as he slowly walked toward the crossing. He needed a miracle.

As Sam drew closer, he recognized one of the guards as his father's friend, one who had visited the family many times. Sam caught the guard's eyes. When the guard recognized Sam and saw the look on his face, he immediately understood what was happening. Suddenly, the guard started yelling wildly and pointing in the opposite direction. The other guard, distracted, turned away. Sam had just enough time to dash across the border and out of danger—and he still had all his bribe money.

Sam made it safely to New York, and he found Gussie. After they married, they used the unspent bribe money to start a successful business. Despite his newfound happiness, Sam never forgot his family back in Polish Russia. Within two years, Sam was able to bring his three brothers to New York, and he and Gussie had a gift waiting for the boys when they arrived: Gussie's single sisters.

This young boy whose future in Polish Russia had been so uncertain lived long enough to see his grandchildren. In fact, I am one of those grandchildren. While Grandpa Sam was still alive, my cousins and I never tired of hearing the story of his courageous journey, or his ingenuity and self-sufficiency. But most of all, we treasured hearing about what brought him to his Gussie: not a stroke of luck or a twist of fate, but a miracle of love.

Eileen Lawrence

BLONDIE

Loving Muriel

I shall love you in December with the love I gave in May.

John Alexander Joyce

Seventeen summers ago, Muriel and I began our journey into the twilight. It's midnight now, at least for her, and sometimes I wonder when dawn will break. Even the dreaded Alzheimer's disease isn't supposed to attack so early and torment so long. Yet, in her silent world, Muriel is so content, so lovable. If she were to die, how I would miss her gentle, sweet presence. Yes, there are times when I get irritated, but not often. It doesn't make sense to get angry. And besides, perhaps God has been answering the prayer of my youth to mellow my spirit.

Once, though, I completely lost it. In the days when Muriel could still stand and walk and we had not resorted to diapers, sometimes there were "accidents." I was on my knees beside her, trying to clean up the mess as she stood, confused, by the toilet. It would have been easier if she weren't so insistent on helping. I got more and more frustrated. Suddenly, to make her stand still, I slapped her calf—as if that would do any good. It wasn't a hard slap, but she was startled. I was, too. Never in our forty-four years of marriage had I ever so much as touched her in anger or in rebuke of any kind. Never. I wasn't even tempted, in fact. But now, when she needed me most. . . .

Sobbing, I pleaded with her to forgive me—no matter that she didn't understand words any better than she could speak them. So I prayed and said how sorry I was. It took me days to get over it. Maybe I bottled those tears to quench the fires that might ignite again some day.

A young friend recently asked me, "Don't you ever get tired?"

"Tired? Every night. That's why I go to bed."

"No, I mean tired of . . ." and she tilted her head toward Muriel, who sat silently in her wheelchair, her vacant eyes saying, "No one at home just now." I responded to my friend, "Why, no, I don't get tired. I love to care for her. She's my precious."

Love is said to evaporate if the relationship is not mutual, if it's not physical, if the other person doesn't communicate or if one party doesn't carry his or her share of the load. When I hear the litany of essentials for a happy marriage, I count off what my beloved can no longer contribute, and then I contemplate how truly mysterious love is.

What some people find so hard to understand is that loving Muriel isn't hard. They wonder about my former loves—like my work. "Do you miss being president?" a university student asked as we sat in our little garden. I told him I'd never thought about it, but, on reflection, no. As exhilarating as my work had been, I enjoyed learning to cook and keep house. No, I'd never looked back.

But that night I did reflect on his question and prayed, "I like this assignment, and I have no regrets. But if a coach puts a man on the bench, he must not want him in the game. You needn't tell me, of course, but I'd like to know—why didn't you keep me in the game?"

I didn't sleep well that night and awoke contemplating the puzzle. Muriel was still mobile at that time, so we set out on our morning walk around the block. She wasn't too sure on her feet, so we went slowly and held hands as we always do. This day I heard footsteps behind me and looked back to see the familiar form of a local derelict behind us. He staggered past us, then turned and looked us up and down. "Tha's good. I likes 'at," he said. "That's real good. I likes it." He turned and headed back down the street, mumbling to himself over and over, "Tha's good. I likes it."

When Muriel and I reached our little garden and sat down, his words came back to me. God had spoken through an inebriated old derelict. "It is you who is whispering to my spirit, 'I likes it, tha's good,'" I said aloud. "I may be on the bench, but if you like it and say it's good, that's all that counts."

People ask me, "How do you do it?" Praise helps—Muriel is a joy to me, and life is good to both of us, in different ways. And we have family and friends who care for us lovingly.

Memories help, too. Muriel stocked the cupboard of my mind with the best of them. I often live again a special moment of love she planned or laugh at some remembered outburst of her irrepressible approach to life. Sometimes the happy doesn't bubble up with joy but rains down gently with tears. In the movie *Shadowlands*, when Joy Gresham reminds C. S. Lewis that their joy would soon end, that she would die, he replies that he doesn't want to think about it. Joy responds, "The pain is part of the happiness. That's the deal."

Muriel hasn't spoken a coherent word in months—years, if you mean a sentence, a conversation—though occasionally she tries, mumbling nonwords. *Would I never hear that voice again?*

Then came February 14, 1995.

Valentine's Day was always special at our house because that was the day in 1948 that Muriel accepted my marriage proposal. On the eve of Valentine's Day in 1995, I bathed Muriel, kissed her good night and whispered a prayer over her, "Dear Lord, you love sweet Muriel more than I, so please keep my beloved through the night; may she hear the angel choirs."

The next morning I was peddling on my exercise bike at the foot of her bed and reminiscing about some of our happy lovers' days long gone while Muriel slowly emerged from sleep. Finally, she popped awake and, as she often does, smiled at me. Then, for the first time in months she spoke, calling out to me in a voice as clear as a crystal chime, "Love . . . love . . . love."

I jumped from my cycle and ran to embrace her. "Honey, you really do love me, don't you?" Holding me with her eyes and patting my back, she responded with the only words she could find to say yes. "I'm nice," she said.

Tha's good. I likes it.

Robertson McQuilkin
Submitted by Kelley Smith

I'll Be Seeing You

The past is never where you think you left it.

Katherine Anne Porter

Caroline watched the bride and groom glide across the floor in a loving embrace, as the saxophone caressed each note of the ballad. The music awoke a longing in her, and suddenly she wished she had never come.

Why did her son Tony and his wife insist she come? She couldn't help wondering why she was here. Everyone else seemed to be part of a couple and she was obviously single—one solitary individual.

During Frank's illness, Caroline had accepted the loss of intimacy they once shared. Since his death, she had found it harder to adapt to the loss of his friendship: the sharing of a cup of coffee over the morning newspaper, the warm exchange of an understanding smile. Now that she had moved into an apartment in a new neighborhood, she missed Frank even more. What Caroline yearned for most was a friend, someone who wanted nothing more from her than companionship and conversation.

Since the move, Caroline had not listened to the records and tapes she and Frank collected over the years. She packed them away, trying to store out of sight the memories and heartache as well. No purpose was served in remembering how she felt when he took her in his arms and swept her across the floor to the strains of Glenn Miller's "String of Pearls" or Benny Goodman's "Let's Dance." No more sweet melodies resounded in her life.

Now, a slim, dark-haired man approached the microphone on the bandstand. "I'll be seeing you . . . in all the old familiar places . . ." he sang. Nostalgia suddenly gripped Caroline with a crushing ache deep in her chest, and a memory carried her back to late summer 1943. She and her friend Nancy were leaving the Seville Restaurant in Indianapolis. The young man at the piano was reaching out to her with a song, but it was late. She had to go.

During World War II, Caroline's life revolved around the war effort. As a special treat, she and Nancy went to Indianapolis to enjoy one of the big bands appearing at the Circle Theater. The music made the three-hour bus trip worthwhile.

After the stage show, they followed the hostess to a table at the Seville. At the piano, a neatly dressed young man with curly blond hair seemed lost in his music. As though someone had called his name, he turned toward Caroline, and their eyes met. A flicker of a smile appeared on his lips, and his fingers paused on the keyboard. Regaining composure, he began playing "Once in a While."

Conversation faltered as Caroline listened to the songs, "Have You Ever Been Lonely" and "The Way You Look Tonight." Leaving to catch the last bus home, Caroline could not resist a final glance in the pianist's direction. He smiled, and the haunting strains of "I'll Be Seeing You" followed them out the door.

Caroline was jarred back to the present when the best

man in the wedding party approached the tables, cajoling the older guests onto the dance floor. "Come on, you people," he urged. "We found musicians who would play the good music you're always talking about, so you guys better dance."

"My name is James Broadmoor," the gentleman said as he approached Caroline. A tanned face accented his white hair, and a friendly smile put her at ease. She extended her hand.

"Caroline Lawson," she said.

"Would you like to dance? My grandson will be disappointed if I don't dance."

"Yes, that would be nice," she answered. They moved onto the polished floor. The apprehension she felt disappeared as James pulled her gently to him. When the song ended, he kept his hand on her waist. An awkward silence fell between them. But when the music resumed, they communicated without words.

"These kids are great. They can actually play real music," James joked when they returned to the table. When the festivities ended, Caroline left with Tony and Jennifer.

A few days later, James called. "I wanted to call sooner, but didn't want to appear pushy." Caroline was surprised at her excitement when she heard his voice. "They're showing *Casablanca* at the Village Theater. Would you come with me?" he asked.

"I'd love to. That's one of my favorites, too."

In the weeks that followed, they attended movies, church and band concerts. James seemed to have a built-in radar for big band music.

One evening, after a piano concert, James and Caroline stopped at a small ice cream parlor near her apartment. The décor was reminiscent of the 1950s, with pink-and-white striped wallpaper and balloons hanging from the light fixtures. Careful not to scuff her new shoes, Caroline led the way to an empty table.

A petite young lady with a single braid down her back placed chocolate sundaes in front of them. "Do you remember telling me about the young man in Indianapolis back during the war who played 'I'll Be Seeing You' when you left the restaurant?" James asked.

Caroline placed her spoon back in the dish. "Yes," she said, "I remember." She felt a lump in her throat as she fumbled with the spoon.

"You know, I played the piano in a little club back in Illinois when I was in college in 1943. It could have been me who played that song for you."

James paused, and there was a longing in his eyes as he looked at Caroline. "I'm just a sentimental old fool."

She reached across the table and took his hand. Tears welled in her eyes. "Me too," she said.

Louise R. Hamm

The Ideal Invitation

A friend lost her mate several years ago and recently developed a friendship with a man who had also lost his spouse. They seemed a perfect match, and all their children agreed they should get married. While they were excited about the upcoming nuptials, they didn't need more crystal vases, blenders, toasters, etc. So this was their invitation:

Phil, Richard, Karen and Allison
and
John, Matt and Steve
request the honor of your presence
at the marriage of their
Mother and Father.
Because they are combining two households,
they already have at least two of everything.
So please, no presents!
Reception and garage sale immediately following the ceremony.

Del Chesser

Five Dates, Eleven Hundred Letters and Fifty-Five Years Later

The older the violin, the sweeter the music.

C. Putnam

The U.S. Army arranged their brief meeting in September 1944. Nathan Hoffman, a soldier from Texas, was waiting at Camp Shanks in New York to ship out for the war in Europe. He decided to use his first leave pass to visit the Big Apple only thirty-five miles away. Little did Nathan know that what awaited him that night would change his life forever.

One of his fellow soldiers—whose parents lived in the city—wanted to drop in and surprise his parents with a hello. No one was at home, so Donald rang the doorbell at a neighbor's house where his parents often went to visit. Evelyn, the neighbors' twenty-one-year-old daughter, answered the door.

"Where's my mom?" Donald asked.

"She's in Brooklyn with my folks."

Donald nonchalantly said, "Say, I'm on a pass with two of

my friends from Camp Shanks. Care to join us downtown?"

Evelyn and one of her friends agreed to go. The soldiers and the young ladies took off for a night on the town, escorting the Texan on his first tour of New York City. The evening ended with dancing at the Bal Tabarin in Times Square.

Before the evening was over, Nathan asked Evelyn, "Would you see me on every pass?" The vivacious young woman replied, "Sure! I'd love to!" Nathan used each pass to see Evelyn, for a total of five romantic dates.

On date number two, the handsome, serious soldier and the attractive, quick-witted young woman again laughed and danced at the Bal Tabarin. The band played "I'll Be Seeing You." Dates three, four and five passed all too quickly, with Nathan visiting Evelyn at her parents' home each night. They hoped for more dates, but the army intervened again.

Nathan's division was restricted to camp. At the camp P-X, Nathan ordered Evelyn an orchid corsage, and wrote on the card in his neat script, "I'll Be Seeing You." The corsage arrived for Evelyn while Nathan was on the ship to Europe, and she wore it proudly to the high holy day services at her synagogue, thinking, *How nice if he were here with me.*

Before their fifth and last date, Nathan and Evelyn had vowed to write daily. And they kept that vow. For the next sixteen months, the soldier from Texas and the girl from the Bronx sent each other eleven hundred letters.

From the beginning, they were much more than just pen pals. Letters to him were addressed, "Nat dear," while she was "Evelyn dearest." He wrote candidly in his October 26, 1944 letter:

Baby, I am not asking you to make any promise with regard to the future . . . who knows how long it will be before the other end of our round-trip ticket to the States. I do know, though, that I

*want you to feel about me as you do now for a long, long time
because it is mutual and maybe both of our prayers together will
help our wishes materialize.*

The sweethearts identified their favorite passages in books they were both reading and then compared opinions. While Nathan was still in England, Evelyn described the record albums of classical music she bought. She asked him, "What do you think of fine music?" He replied by sending her a program from a concert he attended in an English cathedral. He wrote that he especially enjoyed *Symphony No. 5 in C Minor* by Beethoven.

The Texas soldier turned out to be very special to Evelyn. They enjoyed the same music, books, art and entertainment, had the same religion and philosophy of life.

Despite the German surrender in May, Nathan remained in Germany during the summer of 1945, wondering whether he would be sent to the Pacific if Japan refused to surrender. In June, he wrote Evelyn, telling her he would understand if she chose not to wait for him. It would probably be another fifteen months before he could return.

The courtship continued, and their letters gave life to their transatlantic romance.

Their letters dated August 8 through 15, 1945, record their mutual celebration, a celebration tinged with a somber recognition that the world was forever changed:

August 8, 1945—Nathan [in Germany]

Evelyn, from this day on the world as it has been up to now is through. The A-bomb and its successors could become a Frankenstein eventually destroying its creators and the whole planet.

August 11—Evelyn [in New York]

Now the end is in sight, a matter of days. Shredded paper comes from the office windows at every new announcement. People are touchy and suspenseful. This time they say there will be no unofficial V-J Day. We're all waiting for President Truman's peace declaration.

August 11—Nathan [in Germany]

I've just heard the good news about the war. Honey, I'm so happy I could holler, shout, raise hell, cry and do anything. If someone tells me it's a false alarm, I will keel over and drop dead. Hopefully, now the whole damned war is "kaput" and this wholesale slaughter can be brought to an end.

August 15—Evelyn [in New York]

The sirens are wailing. The noise and celebration in the streets are deafening. I can hardly steady my hand. I have a deep peaceful feeling and a million prayers of thanksgiving. I can't remember what peace was like. Most of all, it means our husbands, fathers, brothers, boyfriends and relatives are coming home. We can start our lives again. Pray there will be no more wars.

After the peace declaration, Nathan had to wait his turn, while the soldiers who had fought in Europe the longest went home first. September, October and then November dragged on. The sweethearts grew impatient with their matchmaker, the army. In all their letters, an electric undercurrent of anticipation for their sixth date grew stronger.

Everywhere his unit was sent, Nathan carried with him in his one duffel bag the hundreds of letters Evelyn had sent. Before he finally received orders to go home, he needed to lighten his duffel bag for the trip. He sent the letters home by mail in a twenty-three-pound package.

Nathan's final correspondence of the war, penned on the last day of 1945, reads like this:

. . . This should be the last letter that I shall write to you from

here. When you next hear from me it will be by phone or in person. . . . S'long, honey, pucker up, 'cause here I come . . . with love.

When Nathan returned home in January 1946, Evelyn was there at the Discharge Center to meet him. A month later, on February 24, 1946, they were married in Nathan's family's synagogue.

* * * * *

Fifty years later, as they renewed their vows in the same synagogue where they were married, Nathan shared: "After fifty golden years, I can say that our years together seem to me but a few days because of the love I have for her. And I would wait for her all over again."

"World War II brought us together," said Evelyn. "In Hebrew, we have a word *beshert*—divinely appointed, meant to be. That is what Nathan and I are, *beshert*—we are each other's perfect soul mate."

The twenty-three-pound package of letters Nathan had sent home from the war, along with the letters Evelyn had lovingly saved, are now preserved within two large, bound volumes. The Hoffmans compiled these letters in book form as a labor of love to pass along as a special legacy for their children, grandchildren and friends.

On September 9, 1944, among eight million people in New York, Nathan and Evelyn fatefully crossed paths.

Five wonderful, whirlwind dates, eleven hundred letters and fifty-five years later, their love that endured a war is still going strong.

Amy Seeger

THE BORN LOSER. Reprinted by permission of Newspaper Enterprise Association, Inc.

Love's Cross-Stitch

The purpose of life, after all, is to live it, to taste experience to the utmost, to reach out eagerly and without fear for newer and richer experience.

Eleanor Roosevelt

"Now if you want to change your mind—" Del glanced from the road to read my expression, then faced back to the freeway traffic. "Remember, I'll understand if you'd just like to drive by the house. Not even get out. Or, at the front door, if you decide that's it for the first time, fine. The most important thing is that I care about you. More than any house or the things in it."

I smiled, nodding, hoping my eyes and the tiny muscle tugs around them wouldn't betray me. I didn't want to disappoint this man who was now the very center of my life. But how might I react when I saw for the first time the house he had lived in for the past twenty years, eighteen of them with his Lib?

I knew them both, but that was thirty-five years ago, when we lived in the same town. Lib and Del raised their two girls, then grew older in the house, the house which until now had been to me simply the address I wrote on envelopes of annual Christmas cards.

Then, a little over two years ago, when Lib was near the end, she had asked Del to write me. After her passing, I wrote to him. I shared with him a few of the helps that had served me when I lost my marriage mate of many years, assuring him I recognized our losses were not to be compared, yet believing them similar in a very real way. We corresponded for almost a year before he asked if he might come to see me.

Del signaled to take the off-ramp. I could still change my mind, but we would soon swing into a driveway somewhere to the right. I knew the area, though not in detail. He had driven the many miles to visit me countless times, but until now he had never suggested I visit him.

"Seeing me in your home could be difficult, Del," I warned. "Have you had many people in since you've been alone?"

He pulled to a stop at a light. "Neighbors. The girls, of course, and their families. The grandkids come over pretty often." He smiled at me.

"I mean outside of family and neighbors."

Still smiling, he shook his head no and pulled from the stop. "I want you to see my house. I've been looking forward to this evening. But the decision is still yours."

I tried to busy my mind on anything but the impending, immediate future. Crossing the bridge at the little creek woke the sleeping butterflies in my stomach; the house would be less than a block away. My heart banged against my chest. I hadn't felt this confused or just plain nervous since I was a teenager.

Del slowed for the turn onto Woodhurst, the street I had written on envelopes for years, then braked to a crawl. "Cold feet?"

"Clammy cold."

"Understandable," he said in the gentle, measured tone I'd grown to love. "But we've come a long way."

True. A long drive, and a remarkable length of time as friends. We had kindled from a resurrected, couples acquaintanceship a strong, sweet attachment. To enter Del's home now would ratify our closeness. To refuse would be to minimize our importance to one another.

I breathed in long, deep. "I'm ready, Del."

"Sure?"

"Sure." After all, I told myself, I must confront my fear. Too often I lectured to my daughter: How we handle our fears can determine the rest of our lives. Del and I were older, but we still had the rest of our lives.

The car turned into the drive of a modest, but freshly painted, tan house, the lawn around it cropped neatly; the shrubs near the entry were trimmed and welcoming.

He turned off the ignition and watched me. I smiled and took his hand. "Yes," I said.

Relief washed over him. He grasped my hand in both of his, then returned it to my lap and, like a boy, bounded out of the car.

Neither of us spoke as I walked into the living room, my knees loose-hinged, my mouth dry. My breath caught, and I felt suddenly light-headed. Del was at my side. "You okay?"

"I think so." I wanted to melt into his shoulders, feel his strength around me. But not now, not here.

He guided me to the dining room and said, "I'll just call the Chinese Palace. Shouldn't take them long to deliver. It's been too long since we ate." He slipped around the corner to the kitchen. How could I tell him nothing was going to help? Certainly not eating.

Alone now, I looked around the room. Pretty china in the hutch. I remembered one of the serving pieces from those long-ago dinner exchanges Lib and I used to do. A miniature tea set of rather coarse pottery was displayed at one end of the buffet. Probably belonged to the girls, but meant more to mother than daughters. On the opposite wall hung a lovely oil in a deep frame—a young girl sitting primly near a woodland stream. Lib's art selection. Here, there, her fancies, her expressions, all in affirmation of Lib.

Perhaps I might slip out while Del was still on the phone. I could take a cab to the bus station. I could be home by midnight. Later he would understand. He'd realize I simply wasn't ready to face the many Libs who still lived here. Or, I admitted to myself, I was still not prepared to confront my fear. Of what I wasn't sure. Fear of not measuring up to Lib? Fear that what Del and I felt for each other was less love than need? Did I merely need to feel loved? Did Del simply need a woman to fill the other chair at the table?

"Oh, and lots of rice. We like rice," he said around the corner, and his voice sent the usual prickles up my spine.

On the narrow wall between the hutch and the large window hung a framed sampler done in fine cross-stitch. I stepped closer to read the words: "To experience life? Or to be limited by the fear of it?"

Slowly, I read the sampler again. Lib's painstakingly crafted quote held meaning for her. But its message this evening was for me. Oddly, my breath evened.

Del rounded the corner, his eyebrows lifted in question. A glance took me in, and he smiled. "They'll deliver in a few minutes. Let's go see the rest of the house. Hungry?"

"Starved," I said honestly.

His hand slipped around my waist, and we walked down the hall. Side by side.

Evelyn Gibb

The Golden Gift

"Our Golden Wedding Day draws near," the husband said.
The elderly woman, smiling, raised her head,
"Will you write me a poem as you used to do?
That's the gift I'd like most from you!"

The old man, agreeing, limped from the room,
Went out on the porch in the twilight's gloom,
Leaned on the railing and reminisced:
"Often we sat here, shared hopes and kissed.

"Dear Lord, how the years have hurried by—
Those memories of youth make an old man sigh!
Now we grow weary and bent and gray,
What clever words can I possibly say

"To show that I love her just as much
As I did when her cheeks were soft to my touch,
When her eyes were bright and her lips were warm,
And we happily walked with her hand on my arm!"

So the husband stood while the evening breeze
Echoed his sigh through the nearby trees
Till the joys they had shared in days long past
Merged into thoughts he could voice at last,

And he went inside and got paper and pen;
Sat down at the kitchen table and then
Carefully wrote what his wife had desired:
A gift as "golden" as a love inspired.

"Sweetheart, dear wife, my closest friend,
With you my days begin and end.
Though time has stolen strength and youth,
It cannot change this shining truth:

"Our love has lasted all these years
While hardships came with sorrow's tears.
We've met each test and gotten by,
And I will love you till I die!

"We are not rich in worldly wealth
But we own nothing gained by stealth,
And you remain my greatest treasure,
My source of pride and quiet pleasure.

"I wish you all the happiness
With which two loving hearts are blessed;
You were, and are, my choice for life,
My girl, my lady, my sweet wife!"

The poem finished, the husband arose,
Went into the room where his good wife dozed
And tenderly kissed her nodding head,
"Wake up, 'sleeping beauty,' and come to bed!"

John C. Bonser

7

ON
OVERCOMING

Do not pray for easy lives. Pray to be stronger.

John F. Kennedy

A Timeless Tapestry

The best and most beautiful things in life cannot be seen or even touched . . . they must be felt with the heart.

Helen Keller

I watched a tapestry in the making the other night. It wasn't hanging on the wall of a gallery or my den; it was in a hospital room.

The first threads were woven together nearly fifty-three years before when a young woman named Asa Lee applied for a job. The manager who took her application that day was a handsome young fellow nicknamed Mac. Asa Lee and Mac dated, fell in love and seven months later, married.

Together, they reared a son and a daughter and enjoyed the arrivals of five grandchildren over the years. Their lives had been full until a couple of years ago when Mac's health began to fail.

I met Asa Lee as several of us gathered to sing Christmas carols for hospitalized members of our church.

I couldn't help but notice her ready smile and easy laugh.

I was surprised to learn our first stop was to visit Asa Lee's husband at the Veterans Administration Medical Center. Mac suffers from congestive heart failure and Parkinson's disease, which makes speech nearly impossible for him. He also has an eye condition that has robbed him of most of his sight.

By the time we entered Mac's room, our group had quieted, sobered by what we saw around us. Mac was awake, but he didn't seem to recognize his wife, who bent to kiss his cheek and take his hand.

We did our best singing carols, but our songs seemed small comfort to offer. As we sang, Asa Lee leaned over her husband's bed and looked lovingly into his unseeing eyes. Perhaps she saw reflected in them the joys of Christmases past, of their children playing on his lap, of tender moments they had shared.

Our singing ended, and Asa Lee bent nearer to her husband, smiling, to say a few words before she turned to leave. Mac was unable to respond.

We started for the door. I looked back and saw Mac trying to move. With great difficulty, he turned his head and reached toward his wife.

Mac and Asa Lee must have been woven together by some invisible but invincible thread. Just then she looked back at him. Seeing his outstretched hand, she instantly returned to his side and grasped it, bending near to give him another kiss.

The clasped hands and the shared kiss had taken only a moment, yet the love of which it spoke had knit together the joys and overcome the pains of a fifty-three-year tapestry of love and devotion. A tapestry as ancient as creation and as new as tomorrow's sunrise, when once again Asa Lee will return to her husband's side.

Vicki Marsh Kabat

Daddy's Best Birthday

His courage is his legacy, our inheritance.

Nita Sue Kent

My father died a few months before his thirty-eighth birthday. I was fifty-three at the time. How could I be fifteen years older than my own father? Because the most important birth date our family celebrated was Daddy's Alcoholics Anonymous birthday.

I have thought a lot about what it means to me to have grown up in a family that simply didn't work long before the term "dysfunctional family" was coined. When I was little, I learned lessons that helped me survive at the time. I am still unlearning some of those early lessons.

Last summer, while working in the garden, I shifted a large stepping stone over onto a patch of grass and forgot to return it to its place. When at last I remembered to move it, the grass underneath was sickly pale and stunted. The grass still lived, and with time, water and the sunlight it needed to survive, it grew healthy. Had I left the stone there, the grass would have died and been replaced by grubs, snails and bare earth.

Parts of me are like a lawn where stones have been scattered at random. Some patches didn't get what they needed to grow strong and healthy. While finding and moving those stones, I have often been resentful and angry. There are spots where grass will never grow. It hurts to admit there were things I just didn't get when I was a little kid.

But in the course of all that work, I have come to appreciate how much sunshine did fall on me, and even how to grow plants more exotic than grass in the bare spots. And for the first time in my life, I wish I could remember more.

I've tried to remember how I felt in 1958 when Daddy stopped drinking. Instead, I wasn't even aware of what was going on. And when I did begin to realize something unusual was happening, I was skeptical, even cynical. No expectations for me! I had been sadly disappointed too many times before. Even in the beginning, my family was wise enough to realize that stopping one particularly destructive behavior doesn't mean instant cures, only freedom to work on the deeper issues that inevitably underlie "The Problem." So nobody ever promised anything that I remember. I wouldn't have believed them if they had.

As months went by, I slowly suspected change was possible. Then one night, as my mother and I were driving home, we saw my father's beat-up old blue panel truck parked at the neighborhood bar. I knew it was all over. Mother said, "I have to go see." She parked the car and left me sitting outside while she went inside. Through a window I could see Daddy, leaning against the bar, a tall, amber-colored glass in his hand. Everything inside me went into a protective crouch—deep, dark and hidden away.

Mother came out of the bar with a strange new expression on her face. She climbed into the car and said, "He's drinking iced tea. He needed to check up on some of his old friends. He'll be home in a little while." Something inside me was able to relax a little.

After Daddy's best birthday, thank God, and Daddy's hard work, he never did "fall off the wagon." Following the Alcoholics Anonymous slogan "one day at a time," he and mother truly lived one day at a time, working on their problems and helping other people through A.A. and Al-Anon. Daddy never became financially successful, and sometimes he said how sorry he was that he had no inheritance to leave his children. But he didn't brood over lost opportunities. When he turned eighty, he joined a fitness club and worked out on the weight machines to improve his golf swing.

Then at an A.A. retreat, he fell and broke his hip. He and Mother fought his deteriorating condition for three years. A big man, and always physically fit, Daddy hated the indignities of not being able to walk or care for himself. Slowly, slowly his body shut down, and with Mother and a few other family members by his bed, he died. Later, Mother said, "He can walk again. And I know he walked into heaven clean and sober."

At my parents' fiftieth wedding anniversary some years before his death, the reception hall was filled with children, grandchildren, great-grandchildren, nieces, nephews, cousins and hundreds of friends from A.A. and church. How clear that memory is. How different it would have been if he had not been brave enough in 1958 to ask for help.

Daddy was wrong to think he had nothing to leave his children. He gave us over thirty-seven years and nine months of sobriety—almost fourteen thousand days—one day at a time. His courage is his legacy, our inheritance.

Nita Sue Kent

THE FAMILY CIRCUS® By Bil Keane

". . . and say hi to our grandfather
who art in heaven, too."

Reprinted by permission of Bil Keane.

Fear Fouls a Pond

A good scare is worth more to a man than good advice.

Edgar Watson Howe

The great Louis Armstrong told a story about when he was a boy. A woman told him to go down to the spring and get a bucket of water and bring it back to her. So he went down to dip the bucket into the water. There looking at him out of the water was a pair of eyes—an alligator. Scared to death, Louis left the bucket and ran back to the old lady. She said, "Where is my bucket of water?"

He said, "Miss Allie Mae, I went down there and I put that bucket in the water, and there was a pair of alligator eyes looking at me. I ran. That 'gator scared me to death."

She said, "Louis, that alligator has been there for years, and he probably is as afraid of you as you are of him."

Louis said, "Miss Allie Mae, if that alligator is as scared of me as I am of him, then that water ain't fit to drink anyway."

Retold by Bill Floyd

A Plan for You

For I know the plans I have for you, declares the Lord. Plans to prosper you and not to harm you, plans to give you hope and a future.

Jeremiah 29:11

The telephone rang. The familiar voice on the other end belonged to a close friend from California. Her voice caught with a little sob, and then I heard, "My wonderful husband has just died. . . ."

My mind went back many years to when my husband Norman was pastor of the Marble Collegiate Church on Fifth Avenue in New York City. A striking gentleman started coming to the Sunday morning service accompanied by his mother. They sat about eight or ten rows from the back. He visited several churches on Fifth Avenue but left each one after a few Sundays. He kept attending our worship service, and later he was selected to become an elder. He was considered one of the most brilliant attorneys in New York City. And he was single.

Now . . . "the rest of the story!"

Norman and I were taking a tour group of about twelve

hundred people to Hawaii. We persuaded the attorney to go with us. The trip was a wonderful experience. One evening in the seaside hotel in Hawaii, I was planning the seating arrangements for the dinner table Norman and I would host. I had invited a good friend from San Francisco to be seated at our table. I asked myself, "What gentleman could I select to put next to this beautiful woman?" The thought of our attorney came to mind, for I felt he would be a good choice.

You can probably guess what happened. They fell for each other! That evening in Hawaii was a divine appointment. They were married, he moved to California and for fifteen years they enjoyed a wonderful life together. She was the one calling to inform me of his death.

I remember telling my dear, distraught friend what I tell other friends when they lose a spouse, "God had a plan for you when you two met and has a plan for you now." A happy time of her life had come to a close, and she needed to believe that her future was still full of promise. "Throughout the changes in our lives," I said to her, "we all need to be reminded that God has a plan for us. I believe this because I have seen it to be true in the lives of many people."

At the time, I spoke to my friend from secondhand experience. But now I can speak from firsthand experience because Norman died after more than six decades of our being married. I treasure the past, but I enjoy the present, too. I have begun to venture into new areas of speaking and writing that I never took time for when Norman was alive. But now is as good a time as ever for stretching my capabilities. When one of my friends or acquaintances loses a spouse and asks me for advice, I say, "I make it a point to enjoy new, unfolding plans for my life. If this formula works for me, it can work for you."

Ruth Stafford Peale

Two of a Kind

Although the world is full of suffering, it is full also of promises for overcoming it.

Helen Keller

Everyone called them "the two old people." If they weren't battling each other, they were feuding with someone else and then arguing about it later. Unfortunately, they lived in the condominium above mine.

One evening as I prepared to turn in, I made the usual round of locking doors, turning out the lights and checking in on my daughter and her two little kittens. But on this particular night, Pumpkin, the feisty orange-colored kitten, was nowhere to be found. Pumpkin and I had a relationship of tolerance. But the relationship between Jennifer and Pumpkin was unconditional. They were two of a kind: funny, sassy, loving, playful, adventurous. Kitten and child belonged together. So I knew I had to find Pumpkin.

I searched outside our home and decided to walk down the path leading to the central park of the condominium complex. Hearing a kitten's faint cry, I shined my flashlight up into a nearby sapling. There was Pumpkin, her plump little body supported only by a frail branch. Frantically, she pedaled her legs in a futile attempt to regain her grasp of the branch.

I climbed up into the base of the tree to lift the kitty to safety. Climbing down the spindly tree would be tricky. I sat for a moment to ponder my dilemma. It was then that I heard sharp voices approaching.

"If you hadn't . . ." a woman's shrill voice accused.

"It wasn't *me*," a male voice interrupted with an angry shriek. "She would still be alive if . . ."

"If *you* had been a better father, one who . . ."

He interrupted her interruption. "And *you*? Were *you* such a great mother?"

The woman wailed, "She was my daughter! Paula. Oh, my Paula." She sobbed uncontrollably.

"We still have Robby. He's a good son," the old man countered softly.

The old woman cried, "No one can replace my Paula."

"It was a tragic accident," the old man offered. He shook his head and softly said, "It was so many years ago. We must forgive ourselves."

"*Never!*" she screeched.

The voices belonged to the two old people. They stomped out of sight, and I hurried home.

The kitten safely home, life resumed as normal. That little Pumpkin was one mischievous kitten. When the six acres of garden grounds no longer satisfied her, she took to crossing the street and raiding the neighbors' yards as well.

One day Pumpkin met a car that didn't see the little orange-colored cat. We found Pumpkin late that afternoon, her limp body lying lifeless by the side of the street near our complex. My daughter carried her back to the house, crying the entire way.

I knew Jennie needed time to accept her cat's death. I decided to wait until dinner to talk over the cat's death and our intentions for its burial. The dinner hour arrived, and I went to Jennie's room. She wasn't there. Not only was my daughter not there, the cat's corpse wasn't there either. I went looking. As I neared the park, I paused. There on the wooden park bench sat my almost-eight-year-old daughter, cradling in her arms the large blue bath towel in which we had wrapped the dead cat.

The old woman, carrying pots of soil, approached the bench where Jen sat. She hesitated and then joined the grieving young girl on the bench. She scooted cautiously toward Jen and inquired, "So, what is it you have there?"

"My kitty, Pumpkin—she's dead."

The old woman huddled closer to the child. In and of itself this was an interesting sight; the senior had such a reputation for her disdain of children, especially active busybodies like my daughter. But now she sat with the child in distressed sympathy. She placed one hand around Jennifer's shoulder while the other smoothed her old, navy blue skirt. Over her frumpy white blouse she'd draped her standard item of apparel—an old, gray sweater.

"She'll never come back to life," Jennie's voice cracked. Then sobbing, added, "I'll never get to play with her again."

Leaning closer, the old woman dabbed at Jennie's tears. "It'll be okay," the old woman offered.

"You don't understand," my Jennie mumbled, shaking her head from side to side. Agonized, she asked ever so sadly and slowly, "I loved Pumpkin and she loved me. *Why* did my kitty have to die?"

A far-off look came over the old woman's face as she whispered, "If only she had been home where she belonged." I later learned that mother and daughter had another of their explosive arguments. The daughter had run from the house, slamming the door behind her. She was just seventeen at the time.

Jennie said, "If only I had taken care of her this morning like I was supposed to. . . . Probably she got so hungry that she went hunting for food. If only I had fed her this morning. If I . . ." She shook her head from side to side.

The old woman was lost in her own thoughts. *If only I had taken better care of the relationship between Paula and me; if only I had backed off when I knew my daughter was at her wit's end, if only . . . if only . . . then my daughter would still be alive. If only I had taken the time to understand, to talk, to explain. If only . . .*

"If only . . ." Jennie continued and then stopped. Hopelessness took over, and she shouted in an angry voice, "My kitty is dead!"

The old woman reached out and pulled my daughter to her bosom. Then the old woman began crying, too. Startled, my daughter sat upright and asked, "Why are you crying?"

"Because she was so precious to me," the old woman said.

Jennifer was surprised at this response. After all, the old woman had on many occasions yelled at the cat. In disbelief, my daughter said, "But you were always yelling at her."

"Oh, I know," the old woman admitted. "If only I could do it over. If only I wouldn't have said those unkind things, perhaps she wouldn't have gone away, if only . . ."

"It wasn't *all* your fault." Now it was Jennie offering consolation.

"I guess it was both of us," the old woman agreed resolutely.

"Yup," Jennie said with a big sigh. "Mom says blaming doesn't solve problems. It won't bring her back to life."

"Oh, I know," agreed the old woman again. "I'm sure

your mother will get you another kitten," she said.

"I don't want another kitten," Jennifer said defiantly. She rocked the dead kitten she cradled in her arms. "No one can take her place!"

And no one could take the place of the old woman's dearly beloved daughter.

"I just want it to stop hurting," Jennifer asserted.

"Yes, me too," agreed the old woman. "I long for it to stop hurting so much, too."

"Where does it hurt you?" questioned the little girl. "I hurt here the most." Jennifer placed her hand on her stomach.

"My ache lives here in my chest," responded the old woman. "And deep within my heart."

"They didn't stop to see if they had hurt her," my daughter said softly.

The old woman shuddered and put both her arms around herself and rocked back and forth. Her daughter's body had been found nearly six hours after the hit-and-run.

"And no one came to her rescue," my daughter said.

"Oh, I know," the old woman murmured. "If only I could have been there for her."

"I don't think it would have mattered," offered Jennifer. "Nothing could have survived being hit by a fast car."

Jennifer reached out and put her little arms around the, tiny gray-haired woman. They clung to each other, gently swaying back and forth in silence.

Stroking Jennie's head, the old woman asked, "Do you want me to help you bury your kitty?"

I watched as the two of them dug the hole. Jennie carefully unfolded the towel and gazed at her kitten. She kissed Pumpkin delicately before carefully wrapping her again in the towel. As Jennie kneeled to lay her kitten to rest, the old woman stopped her. She removed her trademark sweater and placed it in Jennifer's hand. "Use this in place of the towel," she instructed. "This is the sweater I was wearing when they found her body. Maybe I shouldn't wear it anymore." Her lips trembled. "It's time to bury my grief."

Reverently, as in a sacred ceremony, the two entrusted to Mother Earth their special, though separate, memories.

The incident transformed the old woman. For the next few weeks, she often knocked at my door to ask if Jennifer could go for a walk with her. And the incident definitely changed the relationship between the old man and his wife. There wasn't the same bickering and groaning between them after that day. They actually walked companionably across the condominium's well-landscaped grounds from time to time. And the old woman obviously enjoyed seeking out Jennifer for walks in the late afternoon when school was out.

Walking-and-talking time with Jennie turned into helping-with-homework time. This went on for the next two years, until I bought a house and moved from the condominium complex. Years later, my daughter still calls on her and cares for her.

Perhaps it was this reaching outside of herself to comfort a grieving child—with no other motive than to help someone else in pain—that finally allowed the old woman to begin healing. She opened her heart to a child, and in doing so, left her bitterness behind. And made room for love to grow again.

Bettie B. Youngs
Adapted from "The Two Old People" in Gifts of the Heart,
HCI, 1997

Letters Home from War

Excerpts from letters to his family reflect the passions of a husband and a father for his children. Lt. Cmdr. John E. Bartocci's thoughts, emotions and inner longings are bound by no time, place or profession.

31 Jan. Dearest Barb, It was sad watching you and the children drive out of sight as the carrier pulled out of the harbor. Three years of shore duty were wonderful. The children's characters have really taken shape. I know them so much better now, and that makes leaving so much more difficult.

19 Feb. My birthday. Does thirty-three sound old? It used to, and I think it still does. When I went down to the Ready Room, I found a large birthday cake, and when I went up to man my aircraft, I found "Happy Birthday" written on the fuselage. We've got a good crew. I like them, and they know it.

Tomorrow is your birthday, but you don't age. You're as attractive as you were when you were seventeen years old—only now, more exciting. As I write these words, I'm thinking of you and how you act, sound, feel, smell. I'm so in love with you, Barb.

25 Feb. The time has come. Tomorrow we'll be on the line, and I'm on the flight schedule. I feel like it's the night before an exam, and I'm not prepared. Nervous as a cat. I admit I'm scared of the thought of getting shot at.

27 Feb. A tragic loss today of one of our helicopters and crew. I played guitar with those pilots only last week.

5 March. I'm glad the children like my letters to them. I think it's better if they have a tangible communication from Daddy rather than just a word passed via you. I can just picture Andrew saying you "lost Daddy." Poor little guy. He can't know why the normal order of things is disturbed. I'm not sure I know, myself.

10 March. I'm back from a strike. What a beautiful sight the sea is when you've crossed the coastline on the way back to the ship.

12 March. I'm sitting in the cockpit of an aircraft at 1:20 A.M. Condition I CAP. The sea is calm. Just now, I saw a falling star. It seems almost out of the question that I could go flying at a moment's notice.

16 March. By the time you get this letter you will undoubtedly have heard of the loss of Lt. J. G. Don S. yesterday. Possibly he took an enemy hit, but visibility was poor. He may have just flown into the water. Don had been in the squadron a scant nine days.

23 April. Operations back to a steady pace. Fresh water is low. No showers allowed. After a sweaty day of flight ops, means lots of deodorant and after-shave lotion.

24 April. The dangers of this business hit home today. They bagged another of our squadron pilots. A parachute was seen so he is probably alive. I'm scheduled for a strike tomorrow. I shudder to think of capture. Please pray that I'll have the presence of mind to do my job properly and with honor.

3 May. Going on a big one again tomorrow. Things are hot out here now. It looks as if the war has escalated, but you probably have a better overall picture than we do.

Our airplanes aren't holding up at all, and we can't get parts. It's a frustrating business. My schedule has become disjointed. Up at 3:15 A.M. And so it goes. And it's hot.

6 May. Waiting to go on a big strike the past two days but weather has prohibited. Still, life isn't boring—last night one of our aircraft caught fire on the flight deck. A sad note: This morning an enlisted man walked into a propeller. It was pretty messy. Here's a guy who is doing a difficult job—for peanuts—and putting up with long separations and lousy living conditions and he winds up dead.

After the pressures of this air war, I know what a treasure the serenity of the family is. I long to feel the children's arms around me. Tears come to my eyes when I think how I want to be with my children, playing with them, explaining things to them, trying to give them some of myself. And then to think of you, my greatest asset. You've flooded my life with goodness. You are the source of all that's dear to me.

14 May. We're now steaming full speed toward Yankee station [line combat], two days early. Could this be escalation? Stay tuned.

19 May. A bad day for us. The opposition was the worst ever, they say. Two pilots are reported missing. A good chance they were captured. I hope so. As one man put it yesterday, "You can't come back from the dead, but you might make it out of a prison camp."

20 May. I am scheduled for the next strike . . . a tough one. . . . I don't mind telling you I'm scared.

21 May. I went to Mass this morning. We brief for the big strike at noon. Before the strike, Barb, it's important for me to tell you again how much I love you. Without you, my life would be shallow and empty.

31 May. Today was glorious in one way. Received a

wonderful photograph of you and the children. Barb, I can't tell you not to worry or not to be afraid. All I can say is, I hope it's God's will that I return to you in August as scheduled. There is nothing I want more than to go on the camping trip that Barty keeps talking about.

2 June. Thanks for your letter with Barty's tooth in it! I wish I could hear Bart laugh right now. He has such an infectious laugh. I love him so. Tell Allison that I love my little girl very much. And Andrew, too.

3 June. I am sad to report that Dave W. was lost at sea early this morning. Search is still in progress. He took off at 2:30 A.M., and that was the last contact.

Hope you're saying some prayers. My emotions are a mix of self-pity, fear, pride, sadness, anger. I wonder if I have courage—and if I do, what is it all worth? Of course, we must maintain our outward appearance of fearless composure.

4 June. We are inventorying and packing Dave's things. What a depressing job. I liked Dave better than anyone else in the squadron. I still can't get used to the idea he's gone.

P.S. Our flight surgeon just stopped in to give me a cigar. His wife gave birth to a girl. I told him, news of a birth is welcome, indeed.

6 June. Tomorrow I will have been commissioned for ten years, and next week we will have been married nine years. Nine wonderful years to a girl who makes me feel nine feet tall and who has borne me three beautiful children. Without you, my darling, I'd be like an autumn leaf—dry and lifeless.

Again, sad news. Yesterday we lost a photo pilot. Just two days earlier, he and I had made the same run together. They were shooting like mad. Yesterday, they got lucky. Damn war. So depressing.

9 June. Dear Bart: How are you, son? I sure enjoyed the

tape recording you, Mommy, Allison and Andrew made. And I enjoyed your joke, too . . .

Dear Allison: I enjoy getting letters from you. Help your mother and be a good big sister to your brothers. Love, "Daddy-O."

12 June. A quiet Sunday. Only two big air strikes. John M. got shot down east of Haiphong but was picked up. You can't imagine the anxiety of waiting for the Helo to get him. Alfred Hitchcock couldn't have duplicated the suspense. Yes sir, a drama a day.

A new pilot came aboard yesterday—an ensign. Poor kid was in the Ready Room when we got back from the Hanoi raid. Must have been something to see all these pilots come in soaked in their own perspiration, hair askew, with dry mouths, adrenaline still up and breathing heavy. That's a hell of a way to meet the squadron!

I'm looking at the beautiful pictures you sent me of the children. I see such hope in their eyes. I want so much to hold them in my arms, Barb. I want to be there to influence my children, to bring out their good qualities. What greater success can a father ask?

14 June. Awards were given out today, and I got my first air medal. The award that would please me would be a trip back home. Four more days of this line period. The ship expects to arrive in San Diego in August. That means our big camping trip is set for September.

27 June. Tomorrow starts our last line period. Thirty-two more days of combat . . . I want to hold you in my arms, taste the sweetness of your lips, feel the softness of your cheek next to mine, make love to you. How deeply I love you and the children.

25 July. Three more days till we leave the line.

29 July. I can't believe this has happened. This morning at 7:00 I was thinking happy thoughts. Combat flying was over. Bob and I congratulated each other on having

conducted ourselves honorably and with excellence. At
11:00, we got word of a fire on the aircraft carrier Forrestal.
We steamed full speed to give assistance. Smoke was billowing out of her stern section, and the charred remnants
of some aircraft were visible on the flight deck. At least
twenty people killed and a lot more injured.

How does it affect us? We're extended on the line for an
indefinite period.

31 Aug.
My Darling John,
I love you. They're trying to tell me you're dead. You
can't be—we have so much to do together. Remember our
camping trip? Remember how we joke and laugh
together?

Oh, John, I love you—John, you can't be dead. . . .

*Lt. Cmdr. John Bartocci was killed when his aircraft crashed
into the flight deck as he returned from a night mission. His body
was lost at sea.*

*His wife, Barbara, returned to college after her husband's death,
earned a graduate degree, and moved with her children to Kansas
City to join the creative staff at Hallmark Cards. Today, still living
in Kansas City, she writes books and travels the country as a
motivational speaker. Allison and Bart, now called John, each
graduated from college, married and are raising families in the
Midwest. Their children know they are lovingly watched over by
"Grandpa John in heaven." Andrew returned to San Diego, where
the family lived when his father was alive. After earning an MBA,
he now works in management for an international company.*

*As John Bartocci once wrote, "What greater success can a father
ask?"*

Barbara Bartocci

FDR and Me

History has demonstrated that the most notable winners usually encountered heartbreaking obstacles before they triumphed.

B. C. Forbes

In one way, Helynn Hoffa was very lucky. As a twelve-year-old in Warm Springs, Georgia, she got to meet and talk with Franklin Delano Roosevelt, the much-admired president of the United States from 1933 to 1945. In another way, Helynn was very unlucky. The reason she was in Warm Springs was to undergo therapy for polio, the dreaded disease she had contracted four years before.

During the summer of 1928, polio struck several people in the small town of Sunbury, Pennsylvania. Helynn was one of the unfortunate victims. But she was lucky that she survived; many others didn't. At first she couldn't even open or close her eyelids, and for two years she was completely paralyzed. She was told she would never walk again. The cruel polio virus had squelched the young child's dream of ever becoming an archaeologist.

Gradually though, with a reclining wheelchair, Helynn was able to rejoin her third-grade classmates. She was determined even at that young age not to be cut out of what life had to offer. Helynn remembers saying, "I can't write, but I can recite.

"I'll never forget the particular afternoon when I was in therapy at Warm Springs. I was sitting on a step of the pool when FDR came swimming over toward me. We chatted for a few minutes—about my progress—and about the value of this wonderful treatment center for polio he had built for thousands like us," Helynn recalls. Now seventy-nine, Helynn has a faraway look in her friendly, brown eyes as she continues, "Then he stopped talking and looked at me for a minute."

"What do you want to be when you grow up?" he asked finally.

Helynn remembers shrugging and telling him, "I'm not sure I could 'be' anything. But if I had a choice, I'd like to be an archaeologist."

"Just remember," FDR said softly, "if I can be in a wheelchair and be president of the greatest country in the world, you can be whatever you want."

That encounter with FDR has guided Helynn ever since. "Here was a person," she thought, "who had to deal with the same physical handicap I have to deal with. And he had to run the United States, too!" Helynn also credits her parents for her strong determination. Her parents' unlimited love, encouragement and support, and FDR's encouraging words, gave her the resolution to endure years of physiotherapy, enabling her to get around in a regular wheelchair.

Helynn remembers one special highlight during high school, "I was the envy of my girlfriends when the football team was assigned to carry me in my wheelchair up and down the stairs!" Helynn went on to graduate with her high school class, took correspondence courses from the University of Chicago and has never quite quenched her thirst for knowledge—reading everything she can.

Helynn eventually became a nun, free-lance writer, artist, bookkeeper, art teacher, sports reporter—and even ran her own print shop, publishing company, as well as her own radio show. She also worked in Honolulu after World War II.

But that's not all. Helynn has authored three books. One is a novel, one is a volume of her memoirs, which she has just completed, and one is a guide for the physically challenged entitled *Yes You Can*. Of this last book she says, "All the encouragement I received from everyone, including my parents and FDR, made a big difference in my life. I wrote this book to encourage others just as I have been encouraged."

Fifteen years ago, Helynn contracted post-polio syndrome, which affects some 30 percent of the three hundred thousand polio survivors in the United States today. This syndrome involves the gradual loss of muscular strength once regained through physical therapy. For the past decade Helynn has spent up to sixteen hours a day in a 1928 model iron lung, which takes up most of her small living room. She adds, "I call it the yellow submarine in honor of my days as an ardent Beatles fan."

After years of traveling—to England, San Francisco, Baja, Hawaii, Canada and Mexico—today Helynn rarely even leaves her house. But she refuses to let long hours in the yellow submarine slow her down much. She explains, "I spend up to four hours a day dictating my work to an assistant, who then types the text on the computer." Helynn is a remarkable example of the familiar saying, "When life gives you lemons, make lemonade." Helynn has indeed made the best of what life has thrown at her.

Calling herself a "smorgasbord scholar," she comments,

"Education can't be given; it has to be earned—it is just like everything else in life. If it's worth having, it's worth working for. And, believe me, knowledge is worth working for! Without it, we achieve little." Helynn believes so much in education that among other efforts, she was one of the pioneers who helped get Southwestern Community College started. To show its appreciation for Helynn, this Chula Vista school bestowed on her an honorary associate of arts degree.

Because of Helynn's untiring support of education and encouragement of the physically challenged, she was featured on CNN and has received various other awards. "Like FDR and me," Helynn says with a winsome smile, "people should refuse to use their physical limitations as an excuse or an obstacle." She elaborates, "The disability that cripples more people than any other is ignorance. All of us are disabled in one way or another—some physically, some economically—the list is endless. But if you can conquer ignorance, all your other disabilities melt away.

"Simply to live, I have to spend time every day in the iron lung," Helynn says. "But I'm just glad to be alive because life is an adventure—and I don't want to miss any of it!" Helynn's determination, sense of humor and enthusiasm for life get her through the hardest moments.

The only complaint Helynn voices is that she simply doesn't have enough hours in the day to accomplish all that she wants to do. Recently some friends dropped by her house to celebrate yet another one of her accomplishments—and to have a piece of chocolate cake. As Helynn enjoyed being with her well-wishers, her eyes sparkled. Then she said, "I've met so many nice people along the way . . . including FDR when I was only twelve years old. In my life, I have been very lucky!"

Sharon Whitley Larsen

In the Eye of the Storm

*Sometimes our light goes out but is blown into
flame by another human being. Each of us owes
deepest thanks to those who have rekindled this
light.*

Albert Schweitzer

Golden leaves fell across the country in mid-
November, but the autumn beauty would soon not matter to Helen Weathers. For on the night of her fifty-ninth
birthday, her life was swept completely out from under
her. She had just finished celebrating at a restaurant with
some of her closest friends and was getting ready for bed
when she felt like a jagged piece of glass pierced her head.
Then, the lights went out for Helen. For a long time. Most
signs of life disappeared instantaneously when an
aneurysm struck down this vivacious woman.

Five days later, her dearest friends, her husband,
Robert, and the rest of her family waited patiently
through a six-hour brain operation to see if Helen would
survive. Her unopened birthday gifts sat at home on her

table just the way she left them. The gifts would remain untouched for months, for after the surgery, she suffered a stroke.

Helen had always dressed with flair and elegance. This now bald woman lay helpless in a hospital bed day after day. She probably would have been embarrassed had she been herself and able to see the friends pouring in and out of her room. Later, she would be grateful. The endless stream of visits, flowers and food for her family gave her relatives the buoy they needed to survive the icy waters.

Helen believes the love and support also kept her alive in the midst of the storm. Within a few weeks, many friends had a prayer chain going for her, hoping to bring her back from the brink of death. Their hopes and prayers were answered. But Helen could barely recognize herself. "I couldn't remember what I looked like before," she says. "I don't remember when I discovered I had no hair. My cousin Elsa said that when I looked in the mirror and saw I had no hair, I turned to Robert and her and said: 'I have no teeth.'"

Helen's friends continued to send flowers, food and cards. One of her closest friends brought her pictures of all her dogs: Doodles, Ms. Liberty and Taffy.

Robert and their daughter, Sandra, brought her new makeup.

Everyone wanted her back even though it became clear that Helen might never be the same woman again. At times, she was like a stranger. To others—and to herself.

When she started recovering, she had much to learn. How to write her name again. How to walk. How to speak clearly. How to dress herself. Sometimes, she felt like a baby. But her brain surgeon said it was a miracle she was alive.

Helen was almost like a child. Her sentences were gibberish. She giggled uncontrollably. Then she'd cry. She was hospitalized for nearly half a year undergoing rehabilitation and trying to return to her former self.

She was placed in intensive therapy and was given classes in arithmetic, which confounded her and left her trying to count things out on her fingers. Finally, she gave up and started using a calculator. "One of my favorite *bon mots* is: 'In real life, there is no algebra!'"

In therapy, one of the happiest incidents she recalls was being allowed to go out to a Wal-Mart to Christmas shop so her doctors could see if she could make it in the "real world." Helen was delighted, though confused a bit, and finished all her shopping in the first two aisles.

After seven months, she made it home to husband, Robert, and dogs, Doodles, Ms. Liberty and Taffy. Today Helen is restored to her former self and has gained back her abilities to paint, walk and speak.

"I am convinced that the only reason I was spared is to inspire others," Helen says from her home where she receives dozens of calls a day from people seeking help with similar disabilities. "I have been in the trenches with people who have suffered like this. I know lots of people were pulling for me. Now, it's my turn to encourage people to go to rehabilitation and hang in there."

Helen is often asked: "How long did it take you to learn to write again?"

"Seven months," she replies and then adds, "and almost that long to keep from putting lipstick under my nose."

When Helen receives phone calls for help, she never turns anyone away. Because she knows deep in her heart that it was love and caring that guided her out of the storm and helped her wade safely back to shore.

Helen Weathers
As told to Diana L. Chapman

$\overline{8}$

A MATTER OF PERSPECTIVE

We turn not older in years, but newer every day.

Emily Dickinson

Beautiful Day, Isn't It?

Worse than not having sight is having no vision.

Helen Keller

The day started out rotten. She overslept and was late for work. Everything that happened at the office contributed to her nervous frenzy. By the time she reached the bus stop for her homeward trip, her stomach was one big knot.

As usual, the bus was late—and jammed. She had to stand in the aisle. As the lurching vehicle pulled her in all directions, her gloom deepened.

Then she heard a voice from up front boom, "Beautiful day, isn't it?" Because of the crowd, she could not see the man, but she heard him as he continued to comment on the spring scenery, calling attention to each approaching landmark. This church. That park. This cemetery. That firehouse. Soon all the passengers were gazing out the windows. The man's enthusiasm was so contagious she found herself smiling for the first time that day.

They reached her stop. Maneuvering toward the door, she got a look at their "guide": an older gentleman with a beard, wearing dark glasses and carrying a thin, white cane.

Retold by Barbara Johnson

From Here to Eternity

As we get older, our vision should improve. Not our vision of earth, but our vision of heaven.

Max Lucado

Our yellow legal pads were almost full, and our pencils were beginning to dull. For hours now, our music committee had been evaluating the past year. Planning for the future was our next task. As minister of music, I challenged the committee, "Okay folks, we've done some good work here. But to see the results we're hoping for, we've got to have a fresh vision."

Committee chairperson Dorcas Chapman rose from her seat and instructed us, "Put down your pencils. Scoot your chairs back from the table. Close your eyes, and try to clear your minds." Her next statement fascinated me: "We're going on a trip."

We listened attentively as Dorcas continued, "First, I want you to picture yourself on the front steps of the church building. After a good look around, step inside the main foyer." Dorcas proceeded, "Take note of what you see, whom you see, and what they are doing." Finally, we were to "travel" into the sanctuary, up the stairs to the balcony, and then back down to the choir loft.

After our first mental journey around the property, Dorcas asked us to start over. "This time," she explained, "it is three years down the road." We were to walk through all the same locations again, envisioning all the possibilities later turned into realities.

"Once more," Dorcas continued, "but this time, it's five years later."

Then, we began sharing what we had seen. Some committee members had pictured multi-level parking garages and buildings with vivid detail—down to the color of the carpet and the awnings on the windows.

One woman described, "I saw a sea of blue uniforms filling the sanctuary." The following year, we celebrated a special Air Force Salute Day, honoring all the military men and women from our city's Air Force base.

We all nodded in agreement as one man reported, "I saw streams of people from all walks of life coming in and out of the church building, worshipping and being spiritually rejuvenated." Since that time, church membership has grown by about fifteen hundred members.

I had goosebumps as we continued around the room. One lady talked about seeing a single mother seated in the balcony with her two children. Another person envisioned hundreds of teenagers at a rally in the gymnasium. This exercise was producing discussion more exciting than we had ever experienced before.

But a puzzling response came from Tommy Brinkley. He was our church organist as well as the orchestra conductor. When it came his turn to share, I eagerly awaited his response. He announced, "I didn't really see anything—just hundreds of harps."

Harps? All he saw was harps? What about a two-hundred-

voice choir filling the choir loft or a fifty-piece orchestra on the platform? I was less than inspired by Tommy's report. We moved on to the next person.

A few days later, Tommy was admitted to the hospital for chest pains. He suffered a massive heart attack and died within a week. As our church family grieved during the following weeks, I reflected on his life and death. My mind drifted to the time I first met Tommy and then to the countless lives my sixty-plus-year-old colleague had touched as a friend and musician.

Soon after Tommy's funeral, I remembered our last music committee meeting and what Tommy had shared. It struck me that while we were still dreaming about the here and now, Tommy had already glimpsed his hundreds of harps. It was easy to imagine Tommy there, surrounded by rows of golden harps whose melodies make finer music than this world will ever know.

At a later planning meeting, I remarked to our committee, "Tommy may have had more vision than any of us. While our vision reaches from here to the next several years, his stretched from here to eternity."

Michael T. Smith with Kelley Smith

You Can Be Right

No man is poor who has friends.

It's a Wonderful Life

Earl once told his younger sister, Liddy, "If you can hang on my back pocket, you can go anywhere I go, too." So Liddy, six years younger, always tagged along, even on Earl's dates. She once stowed away in the dusty back seat of his truck and popped up when he and his date arrived at the drive-in theater. As Liddy grew into a young beauty, Earl made sure all her suitors met his personal approval.

Even after their marriages, Earl and Liddy remained close. Years later, Liddy's husband, Kirby, when diagnosed with terminal cancer, said, "I won't worry about Liddy as long as Earl is alive."

After Kirby's death, Liddy withdrew from everyone, even Earl. He and his wife, Sue, recognized this as Liddy's way of grieving, but gradually their contact with Liddy diminished. As more time passed, it seemed harder to pick up the phone and call.

One February afternoon, Earl collapsed at work. At the hospital, the doctors told Sue it was a heart attack. They offered what they called a "clot buster" shot to open up the arteries around the heart. The shot worked, and Earl's heart attack lessened. After a successful angioplasty the next morning, the doctors told them, "All is well." Relieved and grateful, Earl and Sue went home to rest and recover.

Within twenty-four hours, Earl's entire body swelled. He returned to the hospital. With sinking hearts, Earl and Sue learned that 1 in 100,000 patients who receive the shot experience a side effect called "cholesterol showering." Instead of breaking up only the clots that caused Earl's heart attack, the medication made all the cholesterol in his body release into his bloodstream. The overload was causing all his organs to slowly shut down. One doctor on the medical team said they would have to amputate one limb at a time to try to save him. "I began wondering how much longer I had to live," says Earl. "Emotionally, Sue and I hit bottom. We were both so scared, we didn't know how to comfort each other."

At home a few days later, Sue and Earl received a special phone call. It was Earl's sister Liddy. "I heard about Earl. . . . I wish I knew what to do. If only Kirby were here. . . ." Liddy's voice broke with little sobs. "May I come over to see you? I'd understand if you said no. . . . Would you ask Earl?"

Sue gently replied, "I don't need to. We both want to see you—as soon as you can get here." Liddy surprised Earl and Sue by arriving at their home with all her children and grandchildren. Sue hugged each one as Earl watched from the couch where he lay. When Liddy greeted him she said, "It's been a long time, brother." Earl replied, "Give me a hug!" Receiving his hug, he whispered to her, "Can we put lost time behind us?"

"I'd like that," Liddy responded softly, tears brimming

over her eyelids and streaming down her cheeks. She sat on the footstool beside him. "Can you forgive me for staying away for so long?"

"You know I can, Sis. I just want us to be brother and sister again, especially now," Earl said, reaching out his hand to wipe away her tears. Liddy grasped Earl's muscular, yet swollen hand and simply said, "I sure missed you."

In the following days, Earl's spirits were up. Not able to leave the house, he had time to rethink what was really important to him. "I realized that if I was going to die, I didn't want anyone I left behind to be angry with me," he says. He began calling friends and cousins he had not seen for years. Some had drifted out of his life for no particular reason. Others, though, carried grudges or hurt feelings. One man, for example, had not talked to Earl for twenty years because of a misunderstanding. Earl called him on the telephone and said, "I don't remember what we disagreed about, but whatever it was, you can be right. I don't want there to be any negative feelings between us." Every person he called came to visit him. One woman, suffering from severe physical pain of her own, came in a wheelchair to visit him during one of his hospital stays.

After many trips to the local hospital for tests and treatment, with only a medical file as thick as a phone book to show for it, Earl and Sue decided to travel to a nearby city to discuss Earl's case with a renowned kidney specialist. The specialist gave Earl a month to live.

Soon after, Earl's niece Ronda, one of Liddy's daughters who worked in the medical field, asked another famous kidney specialist his opinion of what her uncle was going through. This doctor offered a glimmer of hope. He instructed, "Tell your uncle to go to bed; it may take two years, but total rest might allow the cholesterol to filter out of his system naturally." Having exhausted all other options, or so it seemed, Earl agreed to stay in bed for as long as it would take.

Though they had no one to talk to who had survived this rare "cholesterol showering," Earl and Sue found comfort in the renewed friendships that Earl had initiated. Phone calls of support came daily. And since medicine offered no answers, everyone they knew agreed to pray.

Late one night, after months of resting and waiting, Sue begged Earl to try something new. She told him, "We've prayed for your health many times, but I've noticed that the Bible also talks about anointing sick people with oil and asking others to pray over them. Could we at least try?" She nervously awaited his answer, knowing that the Earl she knew before this ordeal would have never agreed. But, she hoped that with all he'd been through, he might be willing.

Sue was not disappointed. With Earl's approval, she called the minister at their church and asked him to come and anoint Earl with oil and pray for him. Though it was nearly 3:00 A.M., the minister and a deacon arrived, ready to do as Sue asked.

The next evening, the entire deacon board came. The members gathered around the bed where Earl was confined, and each took a turn praying. After everyone left, Earl and Sue knelt by their respective sides of the bed to continue praying.

On his knees, Earl realized, "What am I doing out of bed? I'm better!" His arms and legs no longer ached, and the swelling was gone. "When it dawned on us what had happened," Earl says, "we got so excited, we went into our backyard in our pajamas and danced together under the stars!

"I knew in my heart that I had a lot to celebrate: first, all my friends, and now, my health, too!"

Several years later, Earl, now in his late sixties, is in excellent health. More important, though, he says,

"Facing death, I realized more than ever how deeply I care for my friends. And I no longer need to be 'right.' Standing by what I believe will always be important, but it doesn't mean I have to insist that everyone agree with me.

"Reaching out, forgiving and telling others, 'Look, *you* can be right,' didn't cost me a thing. It gained for me one of the greatest treasures this life offers: old friendships. And I got back my sister, too."

Now Earl and Sue talk to Liddy nearly every day. She is hanging on his back pocket again after all these years.

Amy Seeger

"To begin with, you let out too much line,
your backswing is all wrong and your. . . ."

Reprinted by permission of Vahan Shirvanian.

Overnight Guest

No act of kindness, no matter how small, is ever wasted.

Aesop

Greenbriar Valley lay almost hidden by the low-hanging clouds that spilled intermittent showers. As I plodded through the muddy barnyard preparing to do my afternoon chores, I glanced at the road that led past our place and wound on through the valley. A car was parked at the side of the road a little way beyond the pasture corner.

The car was obviously in distress. Otherwise, no man so well-dressed would have been tinkering with it out in the rain. I watched him as I went about my chores. Clearly, the man was no mechanic. He desperately plodded from the raised hood back to the car seat to try the starter, then back to the hood again.

When I finished my chores and closed the barn, it was almost dark. The car was still there. So I took a flashlight and walked down the road. The man was sort of startled and disturbed when I came up to him, but he seemed anxious enough for my help. It was a small car, the same make as my own but somewhat newer. It took only a few minutes for me to spot the trouble.

"It's your coil," I told him.

"But it couldn't be that!" he blurted. "I just installed a new one, only about a month ago." He was a young fellow, hardly more than a boy—I would have guessed twenty-one, at most. He sounded almost in tears.

"You see, mister," he almost sobbed, "I'm a long ways from home. It's raining. And I've just *got* to get it started. I just got to!"

"Well, it's like this," I said. "Coils are pretty touchy. Sometimes they'll last for years. Then again sometimes they'll go out in a matter of hours. Suppose I get a horse and pull the car up into the barn. Then we'll see what we can do for it. We'll try the coil from my car. If that works, I know a fellow down at the corner who'll sell you one."

I was right. With the coil from my car in place, the motor started right off, and it purred like a new one. "Nothing to it," I grinned. "We'll just go see Bill David down the road. He'll sell you a new coil, and you can be on your way. Just wait a minute while I tell my wife, Jane, where I'm going."

I thought he acted odd when we got down to David's store. He parked in the dark behind the store and would not get out. "I'm wet and cold," he excused himself. "Here's ten dollars. Would you mind very much going in and getting it for me?"

We had just finished changing the coil when my little daughter, Linda, came out to the barn. "Mother says supper's ready," she announced. Then, turning to the strange young man, she said, "She says you're to come in and eat, too."

"Oh, but I couldn't," he protested. "I couldn't let you folks feed me. I've got to get going anyway. No, no, I just can't stay."

"Don't be ridiculous," I said. "After all, how long will it take you to eat? Besides, no one comes to Jane's house at mealtime and leaves without eating. You wouldn't want her to lie down in the mud in front of your car, would you?"

Still protesting, he allowed himself to be led off to the house. But it seemed to me as if there was something more in his protests than just mere politeness.

He sat quietly enough while I said the blessing. But during the meal he seemed fidgety. He barely picked at his food, which was almost an insult to Jane, who is one of the best cooks in the state and proud of it.

Once the meal was over, he got quickly to his feet, announcing that he must be on his way. But he had reckoned without Jane.

"Now, look here," she said, and she glanced at me for support. "It's still pouring out there. Your clothes are all wet, and you can't help being cold. I'll bet you're tired too; you must have driven far today. Stay with us tonight. Tomorrow you can start out warm and dry and all rested."

I nodded slightly at her. It isn't always advisable to take in strangers that way. Unfortunately, many people cannot be trusted. But I liked this young man. I felt sure he would be all right.

He reluctantly agreed to stay the night. Jane sent him to bed and hung his clothes to dry by the fire. Next morning she pressed them and gave him a nice breakfast. This meal he ate with relish. It seemed he was more settled that morning, not so restless as he had been. He thanked us profusely before he left.

But when he started away, an odd thing happened. He had been headed down the valley toward the city the night before. But when he left, he headed back north, toward Roseville, the county seat. We wondered a great deal about that, but decided he had just been confused and made a wrong turn.

Time went by, and we never heard from the young man. We had not expected to, really. The days flowed into months, and the months into years. The Depression ended and drifted into war. In time, the war ended, too. Linda grew up and established a home of her own. Things on the farm were quite different from those early days of struggle. Jane and I lived comfortably and quietly, surrounded by lovely Greenbriar Valley.

Just the other day, I got a letter from Chicago. A personal letter, it was, on nice expensive stationery. *Now who in the world,* I wondered, *can be writing me from Chicago?* I opened it and read:

> *Dear Mr. McDonald:*
>
> *I don't suppose you remember the young man you helped, years ago, when his car broke down. It has been a long time, and I imagine you've helped many others. But I doubt if you have helped anyone else quite the way you helped me.*
>
> *You see, I was running away that night. I had in my car a very large sum of money, which I had stolen from my employer. I want you to know, sir, that I had good Christian parents. But I had forgotten their teaching and had gotten in with the wrong crowd. I knew I had made a terrible mistake.*
>
> *But you and your wife were so nice to me. That night in your home, I began to see where I was wrong. Before morning, I made a decision. Next day, I turned back. I went back to my employer and made a clean breast of it. I gave back all the money and threw myself on his mercy.*
>
> *He could have prosecuted me and sent me to prison for many years. But he is a good man. He took me back in my old job, and I have never strayed again. I'm married now, with a lovely wife and two fine children. I have*

worked my way to a very good position with my company. I am not wealthy, but I am comfortably well off.

I could reward you handsomely for what you did for me that night. But I don't believe that is what you'd want. So I have established a fund to help others who have made the same mistake I did. In this way, I hope I may pay for what I have done.

God bless you, sir, and your good wife, who helped me more than you knew.

I walked into the house and handed the letter to Jane. As she read it, I saw the tears begin to fill her eyes. With the most serene look on her face, she laid the letter aside.

"For I was a Stranger, and ye took Me in," she quoted. "I was hungered, and ye fed Me; I was in prison, and ye visited Me."

Hartley F. Dailey

[EDITORS' NOTE: *Names have been changed for privacy.*]

The List

We are not rich by what we possess but rather by what we can do without.

Immanuel Kant

Many times my friend June would say, "If I ever get rich, I'm moving into a bigger apartment and getting a completely new wardrobe." I would listen and think, *Dream on, my friend. Your chances of being rich are about as good as mine.* But, to everyone's amazement, a few years ago June did come into a sizable inheritance.

At first June said very little about the money. As the initial shock wore off, she became excited. June is a great believer in making lists, so I wasn't surprised to find her writing down all the ways she would spend her new wealth.

As time wore on, she started revising the list. What had been midway down the column was now at the top. After hearing these changes for some time, I said to her, "You know, it isn't necessary to spend all your inheritance at once. Take some time; pray about it."

"I know, I know," she answered with a hint of irritation. After that, I sat on the sideline, watching the list change from day to day. Then one morning June called. "I've decided how I want to use my inheritance," she said. "Can you come over? I want to see what you think."

This wasn't something I really looked forward to, but we had been friends a long time. So I would go and keep my mouth shut, no matter how the list read.

As we sat drinking coffee, June spread a sheet of paper on the table. To my utter surprise, she had written only three words in large bold letters: CHURCH, CHARITIES, GRANDCHILDREN—in that order. Though I had vowed to keep quiet, I could not keep from asking how she came to this decision.

"Well," she said, "I took your advice and prayed, not once, but many times." She added, "The church means a lot to me, so I'm hoping this gift will benefit its work."

June continued, "It was a little harder to decide on the charities. But since I've always wanted to help children, I'm giving to those that I feel will carry out my wishes."

"As for the grandkids," June pointed out, "they will share some of the money. But I don't think they should have everything given to them. It's important for them to know what it means to work and save on their own."

I interjected, "But what about that big apartment you always hoped to have?"

"It doesn't seem as important anymore," she answered with a smile.

Then June moved her hand, and I could see a few words written in tiny letters at the very bottom of the page. Pointing with my finger, I asked, "What's this?"

"Oh!" she said, blushing a bright pink. "Just something for me."

Leaning forward to read the small print, I burst into peals of laughter. June had written:

AND one new wardrobe.

Agnes Moench

[EDITORS' NOTE: *Names have been changed for privacy.*]

The Mirror Has Three Faces

I am a reflection of my past generations and the essence of those following after me.

Martha Kinney

I am fifty-one years old. My mother was fifty-one when she died. I remember that last day of her life only too clearly. It was a rainy Monday, and my mother could not breathe.

"It's fluid," the doctor said. "We'll tap her lungs." They sat my mother up in the hospital bed and plunged the long needle through her back into her lungs. Again and again they tried, but no fluid came. And no relief.

"It's not fluid," the doctor said. "It's all tumor. We can't help her breathe."

I remember my mother's desperate words. "I can't . . . breathe. Turn up the oxygen . . . please." But turning up the oxygen didn't help. Her lungs, bursting with cancer, fought to make room for the air. My mother whispered her final words to me, "I want the quickest way."

My mother should have grown old. Her dark hair, peppered with gray, should have become snowy white. The fine lines, etched in her face from her smiles, should have become soft wrinkles. Her quick step should have given way to a slower, more seasoned gait.

My mother should have watched her five grandchildren grow up. She should have had the chance to enfold them in her very special brand of love and to impart to them her considerable wisdom. She should have been arm in arm with my father—she was the only girl he ever loved—sojourning into their shared golden years. She didn't. She wasn't. She never had the chance. She was fifty-one, and she died.

I was twenty-seven when my mother died. Over the years, not a day went by when I didn't think of something I wanted to tell her, to ask her or to show her. I railed bitterly against the injustice of it. It wasn't fair that my mother died at fifty-one.

Now I am fifty-one. I look into the mirror and it strikes me: I have slowly but surely been transformed. There she is with that gray peppered hair, those dark intense eyes, that expression on my face. When I hear my voice, it is her voice. I have become my mother.

I am entering a new and strange stage of my life. I have always looked ahead to see my mother. Ever so briefly, I stood next to her. Now I'm beginning to be older than my mother. The direction in which I gaze to see her will change. Soon I will look back at my mother.

Gradually my mother will become young in comparison with me. I will grow old instead of her—acquire the white hair she should have had but never did. I will develop that seasoned gait she never experienced, see those soft facial wrinkles she never had, and so it will continue on and on until one day when I'm seventy-five, as she would have been today. On that day, the reversal of our roles complete, I will turn around to look at her, but see instead my own daughter, at fifty-one—my mother.

Kristina Cliff-Evans

Ready to Roll

I shall grow old, but never lose life's zest,
Because the road's last turn will be the best.

Henry Van Dyke

My eyes froze on the "age" blank of the form I was filling out to rent the in-line skates. Was recording the number that labeled me a senior citizen really required? On
paper, the number did not look age-appropriate to the
activity. Was there a "correct" age? *What number should I
write down?*

In spite of this slight mental detour, I couldn't resist the
golden opportunity: after more than forty years since
graduation, six high school girlfriends reunited for a
weekend house party in San Diego at Mission Beach, surrounded by smooth, wide, curving sidewalks.

Dorothy had brought along her in-line skates. While
some of us were eager to join her in this activity, others
hesitated. Excuses were forthcoming: hadn't skated since
high school; a bad knee; fear of injury; in-line skates were
not the same as roller skates.

The excitement mounted as one by one we tried on

Dorothy's knee pads, skates and wrist guards (in that order). With her gentle coaching, each decided to take a tentative turn close to the security of a wall. It helped that some of us had learned to ski, as the stopping motion felt similar.

When we began to share our socks with the skater-of-the-moment and to squabble like children over whose turn it was, we knew we were ready to roll. We all were ready to commit to renting skating equipment.

There was no question about my enthusiasm! The feeling in the soles of my feet took me back to my childhood. I can still remember the satisfying click-click-click of racing full speed over the cracks of the cement sidewalk squares that lined the streets of my Midwestern home.

Back then, the streets, sidewalks and empty lots in the neighborhood were our playground. Shaded by a canopy of stately elm trees, the varying group of neighbor kids roller-skated, jumped rope, played hopscotch and rode bikes all summer long. The bigger kids organized more ambitious projects: carnivals, theatrical productions, dog shows and parades. Their little brothers and sisters were willing lackeys.

At twilight we'd gather under the elms to play "I Will Draw the Frying Pan," "Red Light Green Light" or "Ghosts."

But any summer day would find me on my roller skates, the skate key dangling on a grubby cotton string around my neck, scabs on my knees.

We regularly performed our most daring roller-skating feat on the steep hill leading down to the next street at the end of our block. Lickety-split my friends and I would roar down the hill and stop ourselves with a quick jerk to the left at the bottom of the hill. We'd slam with a resounding bang into a conveniently located garage door. The door (much to the owner's displeasure) was permanently imprinted with a row of child-sized handprints.

So now, some five decades later, I gleefully suited up with knee pads and wrist guards, buckled up the rented skates and followed Dorothy (my friend since fourth grade) down the alley to the wide, smooth pavement, where we could really take off. Turning her head, she grinned at me and said, "We're eight years old!"

"Absolutely," I agreed. That was the number I'd been searching for.

Betsy Hall Hutchinson

Cracking Up

Laughter heals a lot of hurts.

Madeleine L'Engle

After fifty years of marriage, her husband died. The widow painfully selected the granite marker to place over the gravesites reserved for them both. She gave instructions to put her name and birth date on the marker and also requested that wedding bands be placed between their names along with the year of their marriage.

The widow wanted the marker finished in time for their fifty-first wedding anniversary only a few weeks away. The marker would be the last gift she would give her husband. As workers at the cemetery monument company, we immediately ordered the special color granite she had chosen in hopes we could finish the marker in time.

The marker was finished ahead of schedule. When we called the widow to let her know, she told us she would like to come in to see it before we took it to the cemetery. The guys in the shop loaded the marker on the straps of the crane to place it where she could see it best. With no warning, the unthinkable happened. The marker slipped off the straps and fell to the ground, cracking in half!

Frantically, we were trying to figure out how we could finish another marker when the widow walked in. There she stood in front of us, fully expecting to see the beautiful marker she had so carefully chosen. Wild thoughts raced through our minds. Even though we knew we shouldn't lie, we wanted desperately to spare the feelings of a woman who had already suffered far too much grief. We stumbled for words and finally simply told her the truth.

We expected anger. We expected tears. We *never* expected laughter. But as soon as she saw the marker cracked perfectly in half, her solemn expression turned into one of amusement and then heartfelt laughter! Seeing our astonishment, she composed herself and explained, "At our wedding reception fifty-one years ago, my husband and I solemnly held the knife in our hands and cut into the wedding cake. The cake instantly cracked down the middle and broke in half.

"How fitting it is," she added, "that this happened to the marker. I really wanted my last gift to my husband to be something special, and it is. I have a feeling he's laughing right along with me, just like we did for those fifty-one years."

Maureen S. Pusch

Get Up and Go

How do I know my youth is all spent?
My get up and go has got up and went.
But in spite of it all, I'm able to grin
And think of the places my get up has been.

Old age is golden, so I've heard said.
But sometimes I wonder as I crawl into bed
With my ears in a drawer and my teeth in a cup
My eyes on the table until I wake up.

As sleep dims my vision, I say to myself,
"Is there anything else I should lay on the shelf?"
But though nations are warring and business is vexed
I'll still stick around to see what happens next.

How do I know my youth is all spent?
My get up and go has got up and went.
But in spite of it all, I'm able to grin
And think of the places my get up has been.

When I was young, my slippers were red,
I could kick up my heels right over my head.
When I was older, my slippers were blue,
But still I could dance the whole night through.

Now I am older, my slippers are black.
I huff to the store, and I puff my way back.
But never you laugh; I don't mind at all.
I'd rather be huffing than not puff at all.

How do I know my youth is all spent?
My get up and go has got up and went.
But in spite of it all, I'm able to grin
And think of the places my get up has been.

I get up each morning and dust off my wits,
Open the paper and read the obits.
If I'm not there, I know I'm not dead,
So I eat a good breakfast and go back to bed.

How do I know my youth is all spent?
My get up and go has got up and went.
But in spite of it all, I'm able to grin
And think of the places my get up has been.

Pete Seeger

Get Up and Go. *Words collected, adapted and set to original music by Pete Seeger TRO—©1964 (Renewed) Melody Trails, Inc., New York, NY. Used by permission.*

9
ON
BELIEVING

*Faith sees the invisible, believes the
unbelievable and receives the impossible.*

Corrie ten Boom

Just One Wish

*The capacity to care is the thing that gives life
its deepest meaning and significance.*

                                                          Pablo Casals

Fox River gave life to the country town of Colby Point,
for the road and the river ran alongside one another.
Colby Point was really the name of a road that crept
between the hills and valleys of McHenry, Illinois. Homes
were scattered here and there—mostly summer homes
and retirement homes. At the very end of the road three
houses all faced one another. Three sisters—all single, all
seniors—lived in one of the homes. Across the way their
widowed first cousin lived in a yellow house. Next to her
lived their brother, Bill, and his wife, Cleo.

Cleo had multiple sclerosis, so the pair had moved to
Colby Point seeking a quiet, relaxed life. Little did they
know when they relocated to this serene area that they
would end up rearing their granddaughter, Margie. Before
long, the once-quiet neighborhood became active with
the sounds of a child.

Margie always looked forward to the arrival of Christmas,

and this year was no different as winter began to settle like a warm blanket around Colby Point. Everyone was in a flurry, for at the church Margie and her family attended, the congregation was preparing to share their Christmas wishes with each other. Since Cleo couldn't make it to church, and Bill didn't like to leave her alone for too long, he was in the habit of dropping Margie off at church early on Sunday mornings; the aunts would bring her home.

As Margie sat in church that morning, she rehearsed in her mind over and over what she would say. She wasn't afraid, for she knew what an important wish this was. The service seemed to drag on and on. Finally the pastor uttered the words Margie had been anticipating all morning, "This is a special time of year when everyone around the world celebrates peace and goodwill toward our fellow man. This year, here at St. John's, we want to hear your Christmas wishes. We cannot fill everyone's wish, but we would like to try and fill a few. As I call your name, please come forward and tell us about your Christmas wish."

One after another, the church members shared their wishes, large and small. Margie was the last and the youngest to speak. As she looked out at the congregation, she spoke confidently, "I would like for my grandma to have church. She cannot walk, and she and my grandpa have to stay at home. They miss coming so much. So that is what I wish for. And please don't tell them, for it needs to be a surprise."

Riding home with her aunts, Margie could tell they were speaking in low tones about her wish. She hoped that they would keep her secret. As the next Sunday came around, Margie was getting ready for church when Grandma asked, "Why are you so fidgety? You haven't sat still all morning."

"I just know that something wonderful is going to happen today!"

"Of course it will," said her grandma with a chuckle. "It's almost Christmas, you know."

Grandpa was getting on his coat when he happened to look out the front window. He saw some cars coming down the dirt road one after another. Now at this time of year there wasn't too much traffic, so this was really amazing. Margie pushed her grandma to the window so that she could see all the cars. Pretty soon the cars were parked all up and down the road as far as a person could see.

Grandpa looked at Grandma, and they both looked at Margie. Grandpa asked, "Just what did you wish for, Margie?"

"I wished that you and Grandma could have church. And I just knew that it would come true. Look! There's the pastor, and everyone from church is coming up the walk."

The congregation arrived with coffee and cookies and cups and gifts. They sang Christmas carols and listened to the pastor speak on giving to others the gifts that God gives. Later that night, Margie slipped out the back door and walked outside to look up at the stars. "Thank you," she whispered, "thank you for giving me my wish."

That was just one of the many wishes granted for Margie as she grew up. Her childhood overflowed with the love of her grandparents, four great aunts and many wise, caring neighbors. Margie was truly a blessed little girl.

I should know—I was that little girl.

Margaret E. Mack

The Patient and Her Encourager

Good actions are the invisible hinges on the doors of heaven.

Victor Hugo

At the age of twenty-one, Susan was diagnosed with breast cancer. Of course, the news devastated this young, vibrant college student. To make matters worse, she had no money to cover the medical expenses. Her father had recently lost his job, and her disabled mother hadn't worked in nearly fifteen years.

With an empty bank account and a heart full of faith, Susan began six weeks of chemotherapy treatments. I accompanied her to her chemo appointment one day, and I was amazed at the strength radiating from her face before and after the grueling treatments. Despite her desperate circumstances, Susan's faith sustained her.

Before long, Susan became very ill, and the intense pain was growing unbearable. Though she received unrelenting prayer and support from her family, friends and professors, the pain persisted. Soon, she had lost all her hair.

"If nothing else," she would tease, "I'll save money on hair care!" Despite her positive outlook and unyielding faith, her financial situation remained grim. She already owed more than ten thousand dollars in medical expenses, and she had no income or savings.

One cold February day while Susan was in the hospital, a visitor came to see her. The elderly gentleman with a sweet countenance asked, "Are you Susan?"

"Yes," she replied.

"My name is Mark White, and I live here in town. My wife was in the bed next to you on your first visit to the hospital, but you weren't here long, and while you were here, you were very sick. My wife and I prayed for you each night before going to bed, and we often wondered how you were." The man continued, "My wife died about two days after you left, and I'm here today to pick up some of her things."

Susan nodded, not sure how to respond.

The man proceeded, "The nurse informed me you were back in the hospital. My wife overheard you talking on the phone with your mom one night about your financial situation. My wife and I wanted to help you, and we knew of no better way than to give you this money. We don't know you well, but we want to help. You were always a joy for my wife to talk to and a great encouragement to her. Please take this check and use it for your hospital bills."

As the gentleman walked away, he turned back, "I know you're going to make it, kid. Just keep believing."

As Susan opened the envelope, she thought, *How nice that this elderly couple gave me twenty or fifty dollars.* But what she found inside the envelope was not a twenty-dollar bill or a fifty-dollar bill; it was a check for ten thousand dollars! Weeping, she read the attached note, "Someone needs your encouragement today. Thanks for encouraging me for the few short days I knew you. Love, Marie White."

Susan did just as Mr. White had said—she kept believing. Susan's cancer was gone in a few months and has never returned. In her own special way, Susan reminded me to encourage someone every day; her story has remained with me, and its message becomes more valuable with time. When I asked Susan how to end her story, she said God had given her what she believed to be the greatest gift of all—life.

And, oh yes, I think the money helped, too.

Scot Thurman
Submitted by Kelley Smith

Bewitched

Look for strengths in people, not weaknesses; for good, not evil. Most of us find what we search for.

J. Wilbur Chapman

When I was a very little girl, I was a believer. I believed in Santa Claus, ghosts and the tooth fairy. But most of all I believed in witches because I knew one. Her name was Chloe.

Chloe's country store was near our house in rural Connecticut. Bats found a haven under its shingles and black widow spiders spun webs behind sagging shutters. A battered sign announcing A-U-N-T-I-E C'S M-A-R-K-E-T creaked on rusty chains over the door.

A one-time glimpse of Chloe was all it took to make her unforgettable. Hairs on her nose unfurled every time she breathed out, and blue-gray hair swirled around her head like a giant moth's cocoon. Furthermore, I had spent hours eavesdropping behind kitchen doors listening to rumors. I learned quickly that the world was indeed a scary place where witches cast spells on little girls—and old men.

"Uncle Grady" was seventy-seven years old and he, too, lived on a nearby farm. In the shade of his glorious peach tree, he told me stories about leprechauns, his years in the navy, sea monsters and a magic faraway land called China. His lusty voice and rolling laughter tickled my tummy, and when he took my small hand in his, gnarled fingers and callused palms made me feel all warm inside. But one thing troubled me. Uncle Grady had a glass eye. The question that haunted me most was, "Can a glass eye see?"

On my fifth birthday Uncle Grady brought me a huge fuzzy peachy from his beautiful tree. But when he bent over to give it to me, a terrible thing happened. His eye fell out!

"Blamed thing don't fit right no more," he muttered. He picked up the eye from the ground where it had fallen and blew off the dirt. Then he wiped it clean with his red-gingham handkerchief. "I guess I'd better buy me a new one."

One day our new housekeeper, Mrs. Swensen, took me with her to Chloe's store. Poor, poor Mrs. Swensen. She didn't know that Chloe truly was a witch. She couldn't hear my small heart hammer as she lifted me over the one-fanged, black cat that crouched on Chloe's doorstep defying the timid to enter.

"Are you going to s . . . s . . . stay for coffee?" I asked Mrs. Swensen.

"For a bit, child. Chloe loves folks to visit for a while."

"Can I go play with my friend?" I asked nervously, and when Mrs. Swensen said yes, I loved her for it. Softly, I slipped away.

The windowless store smelled like wet chickens and mothballs. Dust coated the counters and shelves, and in the center of each aisle, the glow from a single bulb threw goblin shadows on the ceiling and floor. I shivered and hastened to find my friend, for he alone, in all the world, understood why I feared Chloe.

At last, on a top shelf, too high for me to reach, I found my secret friend—a small, stuffed bear—with one eye. I'd named him Honey O'Grady.

I was overjoyed that no one had bought him yet. I longed to hold him and brush away the cobwebs between his ears. I wanted to say, "It's all right, Honey. Don't be sad." But most of all I wanted to plant a kiss where an eye should be and tell him if he were mine, Uncle Grady could make it better.

Suddenly, I heard Mrs. Swensen's voice. "You scared me half to death, child. Why didn't you answer when I called?"

I tried to speak, but my eyes caught sight of a pair of shoes on the floor behind Mrs. Swensen's. Black, pointed shoes!

I blew a good-bye kiss to Honey and then begged Mrs. Swensen to buy him for me.

That's when I heard Chloe's voice, softer than I remembered. "That bear's been settin' on the shelf for years. Two dollars is all I'm askin'."

Suddenly Honey was in my arms, his tiny heart rapping in rhythm with my own. I hugged Honey tight and dared to glance up from the witch's shoes. Large blue eyes shone down at me through dust-fogged glasses. "Thank you, Auntie C," I murmured.

"That's all right, dearie. You bring him to see me sometime, and don't forget to give him a proper name."

"I did already," I said. "I named him Honey O'Grady."

Chloe smiled. "That's a right nice name," she said. "I like it. I like it a lot."

For a moment, I wished we could stay a little longer. I wanted to tell her about Uncle Grady and his beautiful peach tree and how he was lonely, too. But suddenly a voice inside me warned, *Have you forgotten? Chloe's a witch!*

The next day, I ran down to Uncle Grady's house. "Well, who do we have here?" he asked when I held Honey up for him to see.

"This is Honey O'Grady," I said, "and he can't see very well."

Uncle Grady rummaged through kitchen drawers until he found a worn, black velvet box. Inside, smooth and shiny as a marble, lay his old glass eye. "This'll fix the little fella up just fine," he said. "I don't need it no more anyway." Then he reached for a red-satin pincushion bristling with threaded needles.

"How come they're all ready to sew?" I asked.

"I can't get the thread through those tiny holes, but I've got me a friend who keeps 'em ready. Blue to sew up m' jeans, red to sew up m' shirts and black to sew up m' socks."

One needle was threaded in pink. I wondered what he wore that was pink.

With hands shaking, Uncle Grady poked sawdust back in the hole where an eye should be, basted stitches around the hole, filled it up with glue, pressed the glass eye in, pulled the thread tight and bit off the end. "There," his cheeks bunched into a grin. "Now, he can see!"

Honey's new eye glittered! When he looked straight at me, it made me ask Uncle Grady, "What does a glass eye *really* see?"

Uncle Grady ran the pale pink thread across his palm. "All the good things," he said gently, "the things that some folks never see."

The hurricane roared in on Uncle Grady's seventy-eighth birthday, snapping ancient trees and telephone poles like toothpicks. By nightfall the countryside was plunged into darkness. "We don't have any candles," said

Mrs. Swensen. "We better drive up to Chloe's and buy some." She took my hand and put a flashlight in her pocket. "Poor old lady. I hope she's not afraid all alone in the dark."

But witches aren't afraid of the dark. Or are they? I wondered. I tucked Honey inside my jacket.

When we reached the store, Mrs. Swensen turned the doorknob. "Chloe!" she called. We stepped inside the eerie darkness. "Chloe!" Still no answer. "You wait here," she said. "I'll find some candles and be right back."

That's when I saw a glimmer of light, a flicker from the back of the store. I unbuttoned my jacket so Honey could see too, and together we tiptoed down the long, long aisle through the mops, soup cans and dog food.

The closer we got to Chloe's room, the more enchanted the world became. All the while gentle voices, mingled with the sweet scent of wood smoke, drifted through the beaded doorway and filled up my heart.

The witch was destroyed. Beneath a stained-glass light hovering over a chess board, Auntie C looked beautiful in her soft-pink sweater and a rosebud tucked in her thistle-down hair. Across the chess table, Uncle Grady sat straight and handsome in a green plaid shirt and new red birthday suspenders. Uncle Grady and Auntie C were smiling at each other—and holding hands.

I buried my face in the lingering scent of peaches between Honey's ears feeling happy inside. At just that moment, I learned I didn't need a glass eye to see what lots of people never see—"all the good things."

Penny Porter

The Man Without a Name

Gratitude is born in the hearts that take time to count up past mercies.

Charles E. Jefferson

"Get out, get out! You're on fire!"

Jerked awake by a voice I did not recognize, I sprang from my bed. *Hurry! Hurry! Wake up! Wake up!* were the only words I could think or say as I bolted through the apartment, rousing sleepy children and grandchildren.

The warning came in time for all of us to get out. On that cold Thanksgiving morning my husband, Bobby, two of our three grown children, my husband's twin brother and his two grandchildren huddled outside and watched our apartment and restaurant burn to the ground. By dawn, only the brick fireplace remained standing.

But we were grateful to be alive. Who had awakened us? How could we ever thank that person?

The 124-room hotel next to our restaurant, also part of our business, was undamaged. The desk clerk, who had not seen the fire at first, told us that a man in a pickup truck stopped in the middle of the deserted highway, ran into the hotel lobby, told her to call the fire department and began banging on doors.

Who was the man? We asked everyone—the firemen, police and hotel guests. No one had seen him except the desk clerk. We put an article in the newspaper asking for information. We could never fully thank someone for saving the lives of our family, but we wanted to express our gratitude in some way.

In the following years, we thanked God each Thanksgiving for this person, known only to him, who had done so much for us.

Twenty-five years went by. During those years, we rebuilt our apartment and restaurant, then sold them and the adjacent hotel. We had become volunteers with a group traveling throughout our state, other states and various countries, building churches, dormitories and camps.

On Christmas Day, 1994, my husband Bobby and I and our three children, their spouses and our nine grandchildren gathered at our oldest son's home. Once again we remembered the man who had saved our lives and without whom none of our grandchildren would have ever been born. We prayed for God to bless him and asked that someday we could meet him.

A few days after Christmas, Bobby and I met Ray Horton, one of our group's lead carpenters, to pick up a tool trailer. He invited us into his home for coffee, and we began exchanging experiences and telling about places we had been and things we had done.

Ray told us about building houses in Portland, Texas, in 1969 and 1970. We shared that we used to own a restaurant and hotel there.

Ray turned to his wife. "Do you remember me telling you about a fire at that hotel?

At the same instant Bobby and Ray realized that Ray was talking about our hotel. They stood up, facing each other, and started crying and hugging. Then we all hugged and cried, knowing that we had found the person God had sent to save our lives. At that moment, we finally got to say thanks to the man who had remained nameless for twenty-five years.

Naomi Jones

Sophie's Seascape

God moves in a mysterious way.

William Cowper

Splashes of rich shades and delicate tints of blue, green, gold and other vibrant colors graced each canvas Sophie touched with her gifted paintbrush. Her sunsets were magnificent, and her seascapes so realistic that one could almost hear sounds of waves breaking off the shore. She had studied the sea, the sun, the sand, the shore, the sky. Sophie excelled as a student, and she enjoyed a well-earned reputation and membership in several art guilds from New Mexico to South Carolina.

As a hospice volunteer, I met Sophie a few years later when she was in the final stage of terminal cancer. One Saturday she called to ask me to come to her house and help her "freshen up."

While driving to Sophie's home, I wondered what she meant by "freshen up." Her head was completely bald from the chemotherapy treatments, so I knew she wouldn't ask me to shampoo her hair. I was apprehensive because I thought she might want me to bathe her, and my hospice training had not included that type of patient care. I prayed as I drove to Sophie's home that I would be able to respond with sensitivity.

When I entered Sophie's bedroom, I felt the usual grateful, sweet spirit she always exhibited in spite of her cancer-inflicted pain. I surprised myself when I asked, "Sophie, would you like for me to bathe you?" With an obvious sigh of relief, she replied, "Yes." As I bathed Sophie, a welcomed wave of peace and serenity enveloped her—and me. I was reminded of Jesus' command to wash one another's feet. My prayer was clearly answered—even magnified.

I had been in Sophie's bedroom many times, but I had never noticed the beautiful painting above her bed. It was a resplendent seascape with an almost mystical appearance. "This painting is beautiful . . . !" I commented. Sophie quietly replied, "It's my favorite." Then she explained why.

Several years before, Sophie and her husband, Eddie, moved from New Mexico to the Texas coast to be near Sophie's adult daughter. "Seascapes," Sophie said, "are my favorite subject for painting—an added bonus to being near my daughter!" They hired a moving van to transport their household goods. But since Sophie wanted to make sure her paintings stayed under her protective surveillance, Eddie rented a trailer so they could personally take the treasured paintings to their new home.

Eddie took special care packing Sophie's favorite seascape and placed it in the safest place, the middle of the trailer. When they were only about sixty miles from their destination, the axle on the trailer broke, turning it over and spilling the contents onto the highway and the nearby field. Fortunately, Sophie and Eddie were shaken but not hurt. Sophie began to frantically assess the damage, praying that her precious cargo would not be ruined. Amazingly, within five minutes a sheriff came by the desolate stretch of road. He radioed for assistance, and a truck large enough to hold the contents of the trailer soon arrived. Sophie and Eddie drove on to Corpus Christi and dropped into bed physically and emotionally exhausted.

The next day they unpacked the paintings, and Sophie suddenly realized the seascape was missing! After they both inventoried everything a second time and then a third, they concluded that the precious painting was gone. They hurriedly drove back to the scene of the accident to make sure everything had been gathered up. Nothing but skid marks, trampled grass and weeds remained as evidence of the mishap. They checked with the sheriff who assured them, "*Nothing* was left in that borrowed truck."

The drive home was difficult. Eddie admitted, "I've let you down, Sophie." She tried to reassure him that it was okay. "I'll just paint another one," she said. Eddie knew that Sophie put a big part of herself into each painting and that it wouldn't be so simple for her to "just paint another one." Gloom settled over both of them, for they knew there would be no replacing Sophie's seascape.

The following week, Sophie stayed in their new home to unpack while Eddie returned to New Mexico to complete his work contract. Several weeks passed when Eddie received a call at work from the priest at St. Paul's Episcopal Church, where Eddie had been a member for over twenty years. "Eddie, you need to come down to the church and pick up a package delivered here to you."

When Eddie walked into the church and saw the package, he stared in amazement: *How could it be? Is it really Sophie's painting?* Eddie's hands and heart trembled as he carefully opened the package. Assisted by the priest, Eddie gently removed the packing material. Eddie began to sob when he realized it was Sophie's seascape! The frame was slightly damaged, but the canvas was in perfect condition. Attached was a note: "I was traveling on Interstate 37 when I stopped to rest from my long drive. I saw a box lying in the field, so I opened it—and found this beautiful painting.

"The only identification" continued the rescuer, "was Sophie's name with Artesia, New Mexico, written on the back of the canvas." The traveler explained that he was familiar with Artesia, for he had lived there several years before. He remembered Eddie's name because Eddie had contracted him to make some signs for St. Paul's Episcopal Church. The rescuer had since moved to Tulsa and was en route to Corpus Christi—a 650-mile drive. Eddie could hardly wait to call Sophie: "Honey you will not believe this—your lost seascape has been found!"

Sophie died shortly after she shared this story with me. Eddie gave her seascape to the church, and Eddie invited me to be one of the first people to choose among all of her other beautiful seascapes. I cherish Sophie's seascape hanging in my home as well as the one at church. Each one reminds me that our Creator has a plan for the entire canvas of our lives, and that there was a divine purpose at work when the weary traveler crossed paths with Sophie's seascape.

Barbara Jo Reams Russell

THE FAMILY CIRCUS.   By Bil Keane

"Grandma says it's okay that this life won't
last forever—the next one will."

Make Me Like Joe!

If you think you can't make a difference, think again.

Paul J. Meyer

Joe was a drunk who was miraculously converted at a Bowery mission. Prior to his conversion, Joe had gained the reputation of being a hopeless dirty wino for whom there was no hope, only a miserable existence in the ghetto. But following his conversion to a new life with God, everything changed. Joe became the most caring person that anyone associated with the mission had ever known.

Joe spent his days and nights hanging out at the mission, doing whatever needed to be done. There was never any task that was too lowly for Joe to take on. There was never anything that he was asked to do that he considered beneath him. Whether it was cleaning up the vomit left by some violently sick person or scrubbing the toilets after careless men left the men's room filthy, Joe did what was asked with a smile on his face and a seeming gratitude for the chance to help. He could be counted on to feed feeble men who wandered into the mission and off the street and to undress and tuck into bed men who were too out of it to take care of themselves.

One evening, when the mission director was delivering his evangelistic message to the usual crowd of still and sullen men with drooped heads, one man looked up, came down the aisle to the altar and knelt to pray, crying out for God to help him to change. The repentant drunk kept shouting, "Oh God! Make me like Joe! Make me like Joe! Make me like Joe! Make me like Joe!"

The director of the mission leaned over and said to the man, "Son, I think it would be better if you prayed, 'Make me like *Jesus.*'"

The man looked up at the director with a quizzical expression on his face and asked, "Is he like Joe?"

Tony Campolo

Kathleen's Piano

Faith makes the discords of the present the harmonies of the future.

Robert Collyer

One cold December morning some years back, my husband, Mark, and I were driving to the airport, headed to the West Coast to speak at a medical convention. As we voiced our anticipation of warm weather and the excitement of the big city, Mark dashed into a convenience mart to purchase some last-minute items. He returned with a small brown package in his hand and a shivering elderly lady at his side.

What a contrast they were—Mark in a gray wool pin-striped suit and the stranger clothed in a green polyester coat with two missing buttons and a stain on the front. Her half-frozen toes peeked out from timeworn sandals.

As the determined lady struggled into the back seat of the car, she flashed a tender smile my way. "My name's Kathleen," she announced boldly. "I understand you folks are headed down Kentucky way."

Her husband, it turned out, was a patient at a nearby nursing home, and was not expected to survive through the Christmas holidays. The two had married late in life, never had any children, and when their small monthly allotment dwindled, Kathleen often hitched a ride to the nursing home. Like so many Appalachian women of her generation, Kathleen was fiercely independent—a survivor. She usually stayed at the nursing home all day, for even though her husband was in a hopeless coma, the facility was warm, the food was great, and there was a piano in the day room where she could while away the hours and her cares at the keyboard.

As we approached the small, brick convalescent center, I remembered the calling cards in my briefcase. I handed my ivory linen card to Kathleen. "Don't hesitate to call us if we can ever give you a lift to the nursing home," I said. Kathleen smiled, thanked us for the ride, then confronted the unyielding wind, her thin coat blowing wildly.

When we returned home after our trip, baking, buying gifts and an endless array of holiday errands consumed our days. Kathleen called a couple of times to chat, but it wasn't until Christmas that our paths actually crossed again.

"Did you take Kathleen anything for Christmas?" Mark asked late Christmas night. How could I have forgotten?

We scurried about the house gathering some remnants of Christmas for Kathleen. As we approached her tiny frame residence, the porch light was still burning. We rang the doorbell and waited. Soon, Kathleen opened the door and invited us in, saying she *just knew* we were coming for Christmas.

As we stepped inside the living room, our eyes took in Kathleen's short-sleeved cotton dress, the tattered sofa and chair, and rugs taped around each window to protect her from the harsh weather. A bare bulb dangled from a ceiling wire, scarcely lighting the room.

"This is 'Honey.' She's an alley cat plus a better breed," Kathleen announced, stroking the animal's soft yellow fur. "And Honey and I have a special present for you." Kathleen picked up a xylophone and methodically plunked out "We Wish You a Merry Christmas" on its rusted, paint-chipped keys. "I found this for a quarter last summer at a rummage sale," she said proudly, "and I've been saving it for just the right occasion.

"Do you have a piano?" Kathleen quizzed. I nodded, feeling uncomfortable about the grand piano in our living room at home and the nice clothes in our closet. Christmas was nearly over, and in my busyness I hadn't even played a Christmas carol. In our pursuit of the things money *could* buy, it seemed we had overlooked many of the things it *couldn't* buy.

"Could you . . . would you go home and play 'Silent Night'? You could hold the telephone next to your piano, and I could celebrate Christmas one more time," Kathleen pleaded. Then she shared with us her dream of finding a piano, preferably an old upright model like she'd played as a child. She had little money, but she had faith that God would send one her way.

After the holidays, I combed the classifieds in hopes of buying a used piano for Kathleen. It became apparent, though, that all the bargains had been snatched up by the area piano dealers. I tried to compensate with other small gifts—a pretty blouse, an African violet, a tin of talcum powder.

On Valentine's Day, Kathleen hardly noticed the chocolates I bought her. "My piano will be here soon," she insisted. And, throughout the winter, Kathleen's faith intensified. Her strong faith in the midst of poverty was an unsettling paradox; it amazed me, yet amused me.

But later that spring, something wonderful happened, and Mark and I dropped by to tell Kathleen about it. Some family members had sold their home and were moving. The new owner's sole request was that the heavy upright piano in the basement be removed from the premises. Soon.

"Can you think of anyone who could use that old relic?" they had asked. "It's theirs if they move it." Could we ever!

Kathleen ran to meet us when she spotted our car. "My piano ... it's coming ... I had a dream last night. It's coming from a little town I've never heard of near Point Pleasant, West Virginia," she squealed.

"God's not too far off," Mark mumbled, maintaining a reserved amazement for God's handiwork. The piano was indeed located in a tiny, postage-stamp-sized town only thirty miles from Point Pleasant.

Mark and I could hardly contain our joy. Kathleen was baffled—not that a piano was coming, but that we were surprised. For she had been joyfully expectant since Christmas night, when she put her faith into action. "I've been playing my piano already in my mind," she explained. "Without faith, we can't please God, you know."

And ever since the massive, oak upright was rolled into Kathleen's living room, music hasn't stopped flowing. Artistic expression hasn't been limited by her advancing age or glaucoma. Kathleen's husband has since passed away. But music—be it the classics, roaring-twenties tunes or gospel songs recalled from childhood tent meetings—connects Kathleen with the world. She accompanies the congregation at her neighborhood church and joined a senior citizens' band. Kathleen doesn't read music, but she beautifully reproduces what she hears.

Before I met Kathleen, I understood faith in my mind; now I understand it in my heart. For as with all acts of faith, Kathleen's miracle happened *not* when she received, but the moment she first believed.

Roberta L. Messner

Grandma's Garden

Every blade of grass has an angel that bends over it and whispers, "Grow! Grow!"

The Talmud

I watched my grandma hoe the clay soil in my garden. "Don't see how you grow anything in this," she mused.

"Colorado soil can't compare to yours in Iowa, Grandma!" I stared at her in awe, capturing the moment in my memory forever. Wisps of her silvery hair sneaked from beneath her headscarf as her thin torso bent down to pull a fistful of bindweed.

"This stuff will grow anywhere," she laughed. "Even in this soil!"

Although she lived alone on the Iowa farm she and Grandpa had settled a half century ago, she still maintained a garden that could sustain most of Benton County! Some of my favorite summer childhood days had been spent in her garden helping her pull up plants she identified as weeds, or planting vegetables and flowers. She had taught me that gardening wasn't only about cultivating

plants, it was about cultivating faith. Each seed planted
was proof of that. When I was seven I asked, "Grandma,
how do the seeds know to grow the roots down and the
green part up?"

"Faith," was her answer.

When I grew up and married, my husband recognized
the impression Grandma's dirt left under my fingernails
and in my heart. He supported my dream to live outside
the city, and our two-acre plot had a horse, dog, cat, rabbit, six hens and, of course, a large garden. I was privileged and overjoyed to have Grandma working in it.

Grandma leaned the hoe next to a fence post and
walked to my flower bed to help me plant the daisies
she'd brought from her garden to mine. She didn't know
I was watching as she patted the dirt around the base of a
plant. Waving her hand in the sign of a cross above it, she
whispered, "God bless you, grow." I'd almost forgotten
that garden blessing from my youth. Ten years later, those
daisies still flourish.

Grandma is tending God's garden now but still influ-
ences me daily. Whenever I tuck a seedling into the earth,
I trace a small cross above it in the air and say, "God bless
you, grow."

And in quiet times, I can still hear her blessing, nurtur-
ing my faith. "God bless you, grow."

LeAnn Thieman

10

LIVING YOUR DREAM

Nothing happens unless first a dream.

Carl Sandburg

A Dream Deferred

Better late than never.

Old American Saying

My friend Rita celebrated her fifty-fifth birthday on January 28, 1998. Forty-five years ago on this date, she was scheduled to be on the local *T-Bar V* television show along with other children celebrating their birthdays.

Rita had anticipated this event for months. The excitement of being on television would have been tremendous for any child, but for Rita it would have been a special dream come true. Rita's father was a violent drug addict long before drugs were a common part of everyday life. They lived in the projects, and Rita was ashamed of it at school. Sometimes she had to ask neighbors for food. Once she had been left on the steps of an orphanage all night until her grandparents decided to come back and get her. By the time she was nine years old, she had already been in and out of numerous foster homes. So the prospect of being on television was truly a fairy tale come true.

Rita's grandmother had arranged the TV appearance

months earlier. She had bought Rita a new dress, coat, gloves and shoes. Her grandmother was the most loving, stabilizing person in her life. She was making Rita's dream a reality.

Months before the big event, social workers came to Rita's home and removed her and her brothers and sisters from an environment deemed unacceptable for children. The decision was permanent; there was no returning to her family this time. Rita and her siblings were sent to a children's center where unwanted children mixed with juvenile delinquents.

Rita did not get to be on the television show on her birthday. Making time for one child to be on a birthday program was not part of the agenda at the children's center. She watched the show on her birthday and heard Randy Atcher, the program emcee, say, "Happy Birthday to Rita, who couldn't be with us today." Rita watched as the other birthday children climbed up on Randy's lap and told their names and what they hoped to get for their birthdays. She listened and watched as Randy sang the *T-Bar V* birthday song. The children's center gave her a doll for her birthday, but she had to return it to the center when she was sent to another foster home. Her heart had never been emptier.

Rita's austere life was filled with a series of institutions and foster homes and eventual adoption. No one wanted all of the children together, so Rita's brothers and sisters were farmed out to various families. As the oldest of the siblings, Rita tried to keep track of them. But eventually she lost contact with all her brothers and sisters.

The opportunity to be on *T-Bar V* did not arise again. The years went by, and the show ended. Rita grew up, married and had her own child, who had grown up. Rita tracked down her siblings. Life went on.

Rita never forgot how close she came to being on the

T-Bar V show. She did not dwell on it, but each birthday the memory reappeared. The emptiness she felt that day as her childhood dream and the memories of having her family taken from her would arise from the dark part of her innermost being and fill her with despair. She did not share her story; it was simply too painful to talk about.

But at age fifty-four, she finally told a friend about these painful parts of her history. The friend grasped the intensity of Rita's feelings and suggested she write Randy Atcher to tell him about her experience and explain how much it would mean to her to simply get a birthday card from him. At first Rita thought, *This is silly. Too many years have passed to bring it up. Randy Atcher would think I'm a nut. It is ridiculous. I am a grown woman with a grown son.* But the idea continued to grip her.

At first Rita drafted her letter thinking she would never send it. She looked at it for a few days and, finally, holding her breath, she addressed and mailed it. She thought, *I'll never hear anything about it.* But she was consoled by telling herself, *At least I tried, at least I tried.* As a child, she had survived many disappointments. But missing her appearance on the birthday program placed at the top of the list. So she simply could not squelch that small glimmer of hope that she might get a response from her letter.

As her birthday neared, Rita became more hopeful. She told no one of her hopes, but prayed she would get a card. It would erase some of the childhood hurt. The days went by, but no card came. Finally, her birthday arrived. *Maybe it will come today,* she thought. But she would not allow herself to believe it would. The mail came on her birthday, but there was no card. *What did I expect?* Rita asked herself. *Randy must have thought I was crazy. It was a foolish idea.*

Rita went to the birthday dinner prepared by her son and daughter-in-law. The food was wonderful, and she tried to enjoy herself. But she simply could not fully enjoy the attention. Her mind kept riveting back to the card that never came and to the television show she didn't get to be on as a young child.

When the doorbell rang, Rita's daughter-in-law answered it. Rita was speechless! Seventy-nine-year-old Randy Atcher and his wife walked in the door. Randy gave Rita a big birthday hug and said, "I understand that you had a childhood dream to be on my television show on your tenth birthday. Would you tell us the whole story?" For an hour they all listened, laughed and cried, as Rita described her family, the ups and downs of their lives, and how important the missed *T-Bar V* birthday had been to her.

Randy Atcher gave Rita an autographed picture of himself and his television partner, Cactus. Rita shed tears of joy as her daughter-in-law brought out a huge cake inscribed with "Happy T-Bar V Birthday, Mom" while Randy sang the *T-Bar V* birthday song:

Happy, Happy Birthday from all of us to you.
Now you'll have happy birthdays all your life through.

Rita smiled through her tears, for she knew the words of the song were true. At last.

Marie Bunce

Never "Too Old"

What becomes fragile when we age is not our bodies as much as our egos. The best time to take some daring steps is when we get older.

Helen Hayes

Many of the world's great accomplishments have been made by people who passed their sixtieth birthday. Those people, some more well-known than others, show that there are certainly no preset age limits for achievement.

At age eighty, owner and former publisher of the *Washington Post*, Katherine Graham, won a Pulitzer Prize for her bestselling autobiography, her first and only book. Taking the reins of the *Washington Post* in 1963, she successfully led the paper in what was considered a "man's world" at the time. Today she is a respected member of the newspaper publishing community and is a role model for women of every age.

John Glenn, the first man to orbit the earth in the early 1960s, trained for another space launch more than thirty years later. During his training, the seventy-plus-year-old joined the rest of his space crew in challenging physical practice exercises. America's oldest astronaut, Glenn blasted toward the heavens once again, this time to help NASA learn more about aging in space.

Alan Greenspan, in his seventies and revered chairman of the U.S. Federal Reserve Board, sends armies of Wall Street traders into frenzied deals based on what he says or implies about the direction of the economy. In addition to proving his theories for keeping the economy healthy, Greenspan is showing that being a newlywed in one's seventies can be a "good deal," too.

Billy Graham, in his early eighties, continues to be one of the most influential men in the world. He is said to have preached to greater multitudes than anyone else alive. In keeping with the times, he recently opened a home page on the Internet.

In her eighties, world-renowned chef Julia Child continues to appear on TV cooking shows, write bestselling books and cookbooks, and has also released her tips and recipes in a computer software program.

Many of the great artists of all time have proven the old saying, "Many a good tune is played on an old violin." When Pablo Casals reached ninety-five, a young reporter threw him the following question. "Mr. Casals, you are ninety-five and the greatest cellist who ever lived. Why do you still practice six hours a day?" Mr. Casals answered, "Because I think I'm making progress."

Goethe completed his immortal *Faust* when he was eighty-three. Verdi completed his well-known opera *Falstaff* when he was eighty years of age.

History also shows that some of the greatest world leaders continued to work for progress into their later years. Winston Churchill did not become prime minister of England until he was sixty-two—after a lifetime of defeats and setbacks. His greatest victories and contributions came when he was a "senior citizen."

Harry Truman was first elected to the senate at the age of fifty and became president of the United States at age sixty-one. He served until he was sixty-nine but continued to be active in politics. He wrote two volumes of his memoirs after he was sixty-nine.

Jimmy Carter, the thirty-ninth president of the United States, became the university distinguished professor at Emory University and founded the Carter Center at age fifty-eight. At age sixty-seven, he launched the Atlanta Project, a community-wide effort to attack the social problems associated with poverty. Today he actively works on behalf of the Habitat for Humanity programs dedicated to providing low-income families new homes built by volunteers.

Ronald Reagan, born in 1911, was elected president of the United States just prior to his seventieth birthday. At age seventy-seven, Reagan concluded two terms as president credited with ending the Cold War and renewing public confidence in enduring, traditional American values.

Sandra Day O'Connor, at age fifty-one, was the first woman to be named as associate justice of the United States Supreme Court. Overcoming cancer, she has continued to serve into her sixties.

Many "firsts" have been accomplished by people sixty and over. Raised in poverty, George Eastman, founder of the Eastman Kodak Company, appreciated money for what it could do, but he cared little about keeping it for himself. At the age of sixty-five, he gave one-third of his own holdings of company stock, then worth ten million dollars, to his employees. He was among the first industrialists to establish "fringe benefits" such as retirement pensions, life insurance and disability insurance for employees.

As for Nobel Prizes awarded to recipients over sixty, there are a number of them, most notably, Mother Teresa.

At age sixty-nine, Mother Teresa received the Nobel Peace Prize for her work with the poor of Calcutta, India.

Enduring organizations and causes have often been established by people over age sixty. At age sixty-five, Dr. Ethel Percy Andrus founded and became president of the National Retired Teachers Association, and at the age of seventy-four, she founded the American Association of Retired Persons. After that she added a pharmacy service, a travel service (first in the country), the Institute of Lifetime Learning, the Retirement Research and Welfare Association and the AARP International.

"Father Abraham" was seventy-five years of age when God told him he would make him the founder of a great nation. As part of the promise, God commanded Abraham to move his entire household from Mesopotamia, where Abraham was a member of the noble class, to Palestine, an unknown land for him. As the father of Isaac and Ishmael, Abraham became the forefather of the three major religions of the world: Judaism, Christianity and Islam. In time, his progeny truly came to a number "greater than the sands on the seashore."

Are you merely growing older or, like so many of these shining examples, are you continuing to be active and useful as the years go by? It is possible, as Jane Brody, health writer of the *New York Times*, puts it, "to die young, as late in life as possible."

Jack Canfield, Mark Victor Hansen, Paul J. Meyer,
Barbara Russell Chesser and Amy Seeger

"I think you'll be interested in the next case, he's ninety-two and accompanied by his parents."

Reprinted by permission of Martha Campbell.

Sweet Petunia

The best way to cheer yourself up is to cheer everybody else up.

Mark Twain

There it was—the advertisement that kept reappearing in her local newspaper, calling out to her. She could no longer resist. Much to the amazement of her family and friends, this rather dignified seventy-year-old woman followed her heart and enrolled in clown school.

Not surprisingly, she was the oldest in her class. She painstakingly mastered face painting and struggled to create recognizable balloon animals. But persist she did, graduating with top clown honors, and Sweet Petunia was born!

Most folks would find it rather strange that a woman of her age—and particularly someone so shy—would long to be a clown. But Sweet Petunia saw this as the perfect opportunity to unleash her long pent-up playful side without fear of disapproving eyes.

The transformation began. Chalk-white face, vivid blue widely-arched brows, cherry red nose and smiling, brilliant red mouth. She chose a baggy blue shirt and a pair of voluminous white trousers which puddled over red floppy shoes. Next came a bright yellow mop of hair topped by a white pork pie hat. In the hat, her signature— two purple petunias.

Out the door she would go, volunteering her services at hospitals, community fairs, store openings or a myriad of other places needing a good clown. "Don't you feel like a fool at your age?" snapped her older sister as they drove to a granddaughter's birthday party. These words served only to make Sweet Petunia more jubilant about her new pursuit. "What? Look at these faces! Smiling, laughing, having a good time. After all, everyone loves a clown!"

One particular afternoon, Sweet Petunia slapped her red floppy feet down the corridor of the downtown hospital. As she turned the corner of the east wing, her ears were assailed by a string of horrible curses and a clanking of metal hitting concrete. She hesitated and started to turn around. But just then a young sobbing nurse darted out of the room and nearly collided with her. Startled to see a clown, the nurse crumpled into Sweet Petunia's arms. Words shot from the young woman's mouth like staccato bullets, "He is awful! He's the meanest patient I've ever met! Sure, he's very ill, but that's not my fault!"

The young nurse was clinging so tightly to Sweet Petunia she could hardly breathe. "Let me see him," Sweet Petunia said.

The two moved slowly through the doorway. A waxen-faced man glared at them. As soon as his mind registered the fact that he was looking at a clown, his mouth fell open and he sucked in a great breath. "What? What is this? You look ridiculous!"

Sweet Petunia's red mouth smiled her brightest. "*I* look ridiculous? You *look* and *sound* ridiculous!"

"Get out! I'm dying, and I don't want to look at either one of you!"

The nurse moved to leave, but Sweet Petunia held her arm and stepped closer to the bed. "If you *are* dying, is this how you want to be remembered?" She pointed to the metal bedpan lying upside down between them where he had thrown it. "Some legacy!"

That was the first visit Sweet Petunia made to Room 226. "This unhappy man is going to be my special project," she resolved. In the following months she stopped by at least once a week. Never daunted by the patient's outbursts, Sweet Petunia was determined to reach that tender side she was convinced all people have no matter how tough the exterior.

Sometimes she would visit as Sweet Petunia and sometimes without the costume. Yet, something of Sweet Petunia remained even after the makeup was washed away and the clown suit was hanging in her closet. She always brought her supply of balloons. Patient 226 became very good at purple giraffes and green poodles. In spite of being very near death, this man's last weeks of life were brightened by Sweet Petunia. As for the young frightened nurse who introduced Sweet Petunia to Patient 226, she said, "Sweet Petunia gave me new perspective on how to help patients!"

Not only did Sweet Petunia change the life of the "meanest patient" and the young nurse, she also changed the lives of many others. But one of the most remarkable transformations took place in her. Once a reticent, shy individual who retreated from the limelight, she easily and happily became the focus of the room as Sweet Petunia. The affirmation she experienced as Sweet Petunia enhanced her ability to experience her "real" life. By the time Sweet Petunia had her five grandchildren, that radiant personality was full-blown and genuine. She was an absolute delight to Kevin, Victoria, Drew, Gabrielle and Gavin. One of their grandmother's favorite antics earned her the name "Grandma Whistle." Whenever she came for a visit, she wore a whistle around her neck and blew it, to the kids' delight.

Sweet Petunia has always been special to me, but one unexpected encounter was especially endearing. It had been one of the worst days at the company where I worked. Budgets were shrinking, files were vaporizing, impossible deadlines were looming. What next? The receptionist announced the arrival of my 4:30 appointment. I was unaware of any scheduled visitor for that time. Reviewing my calendar, I asked, "Are you sure this person has an appointment with *me*?"

"I think you need to see this one for yourself," replied our receptionist. Noting the wide grins of my associates, I headed down the hallway. Standing in our lobby, in all her clown glory, was Sweet Petunia! If I ever needed some love and laughter, it was now. She smiled and hugged me, squeezing out my stored-up misery.

When the onlookers knew it was safe to laugh, one of them asked, "Who is she?" With heartfelt love and admiration, I answered, "This is Sweet Petunia. Her grandchildren call her Grandma Whistle. I call her Mom."

Leon J. Rawitz

Special Delivery

Where there's a will, there's a way.

Eliza Cook

"We need a wheelchair," the familiar voice on the telephone told me. Not an unusual request, because it was Dr. Charles Shellenberger, a retired physician I know who for many years has been living his dream as a volunteer, helping meet medical needs of people of all ages in countries around the world. In my work, he has called on me often over the past years with similar requests.

Dr. Shellenberger explained in further detail, however, what made this request unusual: "This wheelchair is for an older man with no feet and legs, and it needs plenty of room in the back and seat."

As the executive director of an association of more than one hundred churches, I pass requests like this on to individuals and groups in our association who can help. In this case, I called the chairman of our ministry that supplies medical equipment. The chairman, E. J. Culp, is another one of our active, energetic volunteers in the golden age group who take great satisfaction and pride in working for a good cause. Within one week, E. J. and his group had used parts from two older wheelchairs to make one wheelchair meeting Dr. Shellenberger's specifications.

When I delivered the wheelchair, Dr. Shellenberger provided more information. "Paul, I will be taking this chair with me when our group goes to Siberia." I didn't want to appear skeptical, question his enthusiasm or sound like a doubting Thomas, so I simply said, "Great! We'll be praying for you and your church group on this trip to Siberia."

But privately I wondered, "How in the world are they going to get that wheelchair from here to their remote destination?" Since I had traveled to that part of the world, I knew from experience the obstacles, hassles and other "red tape" of taking unusual items through customs.

Their ingenious plan was soon revealed to me. One of the members of the volunteer group was pregnant. Dr. Shellenberger, always known for his resourcefulness, simply wrote out a statement, much like a prescription, for the airline and customs officials explaining that the condition of the expectant mother required her to ride in the wheelchair through the airports between connecting flights, which, of course, would necessitate her having the wheelchair aboard the flights.

All the airlines were very cooperative in meeting the special needs of this expectant mother, as she conscientiously followed "doctor's orders" all the way to Siberia! No one questioned the radiant and rested expectant mother, and getting through customs was an absolute breeze.

After arriving in Siberia, the group traveled to the remote village that was the location of their work assignment. Just to be on the safe side, all the while, the expectant mother took her dutiful place in the wheelchair. As they approached the place where they knew the older gentleman would be sitting on the ground begging for food, excited anticipation filled each member of the group. The expectant mother maneuvered herself up beside him and stepped energetically away from the wheelchair. Several men picked up the double amputee and placed him in the specially prepared wheelchair.

With very little instruction, the overwhelmed man soon was proudly navigating the wheelchair everywhere—his sense of independence and dignity soaring! Now he was as radiant as the wheelchair's prior occupant.

When people ask the Siberian gentleman how he got this wheelchair, he replies with a smile, "Special delivery."

Paul Stripling

Being There

We cannot tell what may happen to us in the strange medley of life. But we can decide what happens in us . . . how we can take it, what we can do with it . . . and that is what really counts in the end.

Joseph Fort Newton

"August twelfth!" they exclaimed, telling us about their wedding plans. Then—with a characteristic grin and twinkle in his eyes—Louis McBurney added: "the twelfth of *never!*" As a longtime friend of both the prospective bride *and* groom, I understood the deep meaning behind those words. For him the wait had been seven long years of *nevers.*

Louis's dream began the hot summer of 1954, when the Morris family moved to a new city. On her first Sunday afternoon venture in her new hometown, Melissa Morris and her date drove by the McBurney residence and waved at Louis as he was working in his parents' front yard. That cheery young lady, swiftly passing from view, made an indelible impression. It made no difference that she was with another young man. Today Louis can take us to the very place he was standing when it hit him. It was love at first sight—albeit from a distance!

"It was her smile," says Louis. In that one fleeting moment, Melissa's radiant smile captured his heart. According to his account, the first thing Louis did was go inside and declare his intentions to his mother. "I don't know who she is, but I just saw the girl I am going to marry!"

Indeed, from that day on, there was never a doubt in Louis's mind. Melissa was the one who made his heart sing! But Melissa was not convinced—despite all of Louis's gentle efforts. Yet patiently and persistently through the years, Louis was always "there."

At times *there* meant sitting in the flowerbed beneath Melissa's bedroom window late at night. Louis would often come for a flowerbed visit after another of her long series of suitors brought her home from a date. Louis became known as Melissa's ubiquitous friend!

The long-stemmed red rose supply became all but depleted in their town—one rose at a time. With long-stemmed red roses as his chosen means to declare his devotion to Melissa, Louis and the florist were eventually on a first-name basis. In addition to "Happy June 2nd" (or whatever date happened to be on the calendar), the flower delivery was usually accompanied by a poem penned by the rose giver. Louis enjoyed sending these quiet reminders of his *being there.*

A Morris family rule at the time seriously hindered Louis in his progress toward his goal. Melissa's parents decreed that Melissa could not have two consecutive dates with any one suitor. So, Louis had to wait his turn. Painful though it was to watch from the sidelines while Melissa dated other young men who also adored her, the biggest challenge to Louis's dream came in the spring before their senior year in college. Melissa had finally said "yes" and accepted an engagement ring—but from someone else! Melissa and Ernie had fallen in love. They were planning a wedding for the following December.

But a car accident in October changed everything. Melissa barely survived the crash with severe lacerations and broken bones. Ernie died three days later, all their dreams and plans gone with him.

Louis was *there* to comfort Melissa while her family and friends attended Ernie's funeral in San Antonio. Louis was *there* at her side to encourage her through the long and painful process of physical and emotional recovery.

In the years that followed, another diversion postponed Louis's long-held dream of marrying Melissa. The arduous demands of medical school prescribed for him long hours and hard work, in addition to writing poems to accompany long-stemmed red roses.

In the fall of 1960, my husband and I were surprised early one Saturday with a knock on the door of our newlywed apartment. We were anticipating a visit from Melissa, for she was coming to attend a football game in our city later that day. But we were not expecting the telegram from Louis that was delivered to our door!

After placing the telegram in Melissa's hand when she arrived, I stepped back to watch the expression on her face as she read it. A response of sheer delight signaled a new day in Louis and Melissa's relationship. At last! The medical student—with a flair for writing poetry—prevailed! The many years of friendship and devotion had yielded a good investment. The dream Louis had held onto for seven long years was finally becoming a reality.

Following their wedding, Louis and Melissa moved to Rochester, Minnesota, for his residency in psychiatry at the Mayo Clinic. During his training, Louis found that the clergy, when faced with difficult personal issues, had no place to go for restoration and encouragement. Furthermore, he observed a tendency by the congregation to place a minister and a minister's family on a pedestal, subjecting them to unrealistic expectations.

From that lofty perch, a minister's family was often unable to admit a need for help. They feared the consequences of revealing their own humanity. Louis was deeply moved by this need. At this pivotal point in his career, he could easily have chosen a more conventional route in private practice. But like his love for Melissa, a new dream took hold of his heart in a way he could not ignore.

Louis and Melissa began to talk and pray together about starting an interdenominational retreat center providing brief intensive therapy for ministers in crisis. They dared to dream in ways people had never dreamed before. Louis had learned well the lessons in patience and persistence for making dreams come true.

Today, in the beautiful Crystal River Valley of the Colorado mountains, sits a monument to the pursuit of dreams. In 1971, obstacles were miraculously removed to make possible the construction of the retreat center Louis and Melissa had dreamed and prayed into existence. By 1977, the dream was fully realized. Marble Retreat, a center for Christian psychotherapy, ministering to ministers, was fully operational.

For more than twenty-five years now, Louis and Melissa have been instruments of healing for more than two thousand ministers and their spouses. To this private place, individuals come from far and near with shattered dreams—with broken lives and strained marriages. They leave with hope for a new beginning—daring to dream again in their relationships and in their places of service.

Louis held onto a dream long ago that has now come full circle. Now in his early sixties but once just a young man in love, he did everything possible to follow his dream, even when all he could do was *be* there. For thirty-six years now, Louis and Melissa have *been* there for others—inspiring them to hold on to their dreams.

Doris Dillard Edwards

Reaching My Impossible Dreams

The greater the obstacle, the greater the glory in overcoming it.

Moliére

I looked across the college campus and shivered as I anticipated the next few minutes. The icy November wind whipped my pant legs as I dug my forearm crutch into the snowy path leading to the college field house. Doubts chilled my heart as I set up the rhythm of walking, trying so hard not to lose my balance and fall. *Am I a fool to cling to my dreams?*

Eighteen months earlier nobody doubted I'd meet my dream and make it through college and graduate as a P.E. teacher. In high school I was Mr. Athlete. I was captain and an all-star player on a league championship basketball team that lost only two games. I played halfback and linebacker on football teams that went undefeated for three consecutive years. I played second base on a championship baseball team. I also ran the mile as part of a track team that took second place in the district.

My family and friends also expected me to meet my other dreams of flying my own plane, golfing, playing guitar in a band and marrying a special girl.

Then one hot summer night in 1955, a few weeks after high school graduation, I came home from farm work feeling like I had the flu. I staggered down to my basement bedroom. All that night my body burned with fever, and I vomited constantly into a bucket by my bed. Unbearable pain gripped my back and neck. My worried parents called the family doctor. Finding no reflexes, he confirmed their worst fears. I had polio.

The new Salk vaccine hadn't yet reached our small town in central Washington. I would be one of the nation's last polio victims.

Within days, all I could move were my left wrist and fingers. I was totally dependent on others—an eighteen-year-old baby. After my fever broke two weeks later, I couldn't even bend. Friends hoisted my paralyzed body like a piece of timber up the stairs to a borrowed station wagon bound for the hospital sixty miles away.

There, doctors grimly assessed my paralysis. Polio destroyed 80 percent of my leg muscles. My right arm was virtually useless; my left arm was over 50 percent paralyzed. One doctor predicted I'd be in a wheelchair the rest of my life.

I didn't want to hear that. I believed that God had made me for a special reason, and I always thought that included athletics. Now, other people had to feed and dress me.

Knowing my family and lots of friends were praying for me gave me courage to keep going as therapists repeatedly pushed me to the edge of my limits to salvage my remaining muscles. Sometimes the pain got so bad I'd scream.

Oh God, I prayed one lonely night, *help me build up the remaining muscles just enough to walk and take care of myself.* A hundred days later, I hobbled out of that hospital with a forearm crutch gripped by my half-good left arm. My balance was still poor, I made a mess eating with my left hand and I could hardly dress myself, but God had brought me a long way from helplessness. For another year, I continued physical therapy at home. But I was restless. I wanted to get on with life and pursue my dreams. And that meant college.

Now I was on campus at what was then called Eastern Washington State College, in Cheney, Washington, with my athlete's heart imprisoned in a paralyzed body. A registration packet stamped "P.E. Exempt" flopped against my crutch as I struggled the quarter-mile walk to the gym and offices of physical education teachers. I fell half a dozen times before getting there, depending on kind students to pull me up and steady me again.

By now I was used to people staring and asking awkwardly how they could help. But I wasn't used to my new identity as a crippled person. (Since then I've progressed from being called handicapped, disabled and physically challenged to mobility impaired!) More than anything else, I wanted to major in physical education. Deep down, I knew I might be rejected, but there was no other career that interested me. I decided to take the risk.

Somebody held open the heavy gym doors so I could "crutch" my way in. I walked the length of the gym, memories flooding my mind as I watched students shooting baskets. Above me I heard the familiar clinks and bumps of the weight room. I passed the equipment room, housing all the game apparatus I knew so well.

Finally, I came to the offices of the physical education professors. The professor assigned to me was Dr. Richard Hagelin. I wobbled into his office, plopped into a chair and dropped my crutch. I looked at this man who held my future in his lean swimmer's hands. Tall, with a strong military bearing, he simply listened as I introduced myself and told him what was obvious.

"I can't run or jump," I said. "I can't do push-ups or pull-ups. I can't climb a rope or jump rope. But I want to major in physical education and become a P.E. teacher." I held my breath. He could see I couldn't lift either arm above my head. I couldn't throw a football or shoot a basket. I wondered if he'd dismiss me by saying, "Danny, I'm sorry, but you're in the wrong department."

All I'd ever wanted in life hinged on his reply.

"Well," Dr. Hagelin said without hesitation, "let's see what you *can* do." Any other professor might have written me off. But God had matched me up with just the right person to encourage me.

Dr. Hagelin started me off with two P.E. courses that essentially extended my rehabilitation program: weight training and swimming. I had to pass eleven P.E. activity classes to graduate, and I made it through all of them. I was even able to lock my legs and jump again on the trampoline! Eventually, I earned my master's degree in physical education, and landed wonderful jobs as a P.E. specialist. I taught physical education and had a lot of fun stretching my creativity to the limit. Teachers came from all over the state to watch my ideas in action and to learn from the innovations I'd developed.

Later, I became an elementary school principal, earning three Washington state awards for excellence. I can't explain why, except that I applied Dr. Hagelin's advice to my relationships with my staff and students, always challenging them, "Let's see what you *can* do." I believed in each and every one of them and wanted them to do their best.

I took Dr. Hagelin's advice in attempting and reaching my other dreams. I risked asking a pretty girl who was a football player's girlfriend to have a soda with me—and ended up marrying her. I played bass guitar in my own band, learned to golf with one arm and earned my airplane pilot's license, a feat most people considered impossible for one so paralyzed.

After I retired with twenty-eight years in public education, I went back to my alma mater to help honor Dr. Hagelin. I told the student body how he encouraged a scared, crippled, but determined college freshman one morning in 1956 who was thinking, *Am I a fool to cling to my dreams?* I never asked myself that question again after Dr. Hagelin gave me permission to try by saying, "Let's see what you *can* do." Those six magic words helped me reach my impossible dreams.

Dan Miller

High-Flying Nun

Ah, but a man's reach should exceed his grasp, or what's a heaven for?

Robert Browning

Gumption and prayers have helped me live my dreams for more than seven decades. As an eleven-year-old, I read a news story about a barking dog leading two nuns to a newborn baby abandoned in the bushes. My dream of becoming a nun and helping others was born. Five years later I joined a convent in Mission San Jose.

After serving as a Dominican Sister for thirty-six years, I began to dream new dreams. Pope John XXIII had announced that nuns should consider leading more contemporary lives. In my early fifties at the time, I remember thinking, *I can do that.* So when I was asked to teach high school science, I wasted no time accepting the offer and tackling the preparation required to teach these courses. I provided the gumption, and I asked everyone I knew to lift up their prayers for me. Despite my "advanced age," I earned two master's degrees, and later finished a Ph.D. at the ripe old age of sixty-seven.

Following the pope's directive ended up being fun. My new "contemporary life" included flying, bungee jumping, sky diving and striving to do other things I had never contemplated. Somewhere along the way I was called "the high-flying nun," and that nickname has stuck.

I took jobs with the Archdiocese in Los Angeles as a curriculum coordinator and then as a director of education for the California Museum of Science and Industry in Los Angeles. A student's comment triggered the beginning of a new dream. The student said, "This is supposed to be a science museum, and there's nothing about space science." My passion for space science was born.

After organizing an Explorer Post Program, I took its sixty-three young members up and down the state of California to visit aerospace companies such as Lockheed and Rockwell. Next came tours on four chartered planes with the museum's docents and their family members to see the astronauts fly into space on Apollo missions from Cape Canaveral.

Another dream was fulfilled when NASA asked if I would teach hundreds of inner-city children about space. With stars and planets twinkling in my eyes, I spent twelve years traveling as an aerospace education specialist, showing children aircraft models, space rockets, astronaut suits and moon rocks, and teaching them about scientific principles from gravity to inertia.

When I was seventy-two, I retired from NASA and refocused. Now I fly just once a month up and down the California coast working for the Jet Propulsion Laboratory to teach elementary students.

Aging hasn't stopped me from doing fulfilling and fun things. With tremendous fulfillment, I traveled to Bosnia and Croatia to help orphans. More recently, I went to Honduras and Guatemala, taking along toothbrushes, toothpaste, T-shirts and learning items such as periscopes and magnifying glasses.

Just for fun when I was seventy-nine, I white-water rafted down the Colorado River, hiked for miles and slept under the stars along the Grand Canyon. And only months ago I accepted the invitation of a pilot at an air show to soar into the sky on a navy training plane to enjoy a few aerobatic twists and turns. He even let me pilot the plane! My only regret is that we didn't turn upside down.

People often ask what has been the most fun and fulfilling dream in my life. Hands down, it's the students. I remember one extremely troubled high school student who was going downhill fast. He wrote me a letter I still have. Evidently my teaching about science and space touched a chord in him, for he wrote, "Sometimes I lie out at night just looking at the stars." When I was eighty, he found out where I lived and came to show me how well he had done. He owned his own company, and he had with him a lovely wife and their baby.

I've loved my career of literally soaring with mind, body and spirit upward to the heavens. But the real thrill has been showing young people how to reach their own stars.

Sister Clarice Lolich
As told to Diana L. Chapman

11

REMINISCING

A joyous occasion is never quite as wonderful as when it becomes a memory.

Jimmy Carter

"Y'know, Grandpa . . . I thinks this is gonna
be one of my good ol' days!"

Mom Had a Beef with Rationing

What you don't know won't hurt you.

Source Unknown

How well I recall that summer day during World War II. I did my housework with a song in my heart.

After all, it was the first of the month, and we'd just received our new supply of ration stamps.

They were blue, for canned fruits and vegetables, and red, for meat. It took ingenuity for a housewife to make the stamps and days of the month come out even—especially red stamps.

In those war days, I bought a huge beef rump roast the first of the month and parted with a goodly supply of red stamps. In the following days, we had hot roast beef sandwiches, cold roast beef sandwiches, beef stew, stuffed green peppers, hash, and on and on. On the last day, we'd enjoy soup, made with the bone I'd carved from the roast on the first day.

Yes, I was feeling good this Monday morning, for yesterday was the first day of the roast, and with careful planning, there were at least ten meals left. No substitute like peanut meatloaf for us!

So happy was I, that I generously said yes when my four-year-old daughter, Nina, came in with a request.

"Mama, there's a dog in our yard and he doesn't belong to anyone. He's hungry. Can I feed him something?"

"Give him the bone in the refrigerator," I magnanimously offered.

I heard the refrigerator door open and close, and then the back door slammed shut. I gave a contended motherly smile and went on with some drudgery cleaning.

Suddenly, God in his heaven sent a small voice to tell me that all would not be right in my world if I didn't have a look-see in that refrigerator!

Sure enough, there sat the bone, all alone. I looked out the kitchen window, and there sat the dog eating my roast. I panicked. *What to do?*

I couldn't afford to spend any more red stamps this week. And it was too early in the month to sell the family on peanut meatloaf.

This called for fast action! I grabbed the bone, ran out the back door and threw it with all my might toward the farthest corner of the lot.

The dog dropped the roast and ran for the bone. I raced for the roast, tucked it under my arm like a football and headed for the house. The dog saw my maneuver and the chase was on.

By now, the neighbors had formed a cheering section over the back fence. "Go, Aiken, go!"

I made an end run around the clotheslines. Behind me was the dog, ahead of me were the kids, holding the back door open and shouting, "C'mon, Mom! You can make it!"

I gave it all I had and dove over the goal line into the kitchen. Sweeter words were never heard than those uttered by my son Bruce, who said, "Gee, Mom, could we ever use you on our football team!"

I trimmed the teeth marks from the roast, washed it and cut off enough to make chili for dinner.

The family, especially Nina, thought it best not to tell Father about the excitement of the day. He was sort of finicky about food sometimes.

But he liked his dinner that evening. In fact, he said it was the best doggoned chili he'd ever eaten.

Marie Aiken
As told to Nina Gordon

My Brush with the Red Cross

*Personally, I'm always ready to learn, although
I do not always like being taught.*

Winston Churchill

During World War II, I was blessed with three things.
First, I was too young to serve my country. Second, I was
a perpetual night owl. Third, I was possessed by a mother,
a war worker, who found escape in books and movies—
movies that changed on Monday, Wednesday and Friday
at our local theater.

On the appropriate night, my younger sister would be
tucked up in bed at our grandparents' home where we
lived, and off we'd go, my mother and I.

Once in the theater lobby, there was, as always, a lady
in a Red Cross nurse's uniform, holding a small box and
standing next to a huge Red Cross sign that said, "Give."
This three-night-a-week spectacle, coupled with
Hollywood war/love movies, kept me in a most patriotic
frame of mind. As well I noticed that everyone happily
donated money to the lady in the nurse's uniform.

In our neighborhood there was a corner store called Ehrlicks. Everyone shopped there, and we were no exception. At my gran's request, I made many a trip for small groceries. During one of my trips, I noticed an amazingly similar, albeit smaller, Red Cross sign in the Ehrlicks window: "Give to the Red Cross." I guess the wheels started turning right then, but nothing much happened until about two months later.

On one of my trips to the store, and being a habitual back-lane traveler, I spied Mr. Ehrlick putting his Red Cross sign in the garbage. You can imagine my feelings and what I took home, along with the butter I'd been sent for by Granny. I hid the sign behind my grandfather's workshop until I could develop my plan fully. First, I had to find that nurse's kit some misguided relative had given me for Christmas. Once found, I realized I had a cap, arm band and apron—an apron with a bib. Perfect. It didn't take long to find a blouse and skirt. Finally, I felt that I really looked like the lady at the show.

Behind our house in Toronto's west end was a huge General Motors dealer, which sold and serviced General Motors trucks, tractors and trailers. It seemed to me hundreds of men and a few women came and went from there. I carefully packed my "rocket wagon" with the sign and my outfit. For protection, I took my grandmother's Boston bull terrier, "Toby." We set out for our trip around the block to Spadina Avenue where I set up outside the General Motors gates. Coincidentally, a streetcar stop was just opposite my stand; it proved a real bonus as people alighted and said, "Oh, how sweet" and "Aren't you a thoughtful little girl."

By five o'clock I was rich! This was an era when people worked for fifty to seventy-five cents an hour. According to the bank clock, five-fifteen had arrived. I reluctantly packed up, as Toby and I would soon be required at home for supper. I had to wake Toby from his slumber, where I'm sure he was dreaming of the liver Granny would be cooking for him.

Upon arrival at home, I took everything but my sign upstairs. Instead of washing up, I sat counting my loot, twenty-five dollars—wow! All of a sudden, Granny was standing over me with a very strange look on her face. "Where in the world did this come from?" she asked, setting down the tea towel in her hand.

"It's mine. People gave it to me," I cried, trying to pull it toward me.

"I see," she said.

I knew in a minute she'd have the whole tale out of me. She always did, even when I really tried not to tell her. As predicted, the whole story was told. She just smiled and said, "Well, look at the time. You hurry and wash for dinner. Grampa will soon be here, and I'm sure he'll know what to do."

"What to do?" My heart sank. I knew what to do. Have fun! Dinner was emotionally painful that night.

Afterward, Granny and I sat down with Grampa, who was a Victorian Englishman. She showed him the money, and I told my story. It was a Friday night I shall never forget.

Grampa was very quiet for what seemed to be forever, and then he began to explain the role of the Red Cross and what it did with the money collected. Then he said that I had two choices. Choice number one: Did I think I could find everyone who gave me money? And if I was sure how much each gave, could I return it?

A very strange knot formed in my stomach, and a big lump blocked my throat when I tried to reply. "Well—no, I don't know who . . . who gave what," I stammered.

"Ah," he said. "Then you have only one possible course."

Somehow I didn't think it was going to be toys, Popsicles

and Saturday matinees. "What's that, Grampa?" I whispered.

"We will complete your plan. You collected on behalf of the Red Cross and a jolly good job you did. Bully for you. And tomorrow, Saturday, when I come home at noon from work, we shall go down on the streetcar, and you shall hand over your contribution."

The impact of his words rushed upon me. Loss and salvation all mixed together. The feeling that one has erred, but somehow has been shown an honorable way out. The punishment, well, that's left to self.

The next day dawned as one of my bleakest. I felt that I was guilty, but as a child I was still having feelings of loss. Somehow I got ready for our trip downtown.

After lunch, Grampa washed and shaved, donned his funeral/wedding blue suit and collar, and off we went to the Red Cross. The gray-haired lady looked like Miss Grundy in the Archie comics, but she was nice and smiled at me when I told her how I collected the money. She called others in and they made a fuss over my story. Grampa looked almost proud of me. I felt ashamed. They gave me a receipt and Grampa put it in his wallet.

We stepped outside onto the street. The sun was hot. Grampa looked at his pocket watch. "Well, we should start home," he said. "No streetcar in sight. Let's slip in here," he said, taking my hand. We stepped into the nicest drugstore I'd ever seen. All sorts of marble, with fans in the ceiling.

Wow! There was a soda fountain. We walked right up to it, and Grampa sat on a stool. So did I. "Two banana splits, please," Grampa said, putting the money on the counter. I almost fell off the stool. He winked at me, "Lesson learned, eh?" The banana splits came. The best I ever ate.

Barbara E. Keith

Mama's Medicines

The heart has its reasons which reason knows nothing of.

Blaise Pascal

Mama never got close to a medical school, but she had innovative ideas about doctoring. Having seven children and living nine miles away from a doctor called for creativity. Many times I feigned wellness so I wouldn't have to take her cures. Whatever the ailment, she always said, "Take something to clean you out."

I can see her now. With a frown on her face and a stern voice, she'd say, "Take this medicine, or you will never get well."

Mama kept her medicines on the first shelf of the cabinet, always convenient and in sight. A prescription for springtime blahs was black draught tea, brewed, strained and lukewarm. It looked black and ugly. It tasted black and ugly. Once she added a spoon of sugar, but that did not help. The gold and black box of tea was a regular medication in the cabinet.

Mama finally gave up on giving me castor oil. She thought it was the wonder drug of the ages and presented a gagging spoonful for any occasion. But it was slick and slimy and nearly always came back up. She stopped buying Pepto-Bismol after I drank a full bottle because it was pretty and pink and tasted good. To this day, I don't drink anything pink and thick.

For the flu, Mama's favorite medicine was Carter's Little Liver Pills. They were small and powerful beyond imagination. Mama said the liver was the most important organ in my body and caused all the other parts to operate. With a glass of water, the pills went down easier than castor oil.

Mama had cures for the outsides as well as the insides. Pinkeye cure was warm water with a bit of salt in it. Kids at school said if we looked at someone's eyes with pinkeye, even across the room, we'd get it. A kid with pinkeye was an outcast.

If I stepped on a rusty nail or scratched myself climbing a barbed-wire fence, the wound was treated with coal oil, called kerosene these days. The odor and fumes were so strong those germs had to suffocate when the coal oil hit them. My aunt gave her kids a spoonful of sugar with a drop of coal oil for sore throats, but Mama said she did not believe coal oil was good for children's stomachs.

A disgraceful disease was the itch, called seven-year itch by kids at school, though it didn't last seven years, just about seven days with treatment. "Nice people" didn't get the itch, but we got it. As the school year drew to a close, my two sisters and I found ourselves scratching little red bumps. We were glad school was out and no one would know we had the itch. The treatment was horrendous. Each day we mixed yellow sulfur powder with lard and rubbed it on our bodies wherever the itch appeared. Despite the bad smell, the sulfur and lard cured the itch.

Years later when I served in the U.S. Navy, I learned the itch had a real name—scabies. A new recruit came on base with orders in his service record to report to sick bay for treatment of scabies.

"What's that?" I asked my coworker.

"Just the itch," he said.

Scabies? That's a more dignified name than "itch," I thought. I don't know how the navy treated scabies, but I bet it was not as disagreeable as the way Mama fought it.

A recent bout of bronchitis sent me to the doctor for a chest x-ray and two prescriptions, costing $107.83. Mama would have prescribed Vick's salve rubbed on my chest with a flannel rag to cover it and, of course, Carter's Little Liver Pills to clean me out.

Perhaps Mama's medicines helped me survive. I certainly survived her medicines. She's gone now, and I miss her. Strangely, I miss her most of all when I am sick.

Lee Hill-Nelson

A Birthday Remembered

A good way to repay a kindness shown is to pass it on.

Martha Kinney

As a child growing up in the Ozark Mountains of Missouri in the 1930s, I didn't know we were poor—in fact, at the age of four, I really didn't know what poor was. But I did know I was getting tired of eating oatmeal and being cold.

One day we heard a sharp, loud knock at the door. I clung to my mother's skirt as she opened the door to what appeared to be a giant in overalls. His face was weather-worn, and his hair was long and poorly cut. His eyes were sharp and piercing.

"You Leonard Presson's woman?" It was more a demand for information than a question.

"Yes," Mother's voice was shallow and frightened. "But he's off hunting."

The giant turned and waved to two boys in a wagon pulled close to the door. "Well, we know y'all didn't get home from out West soon enough to put in a crop, so we brung you food to tide you over."

While he talked, the boys unloaded sacks of flour, grain, sugar, canned food of several varieties and smoked meat. Mother picked me up and stood against the wall. "We can't pay . . ." she began.

"You been gone a long time, Mrs. Eva." His stern face softened. "These is bad times—people comin' home 'cause they lost everything in the crash." He waved the boys back to the now-empty wagon. "Be sure you're in church come Sunday." He swung into the wagon and picked up the reins. "You'll be helpin' feed others next winter." Something resembling a smile split his somber face. "We hill people take care of our own."

That night we feasted, and on Sunday we were in church. My parents were greeted warmly by people I was yet to know.

Winter passed, and in the spring the hills and valleys that made up my world came alive with the promise of new life. Crops were planted and carefully tended. All summer we canned and preserved fruits and vegetables. The fall harvest was more than abundant.

On a bleak December day that was my fifth birthday, my father and two brothers loaded our wagon, and we all climbed up and drove to what had been an abandoned house across the valley. I sat bundled in blankets and boots next to Mother. "This is the most important birthday present you will ever get," she whispered. "I pray one day you'll remember it."

From my vantage high on the wagon seat, I watched my own father and brothers reenact the same scenario that I had seen from the safety of my mother's arms a year earlier. I wanted to jump down and run to the children I watched clinging to their own mother's skirts as I had done. That night in my childish prayer of "Now I lay me down to sleep," I had a feeling of warmth; for what reason I did not know. But in my heart I could see those children, and I knew they slept well—and so did I.

Time passed slowly for a little girl growing up in the hills of southern Missouri in the early 1930s. As I grew older, I helped prepare the food that was taken by wagon to families who had come home to escape the paralyzing hardship of the Depression. I even met the "giant" who had come to our door that cold winter day. He was the father of the girl who was to become "my very bestest friend." Even after we grew up and left the mountains to make our lives in the city, we corresponded and often met at family reunions in the Ozarks.

My mother was right. On my fifth birthday I received the most important birthday present ever. I've never forgotten the kindness and generosity of the simple but profound people who believed that they were indeed their brother's keeper.

Mother's prayer has also been answered—many times. For the past six decades, no matter where or how I celebrate each December 4, my birthday theme has been that act of kindness I witnessed on my fifth birthday. It has truly been a birthday remembered.

Elizabeth Leopard

The Cat in the Bag

Of all God's creatures there is only one that cannot be made the slave of the leash. That one is the cat. If man could be crossed with the cat, it would improve man, but it would deteriorate the cat.

Mark Twain

Aunt Faye and her cat Sophie were inseparable. In fact, though Aunt Faye never had any children, Sophie was like a child to her.

I have to admit that the cat was amazing. Sophie always knew when Aunt Faye wasn't feeling well. In fact, Sophie even knew when Aunt Faye's feet were cold at night. Because that cat would snuggle up at her feet in bed, Aunt Faye used to call Sophie her "bed warmer." My aunt was sort of hard of hearing, so when anyone came to the door of her apartment, Sophie ran to the door to alert her.

Good old Sophie the cat was getting on in years. My aunt would call me from time to time to ask me to drive Sophie and her to the veterinarian. In fact, I think she took better care of Sophie than herself. If Aunt Faye didn't feel well, she wouldn't go to the doctor; she would just take an aspirin. But should Sophie sneeze or cough with a hairball in her throat, we were on our way to the vet almost immediately.

So it came as a bit of a shock when Aunt Faye called me crying hysterically. "Sophie is dead! My little Sophie is dead!"

Between sobs, Aunt Faye explained. "You know I don't sleep so good at night. So the doctor gave me some sleeping pills. I didn't like the way they smelled so he told me to put a drop of vanilla extract into the bottle to make the pills taste like candy. So this morning when I was cooking in the kitchen, Sophie got into my bedroom and accidentally knocked over my bottle of sleeping pills. They must have smelled good to her because she ate almost every last one of them. The empty bottle was on the floor next to her."

Aunt Faye was still crying uncontrollably. "You know how long my Sophie and I have been together?" Not even waiting for my answer she said, "We've been together for twelve years. Yesterday, I even bought her a new cat food. They said this cat food was softer for older cats . . . her teeth have started to fall out like mine. Do you know how much Sophie meant to me?"

I sympathized with her.

"Now what can I do?" she sobbed.

"Look Aunt Faye, there isn't much you can do. Put Sophie's body in a paper bag, and place it in the garbage can in the basement. The sanitation department will take her away."

"What?" she screamed. "My Sophie in a garbage can? She was like my child. Since your uncle passed away, she's been my closest friend for all these years. I can't just put her in the garbage!"

"Okay," I said. "I'm working very late tonight so I won't be able to get over to your house. However, if you'll feel better about it, take a taxi to your veterinarian and ask him to have Sophie taken to the animal cemetery. I'll provide the money for the plot and the burial."

The tears continued. "Will I be able to visit her from time to time?"

"Sure. I'll take you to the pet cemetery any time you want to go."

"How can I take Sophie to the vet? Her carrying case fell apart a few years ago."

"Put her in your old suitcase. It's not too big and Sophie will fit perfectly."

"Will there be a funeral?"

"No, dear. The vet calls the people from the pet cemetery. They'll put Sophie in a little casket and take her to the cemetery."

"Okay," she muttered with a broken heart. "It will be dignified?" she asked.

"Yes, it will," I said.

That was it. I felt bad for her, but there was nothing more I could do.

About six o'clock that evening, Aunt Faye called me at my office. "Arnold, I have something to tell you." Strangely, I sensed excitement in her voice.

"What now?" I asked. "Did you go to the vet?"

"I did just like you said. I put Sophie in my suitcase. I was standing by the bus stop waiting for a cab, so I figured, *why spend money for a taxi when I could certainly take the bus?* So I put the suitcase down next to me and started to look into my purse to see if I had the exact change. While I was looking in my pocketbook, some teenage boys came up behind me. One threw me to the ground and grabbed my suitcase with Sophie inside!"

"Oh no, Aunt Faye! Did you get hurt?"

"Just a few scratches. Nothing serious. I yelled for the police, but nobody came. So what could I do? I figured this was the way my relationship with Sophie was supposed to end. So I went home."

"I don't believe this!" I said, trying to hold back my laughter. "Can you imagine the expression on those kids' faces when they opened the suitcase and found a dead cat?"

She started to laugh. Aunt Faye was actually laughing!

"Wait, wait—that's only part of the story. Sophie came home! She really wasn't dead! I only thought she was dead because she was lying so still when I found her in the bathroom this morning. Being jostled back and forth in that suitcase must have finally roused her. When I got back to the house, she was waiting at my door!

"Arnold, thank you for all your help. I prayed for Sophie to enter heaven, and she came back to me."

The next time I went to visit Aunt Faye, she had a little sign on her front door that read, "This is heaven."

Arnold Fine

"I'll say it again, that cat is spoiled."

Front Porches

Life isn't a matter of milestones but of moments.

Rose Kennedy

"Come on out here and sit a spell with me," my grand-father said to me, rising from the dinner table where we had gobbled down my grandmother's fried chicken, mashed potatoes, cream gravy and green beans—her standard Sunday spread. Taking a wedge of her pecan pie with us, Papa and I headed for the front porch.

As I snuggled up to him on the swing, carefully balancing my pie, I could smell the sunshine in his faded blue-denim overalls that he had changed into after church. They were so worn they were as light and soft as his chambray work shirt.

Side by side, we sat on the porch that spanned the front of our farmhouse, scraped up every last crumb of Grandma's pie, leaned back, sighed contentedly and "sat a spell." To me, it was a perfect way to spend a Sunday after-noon.

To this day, front porches hold a special place in my heart. My grandfather's porch was wide and deep enough to handle tricycle races with my cousins, games of jacks, picnics and the dreams of a little girl gazing up into the summer sky.

The porch also had many practical uses. My grandmother, mom, sister and I would gather there in its cool protection with old washtubs filled with peas, string beans or strawberries just gathered from the garden. As we shelled or snapped or husked, we talked about everything from 4-H projects to boys to what was for supper.

On really hot summer nights, my grandfather would drag a cot out onto the front porch, hoping to catch a nighttime breeze and a little sleep. He would fall asleep to a chorus of locusts and crickets in the glow of a million stars.

The porch served as a haven for all, human and animal alike. After a few rounds of pushing a lawn mower around our big yard, my brother would take a break on the porch. Coming in from a freshly cultivated field before moving on to the next one, Papa would stop a minute for a cold drink on the porch. Hot and flushed from canning vegetables, my grandmother would step out on the porch to catch a bit of breeze. Even the dogs knew the next best place to flop besides under a bush was on the cool boards of the front porch.

And there was no better place than the porch to be when a summer rain swept in. You could sit out there and smell it coming from miles away; feel that first hint of a breeze, first hot and then surprisingly cool; see the first drops of rain plop into the dust that layered everything. Then the full force of the storm would hit, sometimes driving you reluctantly inside as winds lashed the rain farther and farther up under the porch's roof.

I received my first kiss on that porch, painted its swing one adolescent-bored summer, helped my father repair its steps and spent many lazy Sunday afternoons on it.

Front porches serve a real purpose in American life. They are an open invitation to sit a spell, to talk, to dream or to do nothing at all—rare luxuries in today's fast-paced life. Front porches soothe the soul as surely as they shade the stoop.

I'm still sitting on front porches. My own home has one that spans the length of our house. It's not quite as deep as my childhood front porch, but still wide enough to hold the dreams of a grown woman gazing up into a summer sky.

And the invitation is still there, now for a new generation of children: "Come on out and sit a spell with me."

Vicki Marsh Kabat

The World Upside Down

In spite of everything, I still believe people are really good at heart.

Anne Frank

I had just turned sixteen when my mother, sister and I were taken into the infamous Auschwitz concentration camp. I watched with despair as my mother was escorted to the gas chambers. At that point, I felt my world turn upside down.

What sustained me during this time warp of horrors were my mother's words. As she was led away, she appealed to my sister and me to live a full life. Her last words to us were, "Remember, they can take *everything* from you *except* what you put in your mind."

I went from feeling victimized by our keepers to the realization that I quite possibly had the inner resources to outlast them. Somehow, with my determination to live, I would overcome their collective decision to eliminate us.

So even as I put on a striped uniform and submitted

my hair to the razor, I mentally committed to a return to normalcy, home and my training classes in gymnastics and dance.

A Nazi officer came to "welcome" the newcomers, and he asked what "talents" we had brought to the camp. My inmates pushed me forward because of my training in ballet. I was forced to dance. With my eyes closed, I envisioned this grotesque prison of horrors as the Budapest Opera House, and I gave the performance of my life. That evening I discovered the power of "doing within when you are without."

Our barracks received some extra rations the next day from the Nazi officer I had danced for—who was none other than Dr. Mengele, Hitler's "Angel of Death." He was known to send people to the "showers" to die if their shoelace was untied.

Is it any wonder that when life and death become as casual as flipping a coin, a personality would undergo radical changes? The tenets of "good behavior" learned in my sheltered childhood were replaced by a kind of animal instinct, which instantly smelled out danger and acted to deflect it. During a work detail, my sister was assigned to a brigade that was to leave for another camp. I could not allow us to be separated, and I quickly cartwheeled over to her side. I thought I noticed a hint of amusement on the guard's face as he turned the other way, ignoring our clutched hands.

Confronting fear and taking action helped me fight off the numbness that a persistent contact with arbitrary authority can create. Learning to "face the fear and do it anyway" became my way to recapture my self-esteem.

The inhumanity continued and months later, unconscious from starvation, I was thrown on a heap of corpses and presumed dead. Later that day, the American troops entered the death camp. I was too weak to realize what was happening. A GI looked my way as my hand moved. At the infirmary, he watched over me until I was declared out of danger.

After several months in the hospital, I returned to my hometown of Kassa, on the Hungarian-Czech border. Out of fifteen thousand deportees, seventy of us returned. A neighbor greeted me on the street, saying, "Surprised to see you made it. You were already such a skinny kid when you left."

Several years ago, I traveled back to Auschwitz on those same railroad tracks that took countless thousands to their death. I came to mourn the dead and celebrate the living. I needed to touch the walls, see the bunk beds where we lay those endless nights while the stench of the latrines wafted over us. I needed to relive the dreadful events in as much detail as memory allowed, while feeling the emotional and physical response.

The next step in recovery for me was to go public with my story. Recently, when I asked an audience of three hundred University of Texas students how many knew what happened at Auschwitz, four hands went up!

I hope that someday my grandchildren will ask me questions about the time when the world was upside down so that if it starts tilting again, they and millions of others can pour out their collective love and spin the world right side up.

Edith Eva Eger
Excerpted from Chocolate for a Woman's Soul
by Kay Allenbaugh

The Four Chaplains

*Valor is a gift. Those having it never know for
sure whether they have it until the test comes.*

Carl Sandburg

On the evening of February 2, 1943, the U.S.A.T.
Dorchester was crowded to capacity, carrying 902 service-
men, merchant seamen and civilian workers.

Once a luxury coastal liner, the 5,649-ton vessel had been
converted into an Army transport ship. The *Dorchester*, one
of three ships in the SG-19 convoy, was moving steadily
across the icy waters from Newfoundland toward an
American base in Greenland. SG-19 was escorted by three
Coast Guard cutters, *Tampa*, *Escanaba* and *Comanche*.

Hans J. Danielsen, the ship's captain, was concerned and
cautious. Earlier the *Tampa* had detected a submarine with
its sonar. Danielsen knew he was in dangerous waters even
before he got the alarming information. German U-boats
were constantly prowling these vital sea lanes, and several
ships had already been blasted and sunk.

The *Dorchester* was now only 150 miles from its destination, but the captain ordered the men to sleep in their clothing and keep life jackets on. Many soldiers sleeping deep in the ship's hold disregarded the order because of the engine's heat. Others ignored it because the life jackets were uncomfortable.

On February 3, at 12:55 A.M., a periscope broke the chilly Atlantic waters. Through the cross hairs, an officer aboard the German submarine U-2 spotted the *Dorchester*. After identifying and targeting the ship, he gave orders to fire the torpedoes. The hit was decisive—and deadly—striking the starboard side, amidship, far below the water line.

Danielsen, alerted that the *Dorchester* was taking water rapidly and sinking, gave the order to abandon ship. In less than twenty-seven minutes, the *Dorchester* would slip beneath the Atlantic's icy waters.

Tragically, the hit had knocked out power and radio contact with the three escort ships. The CGC *Comanche*, however, saw the flash of the explosion. It responded and then rescued ninety-seven survivors. The CGC *Escanaba* circled the *Dorchester*, rescuing an additional 132 survivors. The third cutter, CGC *Tampa*, continued on, escorting the remaining two ships.

Aboard the *Dorchester*, panic and chaos had set in. The blast had killed scores of men and many more were seriously wounded. Others, stunned by the explosion, were groping in the darkness. Those sleeping without clothing rushed topside where they were confronted first by a blast of icy Arctic air and then by the knowledge that death awaited.

Men jumped from the ship into lifeboats, overcrowding them to the point of capsizing. Other rafts, tossed into the Atlantic, drifted away before soldiers could get in them.

Through the pandemonium, according to those present, four Army chaplains brought hope in despair and light in darkness. Those chaplains were Lt. George L. Fox, Methodist; Lt. Alexander D. Goode, Jewish; Lt. John P. Washington, Roman Catholic; and Lt. Clark V. Poling, Dutch Reformed.

Quickly and quietly the four chaplains spread out among the soldiers. There they tried to calm the frightened, tend the wounded and guide the disoriented toward safety.

"Witnesses of that terrible night remember hearing the four men offer prayers for the dying and encouragement for those who would live," says Wyatt R. Fox, son of Reverend Fox.

One witness, Private William B. Bednar, found himself floating in oil-smeared water surrounded by dead bodies and debris. "I could hear men crying, pleading, praying," Bednar recalls. "I could also hear the chaplains preaching courage. Their voices were the only thing that kept me going."

Another sailor, Petty Officer John J. Mahoney, tried to reenter his cabin but was stopped by Rabbi Goode. Mahoney, concerned about the cold Arctic air, explained he had forgotten his gloves.

"Never mind," Goode responded. "I have two pairs." The rabbi then gave the petty officer his own gloves. In retrospect, Mahoney realized that Rabbi Goode was not conveniently carrying two pairs of gloves, and that the rabbi had decided not to leave the *Dorchester*.

By this time, most of the men were topside, and the chaplains opened a storage locker and began distributing life jackets. It was then that Engineer Grady Clark witnessed an astonishing sight.

When there were no more life jackets in the storage room, the chaplains removed theirs and gave them to four frightened young men.

"It was the finest thing I have seen or hope to see this side of heaven," said John Ladd, another survivor who saw the chaplains' selfless act.

Ladd's response is understandable. The altruistic action of the four chaplains constitutes one of the purest spiritual and ethical acts a person can make. When giving their life jackets, Rabbi Goode did not call out for a Jew; Father Washington did not call out for a Catholic; nor did the Reverends Fox and Poling call out for Protestants. They simply gave their life jackets to the next man in line.

As the ship went down, survivors in nearby rafts could see the four chaplains—arms linked and braced against the slanting deck. Their voices could also be heard offering prayers.

Of the 902 men aboard the U.S.A.T. *Dorchester*, 672 died, leaving 230 survivors. When the news reached American shores, the nation was stunned by the magnitude of the tragedy and heroic conduct of the four chaplains.

That night Reverend Fox, Rabbi Goode, Reverend Poling and Father Washington passed life's ultimate test. In doing so, they became an enduring example of extraordinary faith, courage and selflessness.

Victor M. Parachin
Submitted by Rabbi Earl Grollman

12

AGELESS WISDOM

*K*indness is more important than wisdom,
and the recognition of this is the beginning
of wisdom.

Theodore Isaac Rubin

Making the Rest the Best

The hardest years in life are those between ten and seventy.

Helen Hayes (at seventy-three)

On May 21, 1998, I commenced on an adventure I spent seventy years preparing for—my eighth decade. I looked forward to it with great gusto, and I can already tell I have good news for you. Life begins at seventy!

I thought being sixty was incredible, but being seventy is almost incomprehensible. *Other people* aged, but I simply did not believe it would ever happen to me. Many, many years ago, the very idea that I would ever reach seventy was as remote as the thought that the year 2000 would arrive. The inevitable has finally arrived, though. Now that I have reached seventy, I can relax. People don't generally expect as much of me.

When I was in my sixties, people expected me to retire to a rocking chair on the front porch of a condo, "take it easy" and complain about all my aches and pains. They were always asking questions like, "Do you think you should be doing that at your age?" or "What are you going to do when you retire?" I never planned to retire at sixty, or sixty-two, or sixty-five, even though people expected me to. Fortunately, I didn't feel guilty when failing to meet their expectations. Now that I'm seventy, I still am doing all the fun things I enjoy, including playing tennis, climbing mountains and flying airplanes. I am considering retirement. But nobody asks me about it anymore.

Another benefit of being seventy is having lived long enough to accumulate more than a few gray hairs and smile lines. I go into this season of life with a rich reserve. And I'm not referring to my bank accounts. I'm referring to the reservoir of experiences I've gained. I fully intend to apply the lessons I've learned—first and foremost, to maintain a positive mental attitude. I also plan to keep an open mind to new ideas and to maintain a good sense of humor.

Over the years, my gratitude has grown for the many people I've met along the way—family and friends, as well as thousands of acquaintances. Some I've crossed paths with I like very much. Some I love. I wouldn't go so far as to say that I never met anyone I didn't like. But I am proud to say there were hardly any I simply couldn't stand.

I've always been accused of putting more on my plate than is possible for one human to handle. But my philosophy has always been to bite off more than I can chew—and then to promptly chew it. I have loved living this way. I'm realistic enough to know, however, that I will never be as vibrant as I was twenty, thirty or forty years ago. I am still in good health and capable of living a rich, full life—spiritually, emotionally and mentally. But now if I get carried away and promise to be three places at once, no one thinks badly of me. They just chalk it up to my being seventy.

Being seventy has other pleasant surprises. For example, everybody seems astonished that I'm still going strong. Some are amazed I can still walk without losing my balance and talk without forgetting what I'm saying. Since no one expects someone in their seventies to have perfectly good hearing, I can pretend I can't hear if I want!

Once you reach seventy, people offer to open restaurant doors, help you with your jacket and save a place for you. If you're late, they know you'll arrive eventually. When you're over seventy, you don't need an excuse; people are just glad you make it. During an evening's conversation, people don't rudely interrupt you as often. They tend to treat you with respect just for having lived so long.

Being seventy is better than sixty, and it's significantly better than being fifty. When you're in your fifties, people hold you responsible for things over which you have very little control—the economy, social conditions, increasing crime, and the list goes on and on. Also, by the time you are seventy, your kids are old enough to recognize that you did the best you could as a parent and no longer hold you responsible for their problems. I am grateful my grandkids have taught my kids that important truth.

When you are seventy, you are given more choices. You can act either young or old. If you act too young, people say you're going through your second childhood. If you act too old, they think you're getting senile and smother you with kindness. You do have to guard against people expecting that you have all this time and nothing to do with it. Convincing them otherwise is sometimes a challenge. I keep telling people how busy I am, how I have goals enough to keep me busy until I'm one hundred, but I still have to say a lot of no's. I have noticed that I've had to say fewer since I put up a poster in my company headquarters office saying, "Retired—gone fishing, hiking, golfing, flying, cycling, snorkeling, swimming, reading, napping and smelling the roses. . . .

Meanwhile, have a nice day. Enjoy your work. . . . I've been there and done that."

Being seventy has reinforced a belief and practice I have held tenaciously to all my life. I don't have to be overly concerned about pleasing others. I don't have to wear suits, starched shirts or ties. I can wear tennis shoes, or *no* shoes, for that matter!

I can take a nap whenever I feel like it. I'm only sorry that I didn't start sooner. After all, Albert Einstein and Thomas Edison, so I've heard, took naps throughout the day all their lives and no one was bothered. People, in fact, just considered it part of their being geniuses.

Being seventy also gives me more perspective. I've learned not to sweat the small stuff. It's all small stuff. Time is very precious. It's too often wasted on hate, bitterness, holding grudges, or being unforgiving or vindictive.

Now that I've lived long enough to discern what is noble and what is not, I have recommitted myself to doing more good and also encouraging others to do more with their opportunities. I am convinced that doing good will keep my heart and mind strong and vibrant.

I do not know what the rest of my life will bring, but I am setting goals and planning for it to be a great adventure. I look forward to this new season of life, making the rest the best. I'm convinced right now that life begins at seventy. Of course, when I ask my older friends, they insist that life begins at eighty. I wonder if it really begins at ninety. I'll let you know when I get there.

Paul J. Meyer

CRANKSHAFT By Tom Batiuk and Chuck Ayers

No Ordinary Auction

He who provides for this life, but takes no care for eternity, is wise for a moment, but a fool forever.

John Tillotson

I once attended an auction that was no ordinary auction. The public could bid on unclaimed items that people had left behind in safe-deposit boxes. These items were once deemed so important that people paid money to have them safeguarded in steel.

Diplomas, children's report cards, letters . . .

I remember how we shuffled along, past the coin collections and pocket watches and jewelry to documents and small items sealed in plastic bags.

Boy Scout patches, receipts from a Waikiki hotel, a child's crayon drawing of a bunny rabbit . . .

It was all unclaimed property, waiting to be auctioned; the forgotten or overlooked possessions of owners now dead.

Rosaries, letters, train tickets . . .

Each bag was a mystery, the clues doing more to arouse curiosity than to provide answers. I read the immigration papers of Udolf Matschiner, who arrived at Ellis Island in 1906. Did he find what he was looking for in America?

Two marbles, three stones, and a belt buckle . . .

Why these things? Did they represent some special memory, some special person?

Passports, telegrams, newspaper clippings . . .

A yellowed article from a 1959 Los Angeles newspaper was headlined "Vlahovich's Mother Sobs at Guilty Verdict." A mother's son had been convicted of murder. The mother wept, pleading with the judge to spare her son. "Take my blood," she screamed. "Kill me!" What happened? Did she watch her son die in San Quentin's electric chair?

Undeveloped film, birth certificates, marriage certificates . . .

The official business of life intermingled with the unofficial business of life—a lock of blonde hair, a child's math paper and a poem called "Grandmother's Attic," typed on a typewriter with a sticky *e.*

It was as if those of us at the auction had been allowed entry into hundreds of grandmothers' attics, the attics of unknown people.

Diaries, photographs, the ink print of a newborn's feet . . .

In death's wake, most of the items spoke volumes about life. They also suggested a sense of finality, a realization that life on earth ends, and you can't take anything with you.

So what will we leave behind?

A six-by-twelve box full of mementos can speak volumes about what we valued. But it's only a whisper compared to the legacy of our lives themselves.

Amid our he-who-dies-with-the-most-toys-wins world, perhaps we should dare to leave . . .

An investment in other people.

An example of a life guided not by the capricious winds of culture, but rock-solid principles.

And an inspiration to our children and grandchildren to become all they have been designed to be.

Ah, heaven. The ultimate safe-deposit box.

Bob Welch

When I Grow Up

To know how to grow old is the master work of wisdom.

Henri Frederic Amiel

My father was killed in a car accident when I was eight months old, so my grandparents helped my mother rear me. I learned early that experience often gives older people wisdom.

Three golden souls in my life now are my Aunt Emelia, 103 years young; my dear neighbor, Clara Fentress, 97; and my Rock of Gibraltar mother, Winnie Russell Luttrell, 82. Mining nuggets of wisdom from these *grande dames,* I asked them each to describe their success formula for a vibrant life marked by extraordinary longevity. Their answers provide three gems for enriching life at any age:

1. Live One Day at a Time

Emelia Smith, 103

I began living fully one day at a time as a young girl. "Why?" I've been asked. "Because I didn't think I had a choice," is my heartfelt reply. Always giving one's best every day was required for mere survival on the wind-swept plains of eastern New Mexico. Made wiser by hardship, my parents set a compelling example. First of all, they were happy just to be alive each new day. Those were the treacherous days before miracle drugs, and many people died much younger than people die today. Second, they were grateful for the opportunity to improve their lot in life. They, like pioneers of any era, had with high hopes staked out a homestead in a new frontier.

Giving each hour of every day its best had worked well for my parents and others, and it has worked well for me through each season of my life. Living one day at a time has helped me live with joy during happy times and with strength during tragedy—including the trying years of the Depression, the death of my husband over forty-five years ago and the catastrophic deaths of two of my babies and one of my adult children.

"I love how you always remember my birthday and write an encouraging note to me," my granddaughter recently told me, and others have said similar things about the notes I write to relatives on their special days—birthdays, graduations, weddings. Well, I've never had much money to share with others, but I'm pretty certain from my observations of the few rich people I know that money doesn't bring happiness anyway. What I do know for sure is that people—young and old—need encouragement. My experience has proven over and over the truth in Proverbs 12:25: "Anxious hearts are very heavy, but a word of encouragement does wonders." I try to fill each conversation with words of encouragement and to set a good example of celebrating every day.

Whether you live twenty-five years, fifty years or one hundred years plus as I have, you can live those years only *one day at a time*. From my earliest years, that's how I thought you could *get* and *give* the most in life.

And it still is.

2. Count Your Blessings

Clara Fentress, 97

The death of my young son Joel after he was stricken with polio inflicted on me the most painful anguish of my entire life. Numerous children had gone to a nearby summer camp, and many contracted polio there. But of all the children, my dear Joel was the only one to die. After the initial shock of Joel's death wore off and the unrelenting, raw grief set in, I found consolation in remembering each day the happiness Joel brought me in his short life. I tried to capture my emotions in this poem:

A New Day

Some keys to our past we should throw away
It is foolish to unlock their door,
To behold inside many sorrows,
E'en thought mixed with blessings galore.
Tomorrow will be a new day.
Only He will know what 'twill bring,
As I wake in the morning sunshine,
"It is true 'tis new, I shall sing."

Today, at the age of ninety-seven, I have realized more than ever that *attitude* makes all the difference in how one lives life. For example, I used to plant six or eight tomato plants in a spot I call the gully. To reach it, I had to walk down some stairs, off my patio, and then make a fifty-foot trek to my garden. I did all this for about ten years. Even though my garden spot and I were growing older, it was not tuckered out. But I was. When I was almost ninety-five years old, I planted my tomatoes in my patio garden to avoid the tiring walk downstairs. I tell my friends, "That was one of the smartest things I ever did. One must hire a van to move furniture from house to house. But I moved only the furniture of my mind when I decided to plant *upstairs* instead of *down-stairs*." This kind of flexible attitude is the way to go!

An attitude of gratitude gives me grit and gusto for living. Life is too short to dwell on what I do not have; instead, I focus on what I do have:

Blessings

Altho' I'm old and live alone,
Lonely I will never be.
I simply won't allow it.
To do this I'll discipline me.
I shall talk to myself this way:
"You have books to read, eyes to see,
Pick up the phone, call a friend,
Go for a walk or watch TV.
Think about those who are blind,
Unable to do any of these.
Have you forgotten your blessings?
Try to remember them, please."

3. Don't Worry!

Winnie Russell Luttrell, 82

"Worry helps," I've told many people. Then I quickly explain, "Because most of the things I ever worried about *never happened!*" I identify very strongly with Mark Twain, who put it this way:

I am now an old man and have known many troubles,
but most of them never happened.

Joking aside, the tragedies in my life took me completely by surprise. Never did the thought cross my mind, for example, that my husband and I *would not* grow old together. But he was killed in an accident when he was twenty-seven. I was a twenty-four-year-old widow, and our children were fatherless.

All my children grew into adulthood, but at one time I still worried about their safety. And with good reason, so I thought! Two were serving in the military in the Vietnam War. One had gone through college on a rodeo scholarship and chose to be a professional cowboy; he lived by training wild horses—a dangerous job for someone at any age! Another traveled extensively, flying here and there. I had convinced myself he would be killed in the next airplane crash flashed on the evening news. My oldest daughter was working throughout Africa. I remember with unflappable confidence telling another daughter, "Barbara is going to disappear in deep dark Africa, and we'll never even know what happened to her."

All survived the perils I worried so intensely about.

Never in my wildest worries did I consider the possibility that my children who chose to live in our slow-paced New Mexico town would suffer any calamity. And yet Bill died an insufferable death from cancer, and Janet (my youngest) and her husband both were killed by a drunk driver merely three blocks from their home—orphaning an infant son.

Through it all, I have learned to live so that I never have regrets, and I remind myself daily that God loves me and will take care of me regardless of what happens. And after that, I simply don't worry!

* * * *

I am now in my fifties, so these three golden souls in my life are considerably older and wiser than I. I want to be like them when I grow up.

Barbara Russell Chesser

Rules of the Road

Think big thoughts but relish small pleasures.

Anonymous

Though somewhat younger, my wife and I attend a church that caters to senior citizens. We like it because of the traditional service and very friendly elderly people. One in particular is a lady in her early eighties, who cheerfully greets us at the same door every Sunday morning with a smile and kind words. We look forward to seeing Betty and giving her an occasional hug.

On a Sunday when I went to church alone, Betty handed me a small piece of paper and asked me to read it when I had time. On the slip of paper she had written, "Here are some phrases to think about over an egg enjoyed from an egg cup."

Stay loose—learn to watch snails. Make little signs that say yes. Make friends with freedom and uncertainty. Cry during movies. Swing as high as you can on a swing by moonlight. Do it for love. Take lots of naps. Give money away. Do it now. The money will follow.

Believe in magic. Laugh a lot. Celebrate every gorgeous moment. Read every day. Giggle with children. Listen to those older than you are. Entertain your inner child. Get wet. Hug trees. Write more letters. Eat a soft-boiled egg from an egg cup with a candle on the table. Glory.

One Sunday we got to church and entered without a greeting. During the service it dawned on me that our friend Betty was not at her post on this morning. After the service, we went to the fellowship hall for coffee, and I asked another lady where Betty was. She told me that she had been hit by a car and had been flown by helicopter to the hospital in the south of the county. She was small and frail, but not a bone had been broken. She said that Betty was mad because she had always wanted to ride on a helicopter and she couldn't remember a thing.

I discovered that Betty had been moved to a rehabilitation center near my office, so I stopped in to visit for a few minutes. She was in therapy, but I finally found her sitting at a table alone. I walked over to her and saw that she was horribly bruised on the whole left side of her face and body. She smiled when she saw me walking over to her.

I said, "Betty, do you remember that list you gave me about how to enjoy life?"

She smiled again and said, "Yes I do."

I said, "Well, I have another thing to add to the list."

She said, "What is it?"

I said, "Look both ways."

She broke out laughing and reached out to give me a hug.

John C. Fitts

THE FAMILY CIRCUS®

By Bil Keane

"Grandma says if y'want to leave footprints in the sands of time, you should wear work boots."

Fifty Reasons Why Older Is Better

*The great thing about getting older is that you
don't lose all the other ages you've been.*

Madeline L'Engle

1. You really *have* watched a lovelier sunset, eaten a sweeter peach and seen a more beautiful baby.
2. You can say, "When I was your age . . ." to more and more people.
3. You don't have to feel compelled to know all the answers. Or all the questions.
4. If you want to change your mind, nobody thinks anything of it.
5. When you decide to do something on the spur of the moment, nobody thinks anything of it either.
6. There's nothing left to learn the hard way.
7. You've seen it all before, even if you don't remember where.
8. No more pregnancy scares.
9. People are pleasantly surprised when you know the difference between the Internet and a hairnet, a Macintosh and a modem, a CD-ROM and a sitcom, a

VPI and a VCR, HBO and HMO, the GNP and a GPS, PSI and PSA or PMS and MCI.

10. Senior-citizen discounts—reduced motel rates, airfares, movie tickets, etc.

11. You can relax, quit trying to impress people and be your best self.

12. Enough time to give blood, forget a grudge, eat words you should never have said to begin with, pray for someone you don't even like and do something kind for someone who'll never know who did it.

13. No more frustrating shopping for gifts because checks aren't only socially acceptable, but recipients— especially in-laws and grandchildren—prefer them.

14. Friends who "remember you when," don't.

15. Lying about your age is easier now that you sometimes forget what it is.

16. Gray hair has more body.

17. You don't have a bedtime.

18. You remove mattress tags without fear of legal consequences.

19. Helping you with your computer makes your grandchildren feel important and needed.

20. Instead of counting sheep when you can't sleep at night, you can count your IRAs, your grandchildren, friends with hip replacements and pills you forgot to take.

21. You will probably be among the first hostages to be released.

22. Standing in the shallow end counts as swimming.

23. You don't have to get all worked up about New Year's Eve.

24. Been there. Done that. Now, a new openness to other experiences.

25. You can wear a sombrero and a bathrobe at the beach.

26. Drivers are more likely to stop for you when you're in a crosswalk.
27. Freedom to start a new hobby or resume an old one with no pressure to live by the old unspoken adage, "If you can't do it perfectly, don't do it at all."
28. Finally, *good enough* is really *good enough*.
29. More body parts can be medically replaced.
30. You can wear comfortable shoes, and no one notices—or even cares.
31. You feel comfortable choosing *being kind* over *being right*.
32. Taking time out for a walk is no longer considered a luxury but an essential.
33. Most of life's major disappointments are behind you.
34. You have developed a new appreciation of old things—old friends, old books, old values and ideals, old wine . . . and yourself.
35. You are old enough to realize you are never too old for new beginnings.
36. You have gained the amazing insight that the faults of other people are no worse than your own.
37. Personal experience has proven that spending time with loved ones is far more meaningful than spending money on them.
38. You've learned that enjoying the journey may be just as important as reaching the destination.
39. You've experienced the joy of occasionally taking detours—the road less taken provides immeasurable delights you never planned nor anticipated.
40. You realize that the gifts of life, health and love outweigh anything mere money could buy.
41. You've had at least one experience you wished desperately you'd never had but you wouldn't trade for anything.
42. You're finally accepting the reality that you won't

live long enough to do all the things other people want you to do; so you're beginning to select priorities that matter most in the long run.

43. You know that lighting someone else's candle in no way diminishes yours.

44. You change the things that can be changed, accept those that cannot and pray for the wisdom to know the difference.

45. You minimize preoccupation with the negatives in your life and concentrate on your gratitude for all the positives.

46. You listen more, learn more, laugh more, love more, lend a helping hand more and live more.

47. You know from experience—yours and that of others—that a clear conscience and peace of mind far outweigh fame or fortune.

48. You're learning to put the past behind you, put the future into proper perspective and live each day as if it might be your last, for someday it will be.

49. Leaving a legacy of love, integrity and good deeds is far more valuable than a great estate of material wealth.

50. It's the perfect time for looking inward, outward, forward and upward!

Lisa Birnbach, Ann Hodgman, Patricia Marx,
David Owen, Liz Curtis Higgs and Others

Who Is Jack Canfield?

Jack Canfield is one of America's leading experts in the development of human potential and personal effectiveness throughout the life span. He is both a dynamic, entertaining speaker and a highly sought-after trainer. Jack has a wonderful ability to inform and inspire audiences toward increased levels of self-esteem and peak performance at every stage of life.

He is the author and narrator of several bestselling audio- and videocassette programs, including *Self-Esteem and Peak Performance, How to Build High Self-Esteem, Self-Esteem in the Classroom* and *Chicken Soup for the Soul—Live*. He is regularly seen on television shows such as *Good Morning America, 20/20* and *NBC Nightly News*. Jack has co-authored numerous books, including the *Chicken Soup for the Soul* series, *Dare to Win* and *The Aladdin Factor* (all with Mark Victor Hansen), *100 Ways to Build Self-Concept in the Classroom* (with Harold C. Wells), *101 Ways to Develop Student Self-Esteem and Responsibility* (with Frank Siccone) and *Heart at Work* (with Jacqueline Miller).

Jack is a regularly featured speaker for professional associations, school districts, government agencies, churches, hospitals, sales organizations and corporations. His clients have included the American Dental Association, the American Management Association, AT&T, Campbell Soup, Clairol, Domino's Pizza, GE, ITT, Hartford Insurance, Johnson & Johnson, the Million Dollar Roundtable, NCR, New England Telephone, Re/Max, Scott Paper, TRW and Virgin Records.

Jack conducts an annual eight-day Training of Trainers program in the areas of self-esteem and peak performance. It attracts educators, counselors, parenting trainers, corporate trainers, professional speakers, ministers and others interested in developing their speaking and seminar-leading skills.

For further information about Jack's books, tapes and training programs, or to schedule him for a presentation, please contact:

Self-Esteem Seminars
P.O. Box 30880
Santa Barbara, CA 93130
Phone: 805-563-2935
Fax: 805-563-2945
Web site: *http://www.chickensoup.com*

Who Is Mark Victor Hansen?

Mark Victor Hansen is a professional speaker who, in the last twenty years, has made over four thousand presentations to more than two million people in thirty-two countries. His presentations cover sales excellence and strategies; personal empowerment and development regardless of stages of life; and how to triple your income and double your time off.

Mark has spent a lifetime dedicated to his mission of making a profound and positive difference in people's lives. Throughout his career, he has inspired hundreds of thousands of people to create a more powerful and purposeful future for themselves while stimulating the sale of billions of dollars worth of goods and services.

Mark is a prolific writer and has authored *Future Diary, How to Achieve Total Prosperity* and *The Miracle of Tithing.* He is coauthor of the *Chicken Soup for the Soul* series, *Dare to Win* and *The Aladdin Factor* (all with Jack Canfield), *The Master Motivator* (with Joe Batten) and *Out of the Blue* (with Barbara Nichols).

Mark has also produced a complete library of personal empowerment audio- and videocassette programs that have enabled his listeners to recognize and use their innate abilities in their business and personal lives. His message has made him a popular television and radio personality, with appearances on ABC, NBC, CBS, HBO, PBS and CNN. He has also appeared on the cover of numerous magazines, including *Success, Entrepreneur* and *Changes.*

Mark is a big man with a heart and spirit to match—an inspiration to people of all ages who seek to better themselves.

For further information about Mark write:

MVH & Associates
P.O. Box 7665
Newport Beach, CA 92658
Phone: 714-759-9304 or 800-433-2314
Fax: 714-722-6912
Web site: *http://www.chickensoup.com*

Who Is Paul J. Meyer?

Paul J. Meyer is a celebrated leader of the multibillion-dollar self-improvement industry—an industry he pioneered nearly forty years ago when he devoted his career to helping others develop and use their potential for achievement.

In 1960, Meyer founded his first company dedicated to "motivating people to their full potential." Meyer's vision was to provide practical, effective, full-length courses to help people achieve their goals. Today that company has grown into a globe-spanning group of personal and professional development companies, including Success Motivation Institute, Inc. and Leadership Management International, Inc.

Over the past three decades, Meyer has authored more than twenty full-length programs on topics ranging from goal setting to leadership to time management. An oft-quoted statement of Meyer's that summarizes his personal business success says, "If you are not making the progress you would like to make and are capable of making, it is simply because your goals are not clearly defined." His materials have been translated into twenty-one languages and are marketed in more than sixty countries with combined sales approaching $2 billion worldwide.

Meyer has recently released two books. *I Inherited a Fortune!* shares the optimism that has undergirded his lifelong success. *Bridging the Leadership Gap*, with his top marketing executives, Rex Houze and Randy Slechta, provides guidelines for values-based organizational leadership. Meyer is also the subject of two biographies, *The Story of Paul J. Meyer* and *Paul J. Meyer and the Art of Giving*.

Meyer and his family currently own more than forty companies throughout the world. The Meyer Family Enterprises span such fields as personal achievement and professional development, education, publishing, printing, vinyl products, leadership training, manufacturing, finance, commercial real estate, automotive racing, aviation, exotic game ranching and international trade.

Correspondence for Paul may be directed to:

Paul J. Meyer
P.O. Box 7411
Waco, TX 76714-7411
Fax: 254-776-0092
E-mail: *Paul@pjm1313.com*
Web site: *http://www.smi-usa.com*

Who Is Barbara Russell Chesser?

Dr. Barbara Russell Chesser grew up hearing the deep rich chords of storytelling. As a child, she enjoyed her large extended family's heartwarming stories, and that family tradition is still very much alive today. Her academic studies reinforced her fascination with how and why people play out the drama of their lives. After graduating at the top of her university class, Barbara continued to study the dynamics of human behavior.

After earning a master's degree from Mills College and a Ph.D. from Texas Woman's University, Barbara taught at several universities, including the University of Nebraska, the University of Nevada, the University of Arkansas, Texas Woman's University and Chapman College. She also carried out short-term assignments in Greece, the Philippines, Nigeria, Tanzania, Swaziland and Morocco.

Her coauthored books include a marriage and family college textbook and three other books, including *Fatal Moments*, a compelling account of recovery from the trauma of accidentally killing someone. She is the sole author of other books, including *21 Myths That Can Wreck Your Marriage* and *Because You Care: Practical Ideas for Helping Those Who Grieve*. She has written for professional journals and popular magazines, including the *Journal of Religion and Health* and *Reader's Digest*.

Barbara is president of Success Motivation, Inc., a research and development company in a global enterprise of more than forty companies.

Barbara's home life centers on Del, Christi, Michael and Mandi. Dr. Del Chesser is Barbara's husband, a Baylor University professor and a CPA. Christi is their daughter; she is also a CPA and a financial analyst. Michael is Christi's husband and a programmer analyst. Mandi is a devoted black-and-white Lhasa Apso who has spent many happy hours with Barbara working on *Chicken Soup for the Golden Soul*.

Correspondence for Barbara may be directed to:

Barbara Russell Chesser
Success Motivation, Inc.
P.O. Box 7332
Waco, TX 76714-7332
Phone: 254-776-0956
Fax: 254-776-6331
E-mail: *product@meyercompanies.com*

Who Is Amy Seeger?

Amy Seeger is vice president of Success Motivation, Inc., a product development company serving Paul J. Meyer and many of his companies in the personal and professional development field. Along with a bachelor's degree in professional writing, Amy also holds an executive MBA degree from Baylor University. With her husband, George, she is the proud parent of a little girl, Anna Joy.

In her position at Success Motivation, Inc., Amy's editing skills and business insights have contributed significantly to the new and existing products developed, designed and produced for distribution throughout the worldwide Meyer Family Enterprises organizations.

Amy brings to her position in Paul J. Meyer's companies a combination of professional expertise and personal commitment to helping others. When Paul and Barbara involved her as a coauthor for the *Chicken Soup for the Golden Soul* project, Amy had just completed editing and producing for Meyer a comprehensive anthology of success stories from the thirty-plus years of his companies' influence worldwide. The *Chicken Soup for the Golden Soul* book offered yet another challenging, worthwhile endeavor.

Amy has always had a deep respect for people who have experienced fullness and enjoyment of their golden years. During her college years, one of the highlights was when she occasionally volunteered for Sunday worship services at a local nursing home, singing hymns for the residents and encouraging them to sing along. Amy's concern for others is also reflected in past service as a volunteer counselor at a crisis center and as a board member of a local citizens' group.

Commenting on the mentoring influence of actively involved people in the sixty-and-over age group, Amy says, "I enjoy seeing the example of those who are involved as mentors, givers and participants in life as they grow older. One thing I've realized is that through my choice—my willingness to grow—I can begin to learn the lessons of the golden years now," says Amy. "In fact, research shows that your personality and outlook at age thirty will likely be the same in your eighties."

You can contact Amy Seeger at:

Amy Seeger
Success Motivation, Inc.
P.O. Box 7332 • Waco, TX 76714-7332
Fax: 254-776-6331
E-mail: *product@meyercompanies.com*

Contributors

Marie Aiken of Seattle, Washington, is a mother and grandmother. Her daughter, Nina Gordon, shares her story that illustrates her gift of humor. This story was published in the *Reminisce Magazine* collectible book, *Tough Times, Strong Women*. For more information, write: Reminisce Books, P.O. Box 990, Greendale, WI 53129 or call toll-free at: 800-558-1013.

John T. Baker, a former teacher, government agent and business executive, is now retired. His poems have appeared in numerous literary journals and on the Internet. He has adapted a number of plays and written lyrics for stage productions. He is also coauthor of several books on American idiomatic expressions.

Barbara Bartocci is an award-winning author and speaker. Her latest book is *Midlife Awakenings: Discovering the Gifts Life Has Given Us* (Ave Maria Press, Notre Dame). She speaks before women's conferences and business audiences throughout the United States and Canada. For more information, call toll-free 877-214-9625, or e-mail *Bbartocci@aol.com*.

John C. Bonser is a retired businessman and an award-winning poet. He is a past president of the St. Louis County Community Chamber of Commerce and the Rotary Club of Overland, Missouri. He can be reached at 1535 Horseshoe Drive, Florissant, MO 63033, or by calling 314-831-5290.

Audrey Bowie is one of Haggai Institute's most popular lecturers. As a pastor's wife she has ministered with her husband, Richard, in India, England, Australia and Singapore as a speaker, teacher and counselor. She can be reached at 16 Weyba Close, Forest Lake, Queensland AUSTRALIA 4078, or by calling 617-33729469.

Marie Bunce lives in Greenville, Indiana, and works as a physical therapy assistant with elderly patients. Changing careers at age forty was a great decision; she loves working with her patients and hearing their stories.

Muriel J. Bussman and her husband live on a farm in Oregon. They enjoy horses, Christmas trees, an apple orchard and six grandchildren. Muriel earned her college degree after turning fifty.

Dudley Callison lives in Waco, Texas, with his wife Laura. As president and director of Face To Face Ministries, he seeks to reach university students for God. Author of *For Seniors Only!*, a Bible study guide for high school graduates, he can be reached at P.O. Box 6335, Waco, TX 76706.

Martha Campbell is a graduate of Washington University School of Fine Arts and a former writer-designer for Hallmark Cards. Since becoming a freelancer in 1973, she has published over twenty thousand cartoons and illustrated nineteen books. You can contact her at P.O. Box 2538, Harrison, AR 72602, or 870-741-5323. E-mail: *marthaf@alltel.net*.

Nardi Reeder Campion, a freelance writer living in Hanover, New Hampshire, has published articles in *The New Yorker, The New York Times Magazine, Reader's Digest* and *Family Circle.* Her column "Everyday Matters" appears regularly in the *Valley News* of West Lebanon, New Hampshire. She is the author of seven books. Her book about the devout woman who founded the Shakers, *Mother Ann Lee: Morning Star of the Shakers,* can be purchased from The University Press of New England, 25 S. Main St., Hanover, NH 03755.

Diana L. Chapman is a national, award-winning writer and a contributor to the *Chicken Soup for the Soul* books. A journalist for fourteen years, she worked at the Los Angeles Copley Newspapers and *The San Diego Union.* She specializes in human interest stories and just completed her first young adult children's book. She left reporting after she was diagnosed with multiple sclerosis in 1992. Diana has been married for eleven years and has one son, Herbert "Ryan" Hart. She can be reached at P.O. Box 414, San Pedro, CA 90733.

Del Chesser holds the Roderick L. Holmes Chair of Accounting at Baylor University. Del often uses humorous stories as illustrations in his teaching. He has published articles in various journals including the *Journal of Accountancy.* Del and his wife, Barbara, have one daughter, Christi Chesser Whittredge.

Dan Clark is a speaker, actor, songwriter, recording artist, video producer and award-winning athlete. Author of twenty books, including *Getting High—How to Really Do It, Puppies for Sale* and *Simon Says,* he also coauthored *Chicken Soup for the College Soul.* You can contact him at P.O. Box 58689, Salt Lake City, UT 84108, or 801-485-5755.

Kristina Cliff-Evans is in her third and favorite career—writing. With many publication credits and several writing awards, Kristina currently writes for children and has completed her first novel. She and her husband, an architect, have three grown children. She can be reached via e-mail at *tinaeva@compaq.net.*

Mildred Cohn was born on September 1, 1925, in Washington, D.C. She and her husband, Murry, have lived in many parts of the world, including China and the island of Guam. They have two daughters and two granddaughters. Mildred enjoys traveling abroad, listening to classical music, attending concerts and operas, and visiting art museums and galleries. She bicycles and has an active social life with many friends.

Jo Coudert is a freelance writer, a contributing editor for *Woman's Day* magazine and a frequent contributor to other major magazines. Her seven books include the bestseller *Advice from a Failure* and more recently *Seven Cats and the Art of Living, The Ditchdigger's Daughters* and *The Good Shepherd.*

Hartley F. Dailey has been writing from his native Ohio for well over half a century. He specializes in stories that speak to the heart. Unquestionably his most famous story is the often-anthologized and dramatized story, "The Red Mittens."

Robert Darden is the author of twenty-five books, including *I, Jesus, Madman* *in Waco* and *The Way of an Eagle.* He edits *The Door,* a popular religious humor and satire magazine, and he's an assistant professor of English at Baylor University. Robert and his wife, Mary, have three children.

Doris Dillard Edwards, a minister's wife and grandmother, teaches English as a second language (ESL) and coordinates the ESL program for the Adult and Community Education Center in Columbia, South Carolina. She is a curriculum writer, consultant and presenter in the fields of ESL and English as a foreign language.

Edith Eva Eger is a well-known clinical psychologist and international speaker. She has been featured on many television programs worldwide, including *Oprah.* Her own journey began in Auschwitz; this place of death and carnage became her greatest classroom. Beyond surviving, she conquered her demons to create a triumphant, joyous and fruitful life.

Arnold Fine taught handicapped children and was senior editor of *The Jewish Press* for fifty years. Honored by the National Committee for the Furtherance of Jewish Education and the Jewish Teachers Association of New York, he is an adjunct professor at City University of New York, a husband, and has three sons and six grandchildren.

John C. Fitts is a chaplain for The Hospice of the Florida Suncoast and also All Children's Hospital, both in St. Petersburg, Florida. He pastored churches in Alabama and Florida for nearly twenty years. John and his wife, Patty, life in Palm Harbor, Florida, and love spending time with their three grown children, their spouses, and their new grandson. John can be reached by e-mail at *jfitts2@juno.com.*

Bill Floyd is a retired United Methodist minister and lives in Dalton, Georgia. He has collected thousands of stories like "Fear Fouls a Pond" from books, magazines, and most often, from real life. He uses these illustrations to bring into sharper focus his messages from the pulpit.

Evelyn Gibb, having reared three children, lives with her husband in the foothills of Washington's Cascade Mountains. Her greatest joys come from natural beauty and sharing her writing in national magazines. Her book-length chronicle of a 1909 bicycle adventure, *Two Bikes and a Billiken,* will be published soon. She can be reached at *evgorgib@ncia.com.*

Randy Glasbergen is the creator of the cartoon *The Better Half,* which is syndicated to 150 newspapers by King Features Syndicate Worldwide. More than twenty-five thousand of Randy's cartoons have been published in magazines, books and greeting cards around the world. Look for Randy's daily cartoons online at *www.glasbergen.com,* or e-mail him at *randy@glasbergen.com.*

Arthur Gordon has been managing editor of *Good Housekeeping,* editor-in-chief of *Cosmopolitan,* and editorial director of *Guideposts* and *Air Force Magazine.* He has also been a staff writer for *Reader's Digest.* His novel *Reprisal* was a Literary

Guild selection. His most popular book, *A Touch of Wonder,* has sold almost half a million copies.

Louise R. Hamm is a retired legal administrator, mother of three, grandmother of two, and recently widowed after fifty-one years of marriage. In addition to stories in other *Chicken Soup for the Soul* books, her works include business articles and personal pieces.

Stuart Hample is coeditor of the million-copy bestseller *Children's Letters to God.* The book, along with many other children's, humor, gift and other titles, are published by Workman Publishing *(www.workmanweb.com).* Mr. Hample is also the editor of *Me and My Dad.*

Tom Harken is a self-made millionaire. Married, he has two sons, is owner of eight franchises of the Casa Olé restaurant chain and received the Horatio Alger Award in 1992. Author of *The Millionaire's Secret: Miss Melba and Me,* he has given more than three hundred speeches around the country about literacy.

Phyllis S. Heinel grew up in Spokane, Washington, where she and her husband now live. They have three daughters and seven grandchildren. Phyllis says writing has always been her passion. She belongs to a writing group.

Vern Herschberger of Cranfills Gap, Texas, works as a freelance editorial cartoonist. His wry wit and critical detachment have brought joy to thousands and a jolt to a few. Herschberger also works in watercolor and oils, with pieces in various collections across the United States. He can be reached at 254-675-4241.

Lee Hill-Nelson is a wife, mother, grandmother and retired church secretary. She began writing in 1986 when her children asked her to record her memories about growing up. She has been published in several newspapers and magazines.

Betsy Hall Hutchinson is a writer and artist whose nostalgic essays about her St. Paul, Minnesota, childhood have been published in *The Christian Science Monitor, The Arizona Daily Star,* Cox Newspapers and elsewhere. She has worked in the book publishing industry as an editor, copywriter and illustrator. Two potential books for children lurk in her computer: a Southwestern folktale and a non-fiction book about prayer. Write her at 5520 N. Camino Arenosa, Tucson, AZ 85718 or by e-mail at: *BetsyHH@aol.com.*

Barbara Johnson lives in La Habra, California, with her husband, Bill. They have four sons (two deceased). Several bestsellers include *Stick a Geranium in Your Hat.* Barbara speaks to numerous audiences every year with Women of Faith seminars and Spatula Ministries.

Mickey Mann Johnson is an accomplished interior designer in Houston, Texas, and an inspiration to everyone who knows her. Mickey speaks for *LIFE GIFT* and other organizations about donor awareness. Two of her three sons are now married, and Mickey has her first grandchild, Jacob Mann Johnson.

She and her husband, Don, are preparing for a long cruise on their boat, "Charisma," this year—a lifelong dream.

Vicki Marsh Kabat is Associate Director of Publications for public relations at Baylor University. She and her husband, Bruce, have three sons. A graduate of the University of Missouri, Vicki writes a weekly column distributed on the *New York Times Wire Service.*

Bil Keane draws the internationally syndicated cartoon *The Family Circus,* which appears in more than fifteen hundred newspapers. Created in 1960, it is based on Keane's own family: his wife, Thel, and their five children. Now nine grandchildren provide most of the inspirations.

Barbara E. Keith was born, reared and educated in Toronto, Ontario, Canada, and was employed for thirty-seven years by the Federal Public Service. She has used her writing skills throughout her career.

Nita Sue Kent describes herself as child, daughter, friend, wife, mother, teacher, student, painter, writer, gardener and grandmother. These words are the bits of glass in the kaleidoscope of her life. She has lived in Texas, Missouri, South Dakota and West Virginia.

Tom Landry coached the Dallas Cowboys for twenty-nine years. Landry's stature in the coaching profession is surpassed only by his efforts to help others, especially at-risk kids like the one in Mr. Landry's story. Contact Happy Hill Farm by writing HC 51, Granbury, Texas 76048, or by calling 254-897-4822 or faxing 254-897-7650.

Sharon Whitley Larsen is a freelance writer/editor and former special education teacher. Her work has appeared in *Chicken Soup for the Soul* books, *Reader's Digest, Los Angeles Times Magazine, Woman's World, Guideposts* and other publications. She can be reached at 5666 Meredith Avenue, San Diego, CA 92120, 619-583-7346 or e-mail *SWhittles@aol.com.*

Eileen Lawrence is vice president of Chadwyck-Healey, an electronic publisher of scholarly works ("The Home of the Humanities on the Web"). A former teacher and educational consultant, she entered publishing in 1980. In 1986 she started a consulting company, Eileen Lawrence Communications. Eileen lives in Silver Spring, Maryland.

Elizabeth Leopard was one of the first women reporters in the South. Later, after directing public relations at the American Red Cross, she became a crisis counselor and coordinator, assisting people after Hurricane Hugo. Retired, Elizabeth and her husband live in South Carolina.

Evelyn Marder Levin has a Ph.D. in human services and has spent the past twenty years working in and writing about health care and its issues. Based on her corporate experience, she's writing a book about women over fifty in and out of the workplace. She recently established It's A Lululinc., a company which creates unique products for children and pets. She can be reached at

212-679-6503 or by email at: *levinseven@aol.com*.

Florence Littauer is an inspirational/motivational speaker, author and teacher of communication seminars. At age fifty she wrote the first of over twenty-seven books, including *Personality Plus*. Florence and her husband, Fred, have three children and three grandchildren. Florence can be reached at 1611 S. Rancho Santa Fe, Ste. F2, San Marcos, CA 92069, or via e-mail at *CLASSpkr@aol.com*.

Sister Clarice Lolich is a member of the Community of the Holy Spirit, San Diego. Her philosophy of life is to merge the marvels of the universe with the life of the spirit. Her commitment to God's creation binds space, science and religion. She communicates this to students of all ages. Sister Clarice's favorite charity work is with former student Sister Tonia Marie, foundress of a religious community in Guatemala, who has been given property to build a home for homeless elder citizens. Building workers get paid only when money is at hand; each gets about $175/month. Senior grandparents are no longer cared for by their children because of the poverty that reigns in Guatemala; therefore they are street bound.

Max Lucado lives in San Antonio, Texas, where he preaches at the Oak Hills Church of Christ. He and his wife, Denalyn, are the parents of three daughters. He has authored more than twenty-five books.

Margaret E. Mack is author of three books, including one of poetry. Currently attending law school, Margie is married and has four grown sons. She was reared in Illinois with her grandparents; she considers them to be "my best friends."

Eric Marshall is coeditor of the million-copy bestseller *Children's Letters to God*, published by Workman Publishing, (*www.workmanweb.com*).

Woody McKay Jr. is from North Carolina, has pastored churches and worked as a campus minister for over forty years. Father of six, grandfather of eleven, and a remarried widower, his experiences add dimension to his writing. Contact Woody at 985 Holly Hedge Rd., Stone Mountain, GA 30083, 404-294-5795 or *WMCKAY@mindspring.com*.

Robertson McQuilkin is a homemaker, author and conference speaker. His most recent book is the more complete version touched on in his selection in *Chicken Soup for the Golden Soul*, "Loving Muriel." Published by Tyndale House in 1998, the widely quoted book is titled *A Promise Kept: The Story of an Unforgettable Love*.

Roberta L. Messner is author of several books and approximately one thousand articles and short stories appearing in one hundred-plus different publications. She is a writer and speaker on a variety of inspirational, health care and decorating topics.

Dan Miller is a humorous/inspirational speaker and author of *Living, Laughing and Loving Life!* Dan has been on Robert Schuller's *Hour of Power* and James Dobson's *Focus on the Family*. To contact Dan regarding speaking engagements, books or videos, call 360-871-8446, write to Box 55, Manchester, WA 98353, or e-mail *danmiller@telebyte.com*.

Anita Cheek Milner is a professional speaker and humorist. She said she had to have a sense of humor to attend law school in her forties. Passing the California Bar at fifty, she now appears as the "Change of Life Attorney." Contact her through her marketing director Susan Guzzetta at 800-607-2535.

Agnes Moench and husband, Del, live on a farm near the Sierra Nevada Mountains. Her interest in writing was sparked when asked to write a handbook for volunteers. She is currently working on a novel with a Nebraska frontier setting.

Eddie Ogan and her husband, Phil, live in a log cabin in the Gillette Mountains at 930 Onion Creek Rd., Coleville, WA 99114. They have one son by birth, eleven adopted children and many grandchildren. They have been foster parents to seventy-seven children over the last thirty-seven years.

Victor M. Parachin is an ordained minister. He has served churches in the Chicago, Washington, D.C., and Los Angeles areas. He is a freelance writer and author of several books. He lives in Tulsa, Oklahoma, with his wife and three children.

Ruth Stafford Peale is founder and publisher of *Guideposts* magazine, the recipient of numerous national awards, and sits on the boards of the American Bible Society, Laymen's National Bible Association, and the Interchurch Center, among many others. She is author of the book *Secrets of Staying in Love*. Ruth is the mother of three, the grandmother of eight, and the great-grandmother of six.

Renae Pick lives in Denver, Colorado. She is a practicing martial artist with a first-degree black belt, who enjoys hiking in the mountains. Raised in Texas and the youngest of three, Renae and her sisters, Jan Johnson and Donna Wallingsford, all share their parents' philosophy that each day is special.

Lee Pitts writes a self-syndicated humor column. His essays have been featured on Paul Harvey News and Comments. Author of seven books including two recent ones, *People Who Live at the End of Dirt Roads* and *Back Door People*, Lee can be reached at P. O. Box 616, Morro Bay, CA 93443.

Penny Porter is mother of six and grandmother of eight. A former teacher and school administrator, and author of four books including *Heartstrings and Tail-Tuggers*, award-winning Penny is a frequent contributor to *Reader's Digest* and a wide range of other national magazines. Her inspiration is rooted in the love of family and human values today's children so desperately need.

Maureen S. Pusch's story is based on memories of working at a cemetery monument company. Recovering from the death of her stillborn daughter, Maureen found that helping others select a monument to "mark" the life of a loved one changed her forever.

Leon J. Rawitz is president of the Rawitz Group, a marketing communications and consulting firm. With articles in numerous publications, he is a professional speaker, coauthor and presenter of two marketing workshops. He resides in North Carolina with his wife and three children. He can be reached at 919-303-8202.

Barbara Jo Reams Russell has been an elementary school teacher for sixteen years. A graduate of Lubbock Christian University, Barbara and her husband, Randall, have four grown children and two grandchildren. Barbara and Randall are active in church ministries.

Harriet May Savitz is author of twenty books and has taught creative writing courses. Cofounder of the Philadelphia Children's Reading Round Table, her books include *A Girl's Best Friend* (children's book), *Creating Your Own Recovery* and *Growing Up At 62: A Celebration*. She lives in Bradley Beach, NJ, and can be reached by calling 732-775-5628.

Vahan Shirvanian went from Air Force gunnery instructor (World War II) to *Saturday Evening Post* cartoonist in 1946. He quickly became one of the world's bestselling cartoonists and three times has been voted Best Cartoonist of the Year. He can be reached at 44 Hanover Rd., Mountain Lakes, NJ 07046, or by calling 973-334-8998.

Sidney B. Simon is internationally known for pioneering work in values clarification. A University of Massachusetts professor emeritus, Sid presents workshops and speeches around the world. This poem is from his book telling stories of people aging gracefully, and sometimes not so gracefully. You can reach him at 9471 Peaceful Drive, Sanibel, FL 33957.

Kelley Smith is an editorial assistant to coauthors Paul J. Meyer, Barbara Chesser and Amy Seeger. A graduate of Baylor University, she works in the product development wing of Paul J. Meyer's family of companies. Kelley joins her father, Michael Smith, for a story in this volume.

Michael T. Smith and his wife, Sharon, live in Wichita Falls, Texas. Minister of Music at First Baptist Church, Mike is a published composer and arranger as well as an accomplished concert pianist. He has two children: Shelley and her husband, Knox Thames, live in Washington, D.C., and Kelley lives in Waco, Texas.

Paul Stripling, executive director of the Waco Baptist Association, enjoys speaking and teaching in universities and seminaries, particularly in the area of church history. He has pastored five churches, is a frequent contributor to *Lifeway Christian Resources* and *The Baptist Standard*, and is author of the book, *From Me to You*. His family includes his wife Roberta, two daughters, Mary and Paula, and Paula's husband Kyle. Dr. Stripling can be reached at 254-772-6500.

LeAnn Thieman is an author and nationally acclaimed speaker, inspiring audiences to make a difference in the world. She coauthored *This Must Be My Brother*, recounting her role in the rescue of three hundred babies during the

Vietnam Orphan airlift. She can be contacted at 112 North College, Fort Collins, CO 80524, toll-free 877-THIEMAN, or at *www.LeAnnThieman.com*. LeAnn will be a coauthor of the upcoming *Chicken Soup for the Nurse's Soul*.

Marlena Thompson has published children's poetry, short stories, articles, essays and reviews in numerous publications. Marlena has never forgotten her experiences as a student living in Yorkshire. She now lives in Virginia with her husband and daughter.

W. E. "Bill" Thorn is a retired pastor, university president and banqueteer. Speaking over three hundred times a year to various groups, Bill has authored fourteen books, including *Bit of Honey, Growing Old with Class* and *Famous for the Gospel*. He can be reached at 902 N. Main, #70, San Angelo, TX 76903.

Scot Thurman is currently an assistant director with the Baptist Student Union in Fayetteville, Arkansas. He graduated from the University of Arkansas in 1992 and from Ouachita Baptist University in 1997. His love lies in helping people grow closer to God.

Helen Weathers was "dancing as fast as I could"—then the aneurysm struck. Her story of survival has encouraged countless individuals; she found her mission as an advocate for stroke victims. Married to Robert Weathers, she has a daughter and two grandchildren.

Bob Welch is the author of the Gold Medallion Award-winning book *A Father for All Seasons* and *Where Roots Grow Deep*. He has been published in *Focus on the Family, Reader's Digest* and *Sports Illustrated*. Welch works for *The Register-Guard* in Eugene, Oregon, and can be contacted at *bwelch1@concentric.net*.

Bettie B. Youngs, Ph.D., Ed.D., is an international lecturer and consultant living in Del Mar, California. She is author of fourteen books published in twenty-eight languages, including the bestseller *Values from the Heartland, Gifts of the Heart, Taste Berries for Teens and the Taste Berries for Teens Journal*. You can contact Bettie at 3060 Racetrack View Drive, Del Mar, CA 92014.

Permissions

We would like to acknowledge the following publishers and individuals for permission to reprint the following material. (Note: Stories that were in the public domain, or that were written by Jack Canfield, Mark Victor Hansen, Paul J. Meyer, Barbara Russell Chesser and Amy Seeger are not included in this listing.)

Risky Business. Reprinted by permission of The Richard Parks Agency. ©1987 by Jo Coudert.

Time Out. Excerpted from *Random Acts of Kindness* by the editors of Conari Press. ©1993 by the editors of Conari Press, by permission of Conari Press.

The Age of Mystique. Reprinted by permission of Anita Cheek Milner. Excerpted from *Chocolate for a Woman's Soul* by Kay Allenbaugh. ©1997 Anita Cheek Milner.

Strike Out or Home Run? Reprinted by permission of Harriet May Savitz. ©2000 Harriet May Savitz.

The Long Ride. Reprinted by permission of Diana L. Chapman. ©2000 Diana L. Chapman.

Annual Checkup. Reprinted by permission of W. E. "Bill" Thorn. ©2000 W. E. "Bill" Thorn.

Daily Prayer. Reprinted by permission of John T. Baker. ©2000 John T. Baker.

The Rich Family. Reprinted by permission of Eddie Ogan. ©2000 Eddie Ogan.

The Secret Benefactor. Reprinted by permission of Woody McKay Jr. ©2000 Woody McKay Jr.

The Door Prize, Kathleen's Piano and *They Call Me "The Umbrella Lady."* Reprinted by permission of Roberta L. Messner. ©1992 Roberta L. Messner.

Uncle Li and Sarah Wong. Reprinted by permission of Audrey Bowie. ©2000 Audrey Bowie.

Greater Than a Super Bowl. Reprinted by permission of Tom Landry. ©2000 Tom Landry.

The Inventive Generation. Excerpted from *My Turn: The Memoirs of Nancy Reagan.* Reprinted by permission of Random House, Inc.

Love Is a Grandparent. FOREVER, ERMA ©1996 by the Estate of Erma Bombeck. Reprinted with permission of Andrews and McMeel Publishing. All rights reserved.

February, 1963. Text reprinted by permission of the author, Garth Henrichs of Sunshine Publications, and Joe Wheeler, Agent for Hartley F. Dailey, Box 1246, Conifer, CO 80433.

The List. Reprinted by permission of Agnes Moench. ©2000 Agnes Moench.

The Mirror Has Three Faces. Reprinted by permission of Kristina Cliff-Evans. ©1999 Kristina Cliff-Evans.

Ready to Roll. Reprinted by permission of Betsy Hall Hutchinson. ©2000 Betsy Hall Hutchinson.

Cracking Up. Reprinted by permission of Maureen Pusch. ©2000 Maureen Pusch.

Get Up and Go. Words collected and adapted and set to original music by Pete Seeger. TRO-Copyright 1964 (Renewed) Melody Trails, Inc., New York, NY. Used by permission.

Just One Wish. Reprinted by permission of Margaret Mack. ©2000 Margaret Mack.

The Patient and Her Encourager. Reprinted by permission of Scot Thurman. ©2000 Scot Thurman.

Bewitched. Reprinted by permission of Penny Porter. ©1999 Penny Porter.

The Man Without a Name. Reprinted by permission of Naomi Jones. ©2000 Naomi Jones.

Sophie's Seascape. Reprinted by permission of Barbara Jo Reams Russell. ©2000 Barbara Jo Reams Russell.

Make Me Like Joe! Excerpted from *Everything You've Heard Is Wrong* by Tony Campolo, ©1992, Word Publishing, Nashville, Tennessee. All rights reserved.

Grandma's Garden. Reprinted by permission of LeAnn Thieman. ©2000 LeAnn Thieman.

A Dream Deferred. Reprinted by permission of Marie Bunce. ©2000 Marie Bunce.

Sweet Petunia. Reprinted by permission of Leon J. Rawitz. ©2000 Leon J. Rawitz.